13-Cubed
CASE STUDIES IN MIND-CONTROL
& PROGRAMMING

By Stewart A. Swerdlow

Expansions Publishing Company, Inc.
P.O. Box 12, St. Joseph, MI 49085 USA

Cover design, typography and book design: Lorraine Sarich
www.lorrainecsarich.com

Editor: Janet Swerdlow

Published by: Expansions Publishing Company, Inc.
                P.O. Box 12
                Saint Joseph MI 49085 USA
                PH: 269-429-8615
                FX: 269-429-8616

ISBN# 978-0-9740144-4-9

website address: www.expansions.com
email: expansions@expansions.com

Books by
Stewart & Janet Swerdlow

Belief Systems Shattered
Blue Blood True Blood: Conflict and Creation
Decoding Your Life: An Experiential Course in Self-Reintegration
Diary of a Monarch
Healer's Handbook: A Journey Into Hyperspace
Hyperspace Helper: A User Friendly Guide
Montauk: Alien Connection
Practical Tips for Everyday Living I, II, III
Stewart Says...
True Reality of Sexuality
White Owl Legends

Dedication

*To humankind so that all victimization may be removed from
every mind-pattern causing all oppressors and tyrants
to be removed from the Earth.*

*A special thank you to John V. Booth for his support in
making this work possible.*

Table of Contents

Preface

What you are about to read within the covers of this book is a topic that is so vast and so pervasive, that it spans millions of years and every aspect of life. It did not originate on this planet, but our home world has become ground zero for what is known as mind-control and programming.

Those readers who are interested in the true history of the Earth should read my book, ***Blue Blood, True Blood: Conflict & Creation*** (*Expansions, 2001*) which explains the details. Or, you can watch my ***Mind-Control & Programming*** DVD series.

13-Cubed: Case Studies in Mind-Control & Programming is about those who are swept up in the process due to mind-patterns and genetics, and are making the efforts to deprogram themselves from the control systems in place.

In this book I symbolically discuss 13 separate cases of programming and mind-control to demonstrate programming variations as well as how to correct and balance them within the mind-pattern. I provide my interpretations and suggestions for each of these cases so that you can compare their stories and correction techniques to your own needs. Most participants in this study wrote their own stories in their own words. Some are anonymous with fictitious names.

Included are some brief descriptions of special cases that are program-induced but are specific to a particular type of function. I also describe general scenarios and constructs that are common in the programming world, deprogramming techniques, and supplemental deprogramming modalities.

I have personal and first-hand experience in this field since childhood. I was present at the Montauk Project from 1970 to 1983 where heinous mind-control and genetic experimentation took place. There was also time-travel and weapons testing, and weather control. You may read my autobiography in my book, **Montauk: The Alien Connection** (*Skybooks, 1998*).

I worked under the Illuminati controllers for over 25 years and have worked on my own deprogramming since 1990. I was trained as a psychic/mentalist by the secret government. I was physically blinded by microwave and ELF bombardments of the experiments. I was only able to see the energy fields that emanated from the mind-patterns, DNA, and atomic structures of all that exists. In effect, I could see beyond the scope of physical reality. I consider this type of sight more acute and accurate than what is conventionally accepted.

My physical eyesight is now restored. I spend my days working mentally with others to help analyze their mind-patterns. This allows people to change the experiences and relationships that they attract.

In the past few years to the present, much of my work centers on the deprogramming process as a result of 21st century activations. I also emphasize the need for trained deprogrammers who can properly deal with this pervasive and complicated issue. The emotional and mental rewards are beyond words.

Welcome to my world. I caution all programmed people reading this book that there is a strong possibility that you may be triggered unless you are actively deprogramming. It is my hope that the information contained in this book sparks an interest in deprogramming that escalates and extrapolates to huge proportions, allowing humanity a reasonable chance to reclaim its own individual and species mind. Removal of victimization mentality is paramount. Join with me in this endeavor to free yourself and the world from a mental prison.

Stewart A. Swerdlow

Case Studies & Analyses

Introduction

What is programming? It is a method of altering and adding to the mind-patterns and thought-forms innate to an individual and population for the purposes of manipulating the actions, reactions, and plans of that population ~ in this case, our planet Earth. Programming is the software embedded in the brain to monitor all functions.

What is mind-control? It is the application of the programming software as it steers and directs the activities of the individual in every aspect of life. The individual is not able to discern his/her own thoughts from those which are artificially induced.

The process started aeons ago on this planet with a group calling itself "The Illuminati." The Illuminati consists of 13 families who control and manipulate all things on Earth, as well as the 300 families who work directly for them. This is not conspiracy theory; this is fact.

Throughout historical experience, it is known that the only way for a relatively small group to safely and logically control billions of others, is to control their minds and also their bodies.

Through techniques developed before this world began, it was discovered that when a mind is traumatized by torture, fear, and pain, the individual personality fractures and segments in order to deal with the trauma. When this split occurs, it naturally creates a cube or matrix that is layered 13 x 13 x13. This means that there are 2,197 separate components or compartments of a personality that can be reprogrammed into alter personalities or partial personalities within the same individual. All are pieces of the whole; the programming prevents integration and cohesiveness.

The entire population of the world in the 21st Century is programmed—mostly subliminally via satellite transmissions, television, radio, and ground antennae that transmit ELF and microwave signals. These signals piggyback the brain waves to download information and instruction.

Globally, about 2% of the population, or about 130 million people, are specifically programmed. This means that they were physically taken for programming sessions that involved the use of technology, sexual abuse, torture, drugs, and a host of other methodologies.

In the United States, about 5% of the population, or about 15 million people, are specifically programmed. These people are also known as "sleepers," "Monarchs," and/or "sex-slaves." As you read, please keep in mind that the purpose of this book is to demonstrate case studies and their deprogramming. Deprogramming is a slow and tedious process that is like an archeological dig. You cannot just stick the shovel in the ground because you might damage something. You need to slowly brush away and release each little layer until the buried artifacts and treasures are revealed. Only then can they be saved intact and preserved.

In deprogramming, each layer of the control system must be carefully examined, cleaned, and merged back into the original personality so that the end result is a whole and cohesively functioning total human being with all the faculties, memories, and mind-patterns operating perfectly. This is the goal of what I do.

Alters are surfacing in many programmed people. Some lead to suicide programming and other functions that are malevolent. If you can consciously download the programming before it is externally triggered, then you can effectively preclude the programmed functions from occurring, thus giving the individual back control of his/her own life. When programs are triggered, the individual learns to recognize the switch or the anomaly. He/she is then able to work on merging this back into the original personality, which is really centered at the reptilian brainstem before feeding into the left and right hemispheres of the brain.

Working within a programming cube of 2,197 compartments is a formidable task. One must be patient and truly willing to work on the process until completion. Completion which may not even occur in this lifetime, depends upon how old one is when the deprogramming process begins.

In the following section are stories written by individuals who are specifically programmed and have worked with me in deprogramming themselves. The stories are in their own words and are presented as an example of the various types of programming nuances that can exist.

Case #1
Stalker Programming

My soul-personality chose to be born to a twenty-one year old woman whose cultural and genetic background is Germanic. Her mother's paternal family emigrated from Lippstadt, Germany before the U.S. Civil War, at which time their name was changed because they were attempting to escape the repercussions of a family member leaving the clergy for marriage and wanted a better, new life.

They lived in a small, rural community forty miles away from a major American city, where my great-grandparents together started and toiled to support their family on a small, growing dairy farm until the Influenza Pandemic in 1917 took my great-grandmother's life at age forty-two, when her two young daughters were ages nine and seven. So devastating was the loss to my great-grandfather that his family and farm never fully recovered, requiring his mother to move in to help raise the two girls until her own death a few years later.

Both of these daughters, who were my grandmother and great-aunt, were sent to the city while still teenagers to support themselves as domestic help in wealthy, private homes. Initially, they were placed as maids in the same home, sleeping at night in a third floor room after working long days of manually scrubbing clothing on a washboard, cleaning house, cooking, and taking care of the three small children. Little did they realize that almost forty years later, my grandmother and mother would together buy and move into a home just two doors to the east from the very same house that my grandmother and her sister first worked, to raise my brother and I when we were ages seven and eight.

It was during a visit back home to the farm that my grandmother, then in her mid-twenties, met her future husband at the home of a neighbor, and married a short time later. He also lived in the same big city, but was visiting family friends during a weekend getaway when they were introduced. He, too, had lost his mother, who died from being given too much ether in surgery.

My grandfather's background was that of growing up in a well-to-do household presided over by his uncle, who ran a very successful, family owned, industrial metal plating business. My grandfather's father died at a young age, and his three small children and surviving spouse all lived in the same large home with her brother's family. This branch of the family tree had emigrated from Hanover and Osnabruck, Germany in the mid-1800s and traveled back and forth to visit relatives until the outbreak of World War I.

Following his mother's death in the 1920s, my grandfather's sister and brother allied themselves with cousins to deprive, by illegal means, my grandfather's rightful ownership share of the factory; while finding a way to make him financially responsible for all the funeral and hospital expenses of his mother. So deeply overwhelmed with grief regarding his mother's avoidable death and the betrayal by his siblings and cousins, that even after marriage in the early 1930s he could not find the consistent inner strength to deal effectively with the challenges of everyday life. The Great Depression wiped out most of what he owned, except for his small city row house. Employment for my grandfather was not steady, forcing my grandmother to find work in department store sales when their only daughter was old enough to be home alone.

My maternal grandparents shared the commonalties of culture, heritage, and the tragic loss of each of their mothers, who both had the same first name. Their only child, a daughter, was named after her two grandmothers, who also both had identical twin sisters.

The cycle of similar family tragedy repeated itself years later when this daughter, who is my mother, was given little hope to survive double pneumonia when I was age six and my brother was age five. It was during this illness that my father moved out; and my maternal grandfather died from a massive heart-attack following a meeting discussion at the home of my paternal grandparents regarding their son's thoughtless treatment of my mother.

The last words that my mother heard from her father while she lay sick in bed was, "Mrs. — is a real Hell cat, but, don't worry, it's all going to work out." Mother never saw her father again, as he collapsed hours later and died within days in a hospital ward. Despite her severe illness, mother attended the funeral and burial on a bitterly cold winter day. With the help of prayer and sheer willpower, mother's precariously fragile condition slowly reversed and her health returned in the ensuing months, insuring the well-being of her sons in her care.

What helped mother transcend her meager childhood was her steadfast belief in metaphysical thinking that embraced healing, and living life without limitations. Her own mother had a physical healing in her thirties through prayer for a female condition that her doctors said could only be corrected by surgery; and her father was permanently healed of smoking following his reading of literature embracing the idea that man's true spiritual identity meant at-one-ment with God. These spiritual beliefs were also shared by mother's future husband and his family.

At a time when medical science had fewer answers, her future father-in-law was healed of tuberculosis in his youth by changing and realigning his mind-patterns; and his resulting recovery to health could not be explained by his physicians, who advised his family that his death was almost certain. His recovery caused his young wife to leave the Roman Catholic Church and rebuff the reactive harassment and threats of damnation from her parish priests who demanded her return.

Mother was born with the beauty and looks of a model. Her blonde hair, vivid green eyes, and classical Aryan features won her first place in a major, region-wide baby contest sponsored by the city's largest and most influential newspaper. In high school, while being a tom-boy at heart and the only girl talented enough to be allowed to play baseball with the boys, she served on the Fashion Board of a large, respected department store, having many modeling assignments for a number of high-end retailers that included Saks Fifth Avenue. She grew up in the era of Elvis Presley and Gloria Steinem, and her goal upon graduating from public high school a year early was to earn and save enough money from her lucrative hourly job as a book keeper at the union headquarters to relocate to California and attend the Sunset Boulevard campus of UCLA.

Mother was literally bumped into by the man who was going to be my father, forever changing her life direction. He was walking and talking, and not looking; and after being knocked almost to the floor, mother was asked to go out on a date. Together they looked like a Hollywood duo meant for the top billing and bright lights on a theater marquee. She was five-feet six and he was six-feet with black hair and the dashing looks of a screen star. There was a magnetism that brought a thirty-four year old man from a socially prominent family with a twenty year old girl whose life was molded by the school of hard knocks, but having a strong, innate drive to accept all the good that life had to offer, and having a flair and appreciation for culture and fine living.

My father asked his future father-in-law, a fellow Freemason, for permission to marry his daughter after knowing her six months, despite the concerns from his family who perceived my mother as merely a social and intellectual inferior. His older sister had married the son of the president of a very large, multi-national oil company living at the Waldorf-Astoria; his older brother married a daughter of a legendary leader in baseball; and another sister was engaged to marry a Harvard-educated professor of international law. My father's hope and expectation was that this marriage was the right decision, having a year earlier canceled an engagement a couple weeks before the wedding; a threat that was made again to my mother shortly before she was married, because he was again having second thoughts.

My father was born the last of four children following the years immediately after World War I into a family that had earned its wealth from metal stamping and fabrication. My paternal grandfather, while in his twenties, took over the helm of the family business founded in the 1870s by his father, and run by his savvy mother because of the untimely and premature death of her young husband. It was under my grandfather's direction that their factories made the first mass-produced state automobile license plates in the years following the invention of the horseless carriage.

With the cooperation and assistance of state officials, prison labor was coordinated to do the finishing process for most of North America's license plate needs. My father claims that this was possibly the first large-scale usage of prison labor in the U.S. to benefit U.S. commercial and government purposes. During World War II the same factories made mess kits for soldiers, and fabricated parts for vending machines in the 1950s.

My father's background is Welsh, Irish, and English. His mother commissioned a genealogy tracing the family tree to America's founding fathers, U.S. presidents, and the British Royal Family. Their family residence was in a well-known neighborhood of impressively large and stately homes that had one of the world's largest concentration of wealth in the years surrounding the turn of the nineteenth century. They had a full-time household staff comprising of cooks, maids, and a chauffeur. The home's large entrance hall had a grandfather's clock over six feet tall that reached up to the massive stairway landing level where my father and his siblings would like the daring thrill of climbing over the handrail and standing on top of the clock's flat surface, while maintaining their balance.

The succession of nannies employed to help with the care for the children learned quickly of the "sport" directed their way and the carefree lifestyle having little regard for cost . Once, on a family trip to Atlantic City in the Packard limousine, the children so incessantly made fun of the nanny's uneducated diction and stuck her with so many pins, she had to be rescued by being sent home by my grandparents. When my father was in his early teens he went out to the carriage house, got into the limousine, started the engine, put the car in reverse; and slammed hard on the accelerator to lunge the car speeding backwards, wrecking the driver's open door and demolishing the back half of the car, while taking out his home's large back door porch. During winter, rides on snow sleds were made a little more exciting by racing down hills instead on large, silver banquet trays.

My father had a nervous habit of taking a long, metal rod and hitting the leather couch in the family room while alone and conversing with others; the result of which, over time, was a gashing, gaping hole, that was finally patched in scarlet red fabric. Violin lessons for my father in his youth ceased when his Italian teacher, out of unbearable frustration for his young student's smart mouth and refusal to practice, pulled especially hard on my father's fingers to correct their misplacement; only to get in return a fast fist in the teacher's face. What would possibly be considered a little unusual and unexpected is that all of these stories and behaviors were greeted and enjoyed by these children and the parents.

My paternal grandfather was tall at over six-feet three, having the demeanor, personality, and appearance of a cross between Hollywood director Alfred Hitchcock and Lurch, the stiff butler from the 1960s television show, "The Addams Family." He took a kind of sadistic pleasure in getting my brother and I screaming in protest in response to his calling us "the little girls". Whenever we visited, my mother's attempt to calm us down by telling us to just ignore the teasing, was something neither my brother nor I could comprehend in our three and four year-old heads; and my attempts to correct my grandfather's taunting and get him to change his words was always responded to with even more teasing and name-calling.

I took special pleasure on one particular Sunday afternoon visit when I saw my three-year-old brother climb up on to the seat of my grandfather's large wing chair, upon which no one other than my grandfather was allowed to ever sit. When my grandfather saw that my brother was sitting on his chair, he walked over, reached out his long arms as if to simply shake hands, pulled off my brother quickly, sat down, and then yelled. My brother, in all his toddler wisdom had taken the occasion as a once-in-a-lifetime opportunity to empty his very full bladder to saturate the down feather cushion with warm urine. My grandfather had to be physically blocked by my father, grandmother, and aunt; all of whom were biting their lips to prevent hysterical laughing out loud, so that he could not take revenge.

To this day I don't know why my paternal grandfather was called, "Grand Rox," unless it was perhaps a possible reference and description of certain body parts. Fortunately for me, the paternal male, family genetic trait of not being able to easily smile is something I have never experienced, as my smile and laughter is remembered by all who meet me

Affection, hugging, touching was not something commonly demonstrated to my father and his siblings by his parents. Compliments, when verbalized, were often accompanied with a teasing put-down remark. However, world affairs, politics, cultural and current events were topics of discussion during formal meals served by attentive kitchen help. Two scoops of vanilla ice cream topped with chocolate sauce, called "Black and White", was served every evening as one of the choices for dessert. Guests not on the same playing field to return the volley of discussions at the table with the same aggressiveness and thought, were at risk of being made into a mincemeat of subtle forms of verbal put-downs and humiliation; and my mother, who was quiet, timid, young, and in an overwhelmingly foreign culture to her own, became an instant target, not receiving any help, consideration, or verbal protection from my father; because he shared in the same sport and humor.

Mother was treated in her marriage like a maid, having strict instructions regarding her household duties and chores, including the mandatory closing of the draperies prior to my father's arrival back home in the evening; along with the requirement that dinner be prepared and be waiting for serving. There was also a directive that my brother and I were to be seen and not heard at the table. Only mother saw to the needs of my brother and I, and if circumstances or scheduling prevented mother from preparing dinner, we went out to white tablecloth restaurants; which happened at least once or twice a week.

In addition to the list of expectations required for her to fulfill at home, mother had the duties of volunteer work in the community to benefit the family name and reputation, as demanded by her father-in-law. She juggled the home life of caring for two small boys, with chairing the junior division of the symphony orchestra, volunteering at the historical society, and doing the decorating for social events at her city club that had the notoriety of being listed in "The Social Register."

Despite working daily from morning to late at night, mother was blamed as being the source for all of my father's problems, including his lack of any business success. The fact that my father did almost nothing productive was a fact that he wasn't able to see as the possible cause. My mother soon had bleeding stomach ulcers and a complete inability to change her treatment by my father, despite frequent discussions with my father ending in loud arguments without resolution that I quietly listened to from the top of the stairs on the second floor, or from my room where I pretended to be sleeping.

Mother sought a marital separation because being stepped on every day like a doormat was no longer tolerable. My paternal grandparents thought that by stopping payment for private pre-school for my brother and I, forcing our withdrawal, would be the kind of pressure that would make my mother again submissive and obedient to my father's orders. However, they were all to find out that mother's strength was greater than anticipated; along with the surprise to them that my brother and I never appeared bothered about our father's absence, as we never asked where he went or if we was going to return home.

After a couple years of unchanged behavior by my father, even in separation, mother filed for and received a divorce. Most of her "friends" disappeared during the months of the ugly proceedings. Even her attorney, who was selected to represent mother after expressing his desire to provide outstanding representation as a means for settling a grudge he had with her in-laws; double-crossed my mother by charging her higher-than-agreed-upon attorney fees, and had my father write the divorce settlement check directly to himself so that all his fees would be immediately paid first before my mother got the remaining balance.

The divorce brought my grandmother, mother, brother and I together under a different roof. Mother sold the tiny house she never wanted and bought another larger, fixer-upper three blocks away, offering each of us our own bedroom and a bigger urban yard, thanks to the fact that the adjoining lot had never been built on. Luckily for my mother, her father was the real estate agent who sold to my parents their home, and placed my mother's name as joint owner on the title, thinking that my father's verbal instruction of it being placed solely in his name was simply a joke. Upon the day of closing, my father signed the paperwork stating equal co-ownership, too embarrassed to have it changed back to what he originally intended, but very angry. This single action by my maternal grandfather helped my mother to be awarded sole ownership of the house; making it possible to trade it after the divorce settlement for a home better suited to our changing needs.

In the divorce settlement, mother was awarded a small monthly amount for child support because my father had no employment; and my father's share from the sale of the family business conveniently wound up in a trust fund account set up by his parents who told my father that they were doing this only to prevent my mother from getting any of his money. The viciousness and resentment for having to go through the divorce resulted in my father attempting to make life miserable for my mother by having little visible financial means. Every verbalized need that my brother or I expressed was given the standard response of, "That's up to your mother, because this is what she wanted."

Gifts for Christmas and birthdays were another matter. Presents were stacked high at the home of my paternal grandparents; and gifts from my father were fun and frivolous and not there to address the daily requirements for living. Several years later, though, private school education was resumed by my father, which was gratefully accepted and appreciated by my brother and I. When my father's family and social circle found out that we were attending a city public school where the academics were minimal, and the racially provoked fights were daily, the cost to my father's personal embarrassment and prestige for allowing this was greater than the financial price of "somehow" finding the money for paying tuition.

On the exact third anniversary date of my maternal grand father's abrupt and unexpected death, my paternal grandmother died. My mother, grandmother, brother and I found out only after her memorial service, and we believe that it was intended that we not know or attend. It was my paternal grandmother who had instructed her son, my father, to knock on my maternal grandmother's door and try to hand her an envelope following the sudden death of her husband after his "in-law discussion." My maternal grandmother responded by saying to my father that she would gladly scrub floors for the rest of her life than to accept a dime of their money, and then shut the door in his face.

About three years later, we only found out about the death and the scheduled memorial service of my paternal grandfather, "Grand Rox," because a family friend called to inform us. My mother, brother and I attended and sat in the chapel on the few remaining seats on the last row of the packed auditorium, and silently watched as my father, uncles, aunts, and cousins walked in at the appointed time to take their reserved seats in the front row. I was about nine years old and as I listened to the scriptural readings I wondered what I had done to not be considered worthy enough to be told of my grandfather's death by my family; and wondered what had I done to be excluded from sitting with my father. It was ironic that the only two blood-line grandsons to carry on the proud family name of the deceased were treated as outcasts. I will never forget the looks of people who avoided our eye contact or said nothing to the three of us following the service, because it appeared to me that our attendance at the funeral and our very existence was intentionally placed on a level of illegitimacy.

Even today, after all these years of my father's inability to share of himself and initiate more than a superficial participation in our lives, there remains a void. Our infrequent get-togethers, only a result of an effort put forth by my brother and I, often serve to re-confirm that emptiness and force us to look at all his wasted years.

Actions speak louder than words when finding out after his lady friends, each of my father's last three hospitalizations; and we have sadly relegated his infrequent presence and involvement in our lives as being a reflection of his own self-imposed irrelevance. The issues of our abandonment are still perplexing as is the nagging wish that he and other family members could have been different, thus avoiding the heartache and tears. Acceptance of people for who and what they are, and the act of being able to completely forgive what I saw and experienced, remains a struggle.

Born exactly mid-year, I share the same name day with Princess Diana and actor Dan Aykroyd. A tarot card reader told me a couple years ago at a party that I was born wise, knowing all the secrets; which is a pretty accurate truth about many things while I was growing up. In trying to understand during childhood the confusion all around me, I quietly listened, observed, pieced together what was happening; not letting on to anyone else my understanding, and keeping it all hidden inside.

Despite my mother's intention that my brother and I not be told about the nature of her serious illness and its prognosis, my grandfather's sudden death, the behaviors of my father, and the insufficiency of the child support checks, I understood much on my own. After partially grasping the magnitude of many issues, it was simply not as interesting to play with toys and other children my own age. I saw that being an adult offered so much more, which is why I wanted instead to be in their company to better understand their world and was what was going on around me, and act like them.

This accelerated level of maturity included my interest in girls at an early age. My mother was more than a little taken aback when I always wanted binoculars for Broadway shows even when having the opportunity of sitting in good seats, so I could better see all the legs and cleavage. Even in pre-school I was often in a state of arousal; and it was during this time period of when I was four or five years old I remember hiding behind a chair in the corner of a room at home, unwinding string, cutting it, and tying it around my waist and other parts of my body; all the while knowing it was of a sexual nature.

It was also during this time frame that I heard my name called out to me by an unfamiliar male voice coming from nowhere in my quiet bedroom at night, when everyone else was sleeping; and even thought that it could be from God. The following morning I told my mother, "An angel spoke to me last night," a comment which I could tell was dismissed as quickly as it was heard. Being often uncomfortable and scared of the night started at a young age, and I often covered my face with the top sheet which allowed me to relax and go to sleep faster. This action on my part was always corrected by my grandmother who quickly uncovered my face when she observed this behavior.

Watching "The Rocky and Bullwinkle" cartoon on television was a daily pastime; and my brother, even today, remembers and repeats the show's Mr. Wizard, who said something like, " Drizzle Drazzle, Drizzle Drome, Time for THIS ONE, to GO HOME!" while the wizard waved his magical wand.

When in grade school I was frequently ill with earaches and other childhood maladies. In the fourth grade I was taking for over a week a prescription from an ear doctor that caused me to sleep excessively, where I was effectively knocked out upon arrival at home from school until the next morning. Mother's complaints to the doctor finally elicited a change in the medications and an admission by the office nurse that I was mistakenly given adult dosages. It struck us as unusual that this change in drugs came days after the doctor was told by my mother that something different had to be prescribed because I was acting strangely at night and was even crawling on the floors.

It was also in the fourth grade that I got my childhood inoculations and shots; and the resulting high fevers and sickness forced my missing at least another two more weeks of school. Seeing needles, smelling the rubbing alcohol, and receiving shots at the doctor's office caused me to go into shock and faint on more than one occasion. Even today, I faint from blood tests and get light headed from being in a medical environment like an ER where there is bodily trauma, despite not feeling or experiencing pain myself.

All during my childhood and young adult life I often felt drained of energy and not feeling much like participating in sports. Often, my thoughts and attention wandered in class in daydreaming and detachment. There were times that I could never catch up from missing the material from being absent. Mother's response to these concerns, while doing everything she could to help me at night, was to tell me that the same Mind that was drawn upon to write my textbooks, was there to answer all my homework and test questions.

The foundation quote that permeated our lives, and one that I still find to be amazing is, "The Scientific Statement of Being" by Mary Baker Eddy in "Science and Health", on page 486 that reads, "There is no life, truth, intelligence, nor substance in matter. All is infinite Mind and its infinite manifestation, for God is All-in-All. Spirit is immortal Truth; matter is mortal error. Spirit is the real and eternal; matter is the unreal and temporal. Spirit is God, and man is His image and likeness. Therefore, man is not material; he is spiritual."

During grade school I was particularly interested in current events, politics, and UFOs; and remember hearing the in-depth interview on the radio of New Yorker, Barney Hill and his wife. Both claimed to have been abducted while driving on a remote highway, taken aboard a flying saucer, and tortured during the examination by extraterrestrials. I can't explain why my reaction was that of sexual arousal when Mr. Hill described what he experienced in the way of sexual torture.

In seventh grade social studies I was asked by the teacher to sit down and cease my presentation of thoughts regarding the cover-up conspiracies of JFK, RFK, Martin Luther King, and UFOs. I learned the hard way that my peers at school were uninterested, and that adults, except for my mother and father, thought my thinking was at the minimum, out of control, imaginative, or just plain crazy. My father, for a while, was the area representative for a national, civilian UFO investigative group, and once advised me that there was definitely a secret government with an agenda; but that I needed to live my life as if this knowledge did not exist.

From fifth grade through my senior year in high school I attended and belonged to "Fortnightly" social dance groups. Most of the children of the city's elite were invited, and my inclusion was a mystery because these exclusive invitations arrived without application or any known sponsorship. Ballroom and contemporary dancing was taught, along with providing us an appropriate venue in a most exclusive, private club to improve our social skills. I really enjoyed the fast dancing and immersing myself in the rock music, along with winning record albums with my partner for learning and demonstrating our skills during the Friday night competitions. There was a part of me that enjoyed being the center of attention in front of an audience where I could demonstrate a level of achievement, and enjoy a bit of what I considered a sense of superiority.

However, my daily routine was that of being picked up by van for private school through my senior year in high school, because having a car of my own was not a financial option; as I lived in two starkly different worlds. At home, my mother and grandmother worked physically hard to earn their money in low-paying jobs to provide for my daily needs so that I had a roof over my head, clothing on my back, and food on the table. At school, the wealth and influence of the families of my classmates was significant; and the knowledge by my peers of major league sports trades and upcoming national events before the general public, was the norm. Everyone enjoyed quite a laugh when I was made the advertising manager of the yearbook, but had no car to get the ads.

I was also different because of my steadfast refusal to smoke, drink alcohol, or participate in recreational drugs. Popularity and inclusion in the fast lane lifestyle was not an option and I focused instead on doing well in school; though loneliness and low self-esteem were always issues. A grudging respect for my personal beliefs was reflected in my being elected president of the student council in my senior year, and receiving the student council senior student of the year award upon graduation.

From grade school through college there were times I would be terrified to go to sleep at night. My bedroom window faced the backyard where a deep-seated, internal fear would compel me to stand and to look out, carefully listen and to wait for something I couldn't explain. The small, narrow alley dead-ended in back of my home, which went directly into a major avenue in the city. Sometimes a car would slowly creep up the alley at night, circle in the back driveway, and then return to the street. There were evenings I would lay listening for an intruder while covering my face with the top sheet, and simply nervously wait.

During Halloween evening in my junior year in high school I gained an insight into a personal ability to focus my thoughts and produce a physical response in myself and on the object that was thought about at a distance. The CBS radio station was broadcasting a show that featured a woman claiming to be a witch, who asked the audience to concentrate their thought energy on a specific item in the studio. I decided to do what was asked, and while mentally focusing on the object with my arms and fingers outstretched and pointed in its direction, I had goose bumps all over my body and felt the energy while seeing the imaginary energy beam connect with the target. The radio host and guest asked that the audience stop what they were doing because of the vibration effect it was having. For the first time I had the first conscious glimpse into knowing that what I was mentally projecting could have an effect.

Also in high school I had a fascination and empathy for people working in the foreign service and black operations. I could see myself as a courier, and particularly liked spy novels by Robert Ludlum and others, and enjoyed movies like "Three Days of The Condor." I mentally merged with the story's protagonist.

On the first day of my first scheduled college class I chose to sit next to a total stranger who turned out to have much in common with me politically. Almost immediately we became good friends and discovered that our views and interests were very similar. We found other students with the same perspectives, and I helped with organizing a new college organization that brought conservatives together for the first time since the end of the Vietnam War, and served as club secretary. While I also shared an equal interest in going into politics, the thought of prostituting beliefs for the purpose of getting financial contributions and elected, was something that I could not overcome to pursue that endeavor. My college chum, though, is now a U.S. senator, and I had the privilege of working with him before his attendance to law school, his marriage, and conversion to "born again" Christianity.

For as long as I can remember, I have infrequent, sometimes yearly episodes at night where it feels like there is an attempt to knock me out of my body. In the hours between 2 and 4 am I wake up in a state of spatial distortion and bodily numbness, along with a feeling of all-encompassing weight. One way or another, though, I have found methods to recover myself; sometimes taking a couple hours. There have been times where I have stared at my face in a mirror not always seeing my reflection, or being unable to recognize who was staring back. Moving my eyes rapidly, or patiently staring into my pupils has brought back into focus who I really am, and the associated mental distortions slowly pass.

Another lifelong condition is the difficulty, on occasion, in swallowing food as it goes down my throat past a certain point. Sometimes the food collects, without proceeding downwards any farther, requiring me to gag and expunge it back out. It's an unpleasant process that can take a while and leave me unable to eat any more food. While it's definitely uncomfortable, it's more scary for an onlooker to see than it is dangerous for me to experience.

Through the years I have had dreams that are particularly memorable that I feel are important enough to share. In the first dream, which occurred many years ago, I am without clothes and engaged in the act of providing oral sex to an unknown male who is lying down on an elevated platform, whose age is similar but whose face I don't see. The dream's next sequence is where I am presented a piece of tin foil by another person, on which is the severed penis that has been baked. I am told to eat it, and my response was to gag and want to throw up. The intensity of what has happened caused me to wake up in a cold sweat and wonder how I could have dreamt this.

The next dream was more recent and is more brief. I am standing at a urinal, and a high profile, well-known son of a nationally known, late politician is standing close by and watching me without saying a word. What is interesting is that I have no recollection of ever meeting this person, even though we have been together at large social functions; and he happens to live within a mile of my house.

The third dream was in the past year, during a full moon, where I suddenly find myself without clothes, kneeling, and providing oral sex to a member of the British Royal Family; who is standing in front of me. Behind him are mirrors, and above the mirrors is a small, red blinking light. This dream happened before the rumors and allegations involving Charles, and is a something I never would have thought up on my own.

What make these three dreams particularly memorable is their vividness in detail and "reality"; plus, interesting because I would not classify myself as being Gay.

Issues of abandonment, self-esteem, fear, have been an on-again off-again struggle since childhood; and there have been times when the internal, negative dialog has caused sadness, bouts of brief depression, and the inability to assert myself when required. There have also been periods when nothing could impair my happiness or ability to achieve personal and career goals. Unfortunately, the times when I was unable to handle the sabotage of self-doubt has cost me a number of deserved promotions, and attracted my willing acceptance of poor treatment in my personal and professional life.

Being able to better handle the negativity, personal insecurities, and better understand my life by helping connect the dots of the big picture; I owe to finding Stewart Swerdlow. I was in my office at work behind a closed door when a strong, voice-like thought came to me and said to go on the Internet and look up "The Philadelphia Experiment." Of course I knew the story, but was compelled to closely read all the entries on Al Bielek's web page.

The stories of Al Bielek, Duncan Cameron, Preston Nichols, and Stewart Swerdlow were all very interesting; but, I was drawn like a magnet to Stewart. After finding Stewart's own web site and reading its entire contents I bought his Montauk book and began sending him e-mail questions that he personally answered in a direct and friendly way. I was so impressed and moved by his life that I set up a consultation, along with having him do my own personal archetype, and in-depth name analysis. Because of his full schedule I had to wait about two months, even though I was very anxious to talk with him and get his assessment of my health and life.

During the initial consultation I was a bit nervous about talking to him on the phone regarding personal subjects, given the unusual manner that I found him. However, I had an innate trust that it was what I had to do. After the small talk, Stewart did a scan and analysis of my chakras, and provided good recommendations on how to improve my health. All was going as expected until he started to discuss my archetype and my name analysis.

I was totally unprepared for the discussion that followed, and to say that my head was spinning was an understatement. The bombshell that exploded was hearing that I had been programmed; my family belonged to the Committee of 300; I had been sexually abused as a child in rituals; I was at Montauk; that Stewart and I had known each other since childhood from shared experience in this lifetime; and finding Stewart at that time was what I had been programmed many years before, to do!!! It took many more subsequent consultations and personal proof to comprehend what he said, and finally conclude that it was all true.

Any lingering doubts were put to rest when Stewart recognized me from a picture that I sent to him of myself; and a second confirmation came two months later at the Montauk Symposium, days after 9/11/01. I rented a car to get to Vermont because all flights had been canceled, and not attending the event was allowing the thought of victimization to triumph. I was also very excited to have the opportunity to meet Stewart in person, as I had received from him two clear mental transmissions about the event and the probability of seeing other people who knew me from Montauk. Just experiencing first hand my telepathic capability was an amazing confirmation of all that I would learn at the conference and in his incredible, future seminars.

Stewart and his family were wonderful in person, and Janet proved to be an important and dynamic speaker at the symposium event. The wonderful surprise for me, however, was taking my driver's license photo when I was seventeen up to Duncan Cameron, and getting a curious request by him to look at the back of my head. After turning around, Duncan said that he remembered me, and started to cry. I ran over to tell Stewart, and I started to cry, too; because I knew that Duncan was correct, and I felt the connection.

That evening, Duncan came over to me to speak, and surges of energy went through my body from my feet, through my arms, hands, fingers, and up through my head. Duncan stopped our conversation and started pressing the tops of my shoes out of concern that the energy pulsating through my body was resulting in my "flying too high," as Duncan put it. I told him that I was fine and that the pulses of energy were an amazing rush. We must have spoken a couple hours that night, all the while I was thinking how incredibly fortunate it was to be able to find another clue to my own life experience puzzle.

My consultations and seminars with Stewart have helped me get so much stronger, confident, and understand our true capabilities and galactic origins. I have come a far way from a sense of hopeless abandon during our first consultation, to better understand myself and the world; and the means to surpass the rising tide of negativity being thrust on us all. Anyone reading Stewart's material for the first time and thinking seriously about buying a tape or attending a seminar, needs to know that the forces and hidden persuaders in the world that are there to re-mold our thinking and lives is far greater and more powerful than imaginable. The only real hope that we all have is to elevate our thinking and learn how to protect and provide for ourselves, and tap into the infinite wisdom of the God-Mind for every need. It's not easy, nor for the faint of heart; but those who are open to seeing themselves and the world from a different perspective; and actively pursue this knowledge, will see the many benefits in their own lives.

My heartfelt thanks and love go to Stewart and Janet for their help, support, patience, and work; and for the knowledge that Stewart will always be an important part of my life.

Case #1 Analysis
Stalker Programming

When I first saw the name of this gentleman on the email he sent to me, I immediately recognized the programming energy with the Montauk Project flare. At first he was a bit belligerent, which is common amongst survivors of invasive mind-control experiments. At times, it can be difficult for the counselor/deprogrammer to maintain an emotional balance when this occurs.

After some initial emails back and forth, we began our work over the Internet and via telephone. This is an ongoing process which can take many years. It helps when you have an individual, such as this person, who is eager and willing to do what it takes to see it through.

As with all people new to deprogramming, the process must start slowly. I expected the usual sabotage and self-denigration to arise, and it did from time to time. Patience is paramount during these periods for both parties involved.

I quickly determined, based on his memories and mannerisms, that he was a survivor of Montauk, or a Montauk-related mind-control project with heavy emphasis on sexual ritual and male Monarch programming.

In such cases, deprogramming often brings up the reliving of physical symptoms such as nausea, choking, pain in the body, headaches, sexual stimulation, nightmares, and anxiety, to name a few.

Over weeks and months we began to slowly retrieve memories of events and programming sessions that revealed more specifically the functions that this person had programmed into him. His primary functions centered around Sexual Magick Rituals involving mostly other males. This implied male Monarch programming which can be deprogrammed via placing the image of a Monarch Butterfly at the pineal gland to observe whatever comes into the conscious mind. Once awareness is established, everything must be flushed with violet. Finally, this information must be merged back into the Original Soul-Personality using the Brown Merger Archetype.

Because of the relationship that this man has with his mother, and because he has a photographic memory of anywhere he has been, there was evidence of Stalker Programming. This type of function is extremely important to the Illuminati for spying purposes.

With this programming, a person can walk into a room for only a brief moment and then weeks later completely relay with exact accuracy everything that occurred, including the contents of the room, detailed descriptions of the designs, furniture, temperature, who was there, what was said, clothing worn by all present, events leading up to the scenes in the room, etc.

The same holds true for casual conversations. A "stalker" slave can sit next to a person at a dinner party and many years later recall the exact conversation. He/she can tell you everything about the other person, including family history, work experience, finances, and personal relationships. This is truly a remarkable ability that is based on a high IQ level and a social standing that enables the "stalker" to mingle in important circles of upper eschelon society. The individual above happens to live in an exclusive area, attends elite socialite parties, and has vast knowledge of everyone/everything he meets/sees.

This male is successfully deprogramming. He is very energetic and motivated in this process. Occasionally he suffers from bouts of depression as is normal during this process, but continues to move forward no matter what happens in his inner level work.

It is common for a male "stalker" to believe that he is gay or bisexual. This sexual orientation is extremely helpful when attempting to find out or gather information on others, or from groups of people. In this way, there is a versatility in relationships that enables the "stalker" to access all different types of people. He can fit in with any social group and maintains a high level of awareness and observation.

As you can read from the person's story in his own words, there is great detail to minutia. He can often go on tangents away from the main storyline. This is purposely placed in the programming so that if the handler or controller are questioning a particular person or detail from the "stalker," he is able to go follow another line of information without skipping a beat.

For example, if the "stalker" relays information about a person and that person's friend is mentioned, the line of questioning can focus on this piece of seemingly innocuous information leading to details of the friend's life, family history, etc.

The "stalker" is like having a live computer program online. You simply click on whatever information you want detailed and the information is there. Every piece of data, no matter how small or insignificant it may seem, is available to be downloaded and regurgitated by the "stalker."

Most of the time, the "stalker" does not consciously remember all these details that he carries within himself. He must be triggered into a line of thinking for the process to unravel.

Often, even for the handlers and controllers receiving the information, the "stalker" needs to be refocused and kept on track. Otherwise, the listeners would have to wade through a ton of superfluous information to get to the reason of the "stalker's" mission for that particular event.

It is my observation through the years of various persons with stalker programming, that the females tend to be very overweight and extremely opinionated. However, both the male and female "stalkers" have a tendency to be physically unfit and emotionally needy. Most enjoy sexual activity and would like to have an intimate relationship. Yet, they have a difficult time maintaining a relationship outside of their immediate families.

The "stalker" tends to have a heavy laugh, sometimes annoying to others, yet everyone loves them and considers them to be kind, generous, and trustworthy. Now, this is an important factor as it is the trust aspect of the Stalker that enables others to open up to them and allows "stalkers" to access personal environments and residences. Then the "stalker" is able to download every bit of information as if the person and his/her surroundings under observation being minutely dissected and each tiny part catalogued.

As a side-effect, the "stalker" tends to be highly critical of others, have a sensitive personality that is easily hurt, and absolutely must be in charge of any projects in the home or office, or anywhere else if possible.

Because the "stalker" likes the finer things in life, he/she is always renovating his/her home, and making recommendations to others along those lines. They tend to be collectors of such things as fine art, rare books, and antiquities, and they love fancy clothing.

With a deep appreciation and intense knowledge of the material world, the "stalker" finds it easy to observe and comment on all that he/she sees. This is one reason that he/she appears to be highly critical by others. In reality, he/she is extremely observant without missing a beat, and can easily objectively compare people, places, and things from a variety of strata.

A side-effect of this type of programming, because it is so intense, is that the "stalker" often has digestive issues with a tendency to overeat. The "stalkers" may become ill easily. Medicines do not have a strong impact on them. It is almost as if they are not designed to live long lives as they are obviously a liability with all that they know and observe. Plus, how much information can one "container" carry?

One danger the "stalker" faces as he/she ages and is used less, is that much of the programming breaks through to the conscious mind. This can create difficulties for the "stalker" in everyday life situations. He/she may find him/herself unable to focus on daily life as he/she constantly observes and goes off on tangents.

Ultimately, there can be an overload in the brain, causing a mental and emotional collapse. The "stalker" could even be placed in a mental institution. Or, it may be necessary to live with the mother or other close relatives who take care of him/her, taking care of life's necessities and responsibilities.

The individual in this example is doing rather well, but does still display manifestations of these conditions. He is diligently attempting to break free of the mother's control, but falls back due to lack of financial independence and circumstances involving home renovations and illness.

The "stalker" often feels alone and lonely. This is a trap leading into depression that can cause a lapse in deprogramming. Excuses are made for not continuing with the momentum of the deprogramming. If this continues, he/she will find him/herself back where he/she started.

Any deprogrammer working with a "stalker" should work face to face as often as possible and give strong encouragement at all times. The "stalker" needs to be desensitized to details and planning, as well as encouraged to take chances with a new and different lifestyle.

The best idea in deprogramming for such individuals, male or female, is a physical move to another geographic location. The geographic location should always be one that fits the energy of the "stalker" so that the Original Soul-Personality is able to strengthen and flourish.

Case #2
Presidential Model Programming

)—(I was born and raised on the outskirts of Baltimore in a small waterfront community near the western shore of the Chesapeake Bay. Bordered by the Gunpowder Falls State Park and the military installation of Aberdeen Proving Grounds, my family has resided in this area for well over fifty years. Growing up in this ecologically rich and diverse environment, the days of my youth were spent with family and friends enjoying all the recreational opportunities the area had to offer.

I was very fortunate to be living in a community where every day seemed as if I were on a perpetual and never ending vacation. I was truly blessed to have loving parents, an older brother, and a wonderful uncle that doted upon me as if I were his own. This fabulous existence was made complete with my grandparents living next door, and the frequent visits by my many relatives. In fact, for a brief period in the 1960's, my mother's siblings and their families lived directly across the street from us on property owned by my grandparents. Life could not have been more ideal.

It wasn't until many years later that I learned this idyllic childhood of mine was more sinister and evil than anything I could ever have imagined. I was merely lead to believe I lived an abundant and charmed life, but in reality it could not have been further from the truth. It was the betrayal of those closest to me that helped create the total mind-controlled and programmed multiple I am today. Through the insidious manipulation of trauma-based conditioning, I was able to totally dissociate all thought processes, and hence all aspects of both my inner and outer worlds. All that I had trusted and believed in suddenly ceased to exist. In lieu of the one reality I had always known, there were now 2,197 different realities incorporated into the world of my programmed matrix. In the construct of this matrix live each of my alters, programmed by an ingeniously perfected system of torture and trauma-based conditioning to permanently split my consciousness through a process of total dissociation.

Growing up in the mid 1950's and 60's, many fun-filled hours were spent being entertained by the popular television shows of the time. "I Dream of Jeannie," "Bewitched," and the science fiction genre of "Star Trek" were a few of my favorites. I thoroughly enjoyed these purely fictional characters and other worldly themes. It wasn't until many years later that I learned these shows were based more in truth than fiction. In fact, it was the Star Trek movie "Nemesis" that prompted me to seek out Stewart Swerdlow for a consultation in the winter of 2002, and suddenly realize that my life as I had known it never truly existed. Instead, I found it to be a manufactured fairy tale used to control and manipulate the mind-patterns of those attracted to this world of trauma-based programming and mind-control. It wasn't until my first consultation with Stewart, that I learned the truth behind my existence and the subsequent revelations that followed. Suddenly a light went off in my head allowing me to find answers to questions that have eluded me for years. Finally, the pieces of the puzzle began to fall into place.

The period between 2000 and 2002 had been one of the most stressful and trying times of my life. My daughter revealed in the winter of 2001, that her father had been abusing her for many years. Suspecting the abuse since early childhood, I attempted to restrict contact between the two of them through the judicial system, although it was to no avail. In August of 1997, the Circuit Court of Maryland gave him unsupervised visitation, thereby allowing overnight visits with my daughter in Maryland and in his home state of Texas. Little did I know at the time there was nothing I could have done to prevent my daughter from being abused. Unbeknownst to me, we were pawns of a legal system that deliberately manipulated and sanctioned the abuse of innocent children to further facilitate the Illuminati's agenda.

The toll it took on both of us was tremendous. My daughter was admitted six times within an eight-month period to the Sheppard Pratt Hospital (a renowned mental health institution) for severe depression and attempted suicide. It nearly destroyed us both, and our relationship. She was diagnosed with more mental and emotional disorders than I could possibly remember. With each admission there was yet another disorder uncovered in an attempt to explain her emotional and psychological deterioration. The likelihood of a recovery seemed hopeless by every passing day. Medication was the treatment of choice only adding to the severity of her illness. We were both at one of the lowest ebbs of our lives, with no apparent relief in sight. I was losing my child and I did not know what to do. It was only a matter of time before I would have to place her in the custody of the state, to be housed in a residential treatment center for the protection of us both. All appeared to be lost.

I didn't think life could get much worse, but I was wrong. During this difficult period I started to experience sensations throughout my body that I could not comprehend. Unexplained waves of energy would radiate up and down my entire body with such intensity, that at times I thought I would go out of my mind. I could not understand what was happening to me, but whatever the cause I knew there was no cure utilizing traditional modalities. I began consulting psychics for answers in an attempt to determine the cause of my discomfort, although this resulted in merely limited success. There was only one woman I contacted that could even put a name to the reaction I was experiencing. She thought this to be a kundalini activation, which meant that the chakra centers along my spinal column were beginning to open, thus creating the undulating waves of energy I felt throughout my entire body. That is the only answer I received, at least it was something or so I thought.

During this time I also began to develop a heightened level of psychic ability and intuition. This intuition allowed me to see and feel things that I never previously imagined were possible. The degree to which this happened was astonishing. I even experienced the role of a medium, in which the deceased would contact me to relay messages to their surviving friends and loved ones. The information was very accurate, and targeted so specifically for the receiver, that it's source was never questioned. I didn't realize until speaking with Stewart that these messages emanated from satellite transmissions, and were designed to deceive and manipulate me in order to perpetuate my programming.

Coinciding with the above, I also started to have very clear visions of my body astral projecting to a cloistered monastery in Tibet. It all seemed so real I actually felt as if I were being transported physically to a remote location in China's Himalayan Mountains. I could accurately describe in detail being in the presence of Buddhist monks seated in front of an open fire and wearing their traditional red robes as they spoke to me. In one of the visions I was lead to an open doorway by two of the monks. Each of the men held one of my outstretched arms as they accompanied me towards a very large set of open double wooden doors. Upon reaching the doorway, we continued walking forward until we were outside the monastery. Instead of stepping onto solid ground, we hovered in mid-air high above the mountain range below, almost touching the white clouds surrounding us. The monks then let go of my arms so I could be freely suspended without support, and unrestrained to feel the pure exhilaration of the moment. It was incredible, and so realistic were the physical sensations I experienced, it felt as if I were truly there. If anything, it was a respite from seeing my dear child going through a living hell of her own.

It wasn't until one rather frightening astral trip, that I realized I was being artificially manipulated to experience the event that had previously taken place. During one of these episodes I appeared before a council of monks in the monastery. One of the leaders told me I was to listen to him and no other, for only he would tell me the truth and never lead me astray." Immediately I knew something was wrong and quickly came out of the meditation, never attempting it again. I didn't fully understand what I had experienced, although I knew it was not merely a respite from my troubles. Instead, it was my first real glimpse into the darkly sinister realm of programming, and my family's role in the Illuminati's New World Order.

The first I heard of the New World Order was through my brother who attempted to make me aware of the existence of shapeshifting Reptilians and the Illuminati's plan for total world domination through implementation of their diabolical and Satanic agenda. Although I listened to him with an open mind on most subjects, when it came to believing the world was enslaved by a Reptilian race I quickly tuned him out. This however, did not last for long.

It was my brother that introduced me to Stewart and Janet's website with the hopes of finding a solution to the turmoil my daughter and I were going through. He encouraged me to contact Stewart for many months before I made that first call, however I refused to listen to him. I was convinced my daughter had the same mood disorder as her father, and that it would just take time for her to heal emotionally and psychologically from the trauma she had endured. The proper mix of therapy and medication was all that was necessary to put her on the road to recovery. I had enough to worry about, so a hybrid race of Reptilians controlling the Earth was not at the top of my priority list.

That may have been my view until I read Janet Swerdlow's article on "Specific Programming." It piqued my interest immensely. I felt Janet had used my daughter as the role model for her description of a specifically programmed person. It was amazing, absolutely amazing, how accurately Janet described my daughter and our situation in almost perfect detail. I knew after reading her article I had to make contact with Stewart. That is when the e-mails between the two of us began.

I first wrote Stewart in December of 2002 regarding my daughter and the previously mentioned kundalini activation. Shortly after we initiated communication, the movie "Star Trek: Nemesis" appeared in theatres for the holiday season. As I watched the movie, it suddenly dawned on me that I named my daughter after the counselor and psychic from the television series "Star Trek: Voyager." I didn't realize that the character's role of a goddess would hit so close to home nearly fifteen years later. It was such a revelation, that I just had to write Stewart for his opinion.

Through our correspondence I began to realize there was more to my situation than I once believed. This was especially true when Stewart told me the astral vision I experienced was actually a standard Tibetan Monk program, originating from controlled satellite transmissions. Like myself, he was subjected to the same type of programming scenario. Contacting Stewart with this information and his subsequent response, along with Janet's articles on specific programming finally brought me to the point of making the call for my first consultation. I can say without hesitation, that phone call was the most significant turning point of my life.

On February 5, 2003, my whole belief system and sense of reality was shattered forever when I came to realize my life and the world as I had known it never truly existed. That was the day I first spoke with Stewart and learned that I was a specifically programmed Monarch sex-slave, whose last name meant "from the rose." He told me the "rose" he saw at my pineal gland was a symbol of the Illuminati bloodline, indicating my importance as a hierarchy slave.

I really didn't care how important I was, or whose lineage I was from. I only knew I was in a state of shock over this revelation, and had not a clue what to do with the information I just received. At least it was an answer and one intuitively I felt was correct. According to Stewart, my daughter was also a Monarch sex-slave. Born to highly programmed parents (her father is from a "Committee of 300" family), she could not have escaped the same fate as her father and I. Genetically perfect for programming, the combination of my blonde hair and blue eyes and my daughter's red hair and green eyes, further reinforced what I believed upon reading Janet's article.

Stewart continued the consultation telling me there was an etheric "X" on my upper left shoulder, placed there by my original programmer. It meant that I was very important to them and not to be touched or programmed by anyone else. To further emphasize my value and significance to the Illuminati, I not only had Monarch programming, I also had "Twinning" programming as well. The double letters in my first and last name indicated this type of specific programming. It meant there was another child similarly programmed, to carry out a specific function instilled in us from a very young age. Should one of us fail for whatever reason to fulfill the agenda, the other would act as a backup to take over the task. Stewart said I would meet this programmed twin of mine sometime this year.

Going further with the information, he told me that my programming was implemented at NSA. This made sense considering I live only an hour's drive away from Fort Meade where the Agency is located. Conveniently, my mother worked there in the 1960's as a real estate agent, selling homes to soldiers returning from the Vietnam War.

The information that came forth during this session was absolutely amazing. Stewart mentally scanned my entire chakra system enabling him to tell me things about myself that no one, and I mean absolutely no one knew. It was this knowledge that lent credibility to his revelations regarding my programming and that of my daughter. He gave me exercises to ground and balance myself, along with several methods to begin the deprogramming process. Finally, I was given answers that I knew instinctively were true and that I could accept. Now the real work began.

I started deprogramming with the simple grounding and balancing exercises Stewart taught me. The first step was to determine my specific T- Bar, to be placed at my pineal gland for balancing the right and left hemispheres of the brain. I have the upper case "T," which is the symbol specific to my particular genetics. By balancing my T-Bar and spinning my chakras with the correct colors, I achieved almost immediate results. No longer did I feel the undulating waves of energy displacement throughout my body. After all these months, I finally experienced relief. I realized that the programming issues had been the source of my discomfort, and by utilizing these simple techniques I felt better than I had in years. Taking the sea salt baths as he suggested helped purify and cleanse my body of accumulated toxins, adding to the relief I felt.

Although I experienced a considerable amount of physical relief, I was unprepared emotionally for what was to follow. Along with the grounding and balancing exercises, Stewart showed me how to unlock blocked DNA sequences through a series of specific deprogramming techniques. If done properly there is little if any margin for error.

I began by using the <u>Golden Altar of Forgiveness</u> to release myself from those whom I have had negative experiences with in this lifetime. At first I placed only my family and former husband on the Altar, but the more details that surfaced during the deprogramming process, the longer the list grew. Following the techniques I learned from Stewart, and adding a few of my own as I became more proficient, I began to remove and release negativity accumulated since infancy.

Clearing out this emotional debris allowed me to hone and develop my own psychic abilities. It was amazing how easily I was able to access energies of all sorts, and eventually reveal the many hidden talents that have been kept from me all my life. Always being so logical and analytical in nature, here I was accessing those intuitive and psychic energies suppressed within me throughout my lifetime. It made the deprogramming process much easier, once I began releasing myself from the emotional bondage in which I was held.

Interestingly, the more cleansing and release work I accomplished, the more I began to pick up on a connection to Stewart. This connection transcended our initial conversation. I was uncertain of the reason for this feeling, but I could not shake the sense of having known him somewhere from my past. I thought perhaps I was imagining things although I didn't believe this was the case. Finally, I asked him if he knew me prior to the consultation. Feeling this to be a long shot, he admitted that he did know me. Talk about a surprise! Rather puzzled by this admission, I didn't ask for further clarification nor did he offer any. It wasn't until doing the release work in a sea salt bath that I felt compelled to place Stewart on the Golden Altar. Whoa! I couldn't for the life of me fathom why he belonged there. I just knew I had to forgive him for something, and the reason for this was soon to become very clear.

My question was answered the next day while accessing past memories through use of the <u>Green Spiral Staircase</u> exercise. Using this as one of the techniques learned from Stewart, I placed myself in medium green and began the deprogramming process:

I began to descend the staircase until I reached a closed door. Upon opening the door, I entered into a room ablaze in a fire so intense I could literally feel the searing heat on my skin. I didn't know my location, but I knew the man that waited for me on the ritual altar; it was Stewart! Well, here was my surprise. I guess he did know me. The next thing I realized, I was throwing back my head and opening my mouth to engulf a smoky white substance descending from the ceiling above. Immediately I realized this was an astral entity. I didn't know why I knew this, instinctively I just did. Taken by surprise I quickly ascended the staircase, flooded the scene in violet, merged it, and placed myself in brown.

That was enough deprogramming for one day. I was in utter amazement at what just occurred, never experiencing anything like it before. I knew nothing about Satanic rituals but here I was, right in the middle of one with a man I've never met and only spoken with by phone. Of course the first thing I did was write Stewart to verify I was not losing my mind. There were so many questions afterwards that I didn't know where to begin. At least I wasn't losing my mind and I knew I was on the right track. I decided to try and obtain more information regarding the ritual, so again I used the <u>Green Spiral Staircase</u> exercise to delve deeper into this experience:

I was again in ceremony, although details were much clearer this time. An orgy was taking place with participants mostly in human form, though there were many shapeshifting Reptilians present as well. Taking in the demonic astral entity as I had previously, I descended from the altar to address the ritual participants. The voice however was not my own, but that of a demon possessing my body. I announced in an unearthly voice, "It is time for the blood sacrifice to begin." Immediately after uttering those words, a young girl around the age of six, with shoulder length blonde hair was brought into the room. She began to scream as she was raped and dismembered by the participants. After this occurred I went on the altar, whereupon the entity exited my body. That ended the ritual, and as before I ascended the staircase and concluded the exercise.

I could hardly contain myself after this memory surfaced, I was so sick. It was one thing having sex with a man I didn't know, even having a demonic entity possess my body, but the thought of this poor child being tortured and killed was too much to endure. I knew I had to continue with the deprogramming process regardless how incredibly difficult it became. I couldn't live with myself if I didn't do everything I could to absolve myself of those horrors I was actively participating in.

I began keeping a journal of my experiences to help me assimilate and record all that transpired during my deprogramming. There was no set chronological order to the information I received. Some memories are very recent, while others date back to my early childhood. Through the use of the <u>Green Spiral Staircase</u> and the <u>Monarch Butterfly</u> exercises, memories that were suppressed over a lifetime began to surface. From my early years to the recent past, I have recollections where torture and trauma split my consciousness into the fragmented pieces I know today as my programmed matrix. The more work I did, the clearer the memories became. I started to realize exactly how important I was to the Illuminati and their agenda, through the intense and often excruciating process of deprogramming. The more I released past issues and followed Stewart's techniques, the quicker and more detailed the memories became, as evidenced by the following:

Upon descending the staircase, I opened a door to a large room. Entering the room I realized immediately that I was naked beneath a dark velvet robe. The robe appeared to be black or midnight blue, although it was difficult to discern the exact color. An orgy was taking place in the room with participants I did not recognize. Escorted by a naked woman with black hair, I was taken to a bed in the center of the room where two men waited for me. The woman removed my robe, and I began to have sex with both of the men while the orgy participants watched. At the height of orgasm, one of the men shifted into a Reptilian while throwing his head back and emitting loud guttural noises. Unable to go further with the memory, I exited the <u>Staircase.</u>

I could not discern either of the men's identity, although I knew this event took place in the late 1970's when I was in my early twenties. The length and style of my hair also confirmed this, as it appeared exactly as I wore it at the time. I also realized in a subsequent memory, the woman escorting me into the room was a former co-worker of mine from a job I had nearly twenty-five years ago. She attempted to contact me on several occasions over the years, although I have not resumed a friendship with her since our association ended. Fortunately for me I didn't go any further with the relationship.

This next memory put a more definitive name on the type of Monarch programming I soon realized I possessed. It was very clear after recalling this next event, why I was called a "Presidential Model." Using the <u>Green Spiral Staircase,</u> the following information poured forth:

I descended the staircase and upon opening the door, I entered into an exquisitely beautiful room with very high ceilings. Dressed only in my ceremonial robe, I was escorted to a throne elevated in the center of the room by a finely dressed man. It was apparent this was a formal gathering in that all the men were very well appointed and impeccably dressed in tuxedos. There were no other women present than myself. I was treated as a queen holding court over her subjects. Upon being seated on the throne, a procession of elegantly dressed men began showering me with lavish gifts. One of the men actually knelt before me to place a pair of beautiful high-heeled shoes upon my feet. Shortly thereafter, I was lead into another room outfitted with a large bed. In this room there were three men present.

To my utter amazement, waiting for me was George Bush, George W. Bush, and Dick Cheney! The four of us began to engage in ritual on the bed, and as things heated up all three men began shape-shifting into Reptilian form. I vividly remembered having sex with George W., as his father the senior Bush held one of my arms overhead and Dick Cheney held the other. All three men were in Reptilian, not human form. During the ritual I again took in the demonic entity as I had previously, while the men began to emit deep guttural noises. During the height of the ritual, tiny babies were brought into the room and devoured by the men. That was enough for me. I concluded the exercise, flushed the scene with violet, merged it, and went into brown. This occurred on the last full moon prior to February 26, 2003, shortly before the war in Iraq.

I knew my importance after this was greater than I could ever have imagined. Memories continued to surface indicating the elevated status I had obtained within the highest levels of government. Consequently the term "Presidential Model" was quite appropriate for this type of programming.

I also began to recall participating in satanic rituals with several past and present mayors of Baltimore at the Basilica of the Assumption, the Catholic Cathedral of the Archdiocese. My memories went as far back as the age of twelve and thirteen, to my initiation by former mayor Tommy D'Alesandro. The most recent of these memories took place on September 19, 2003, the night Hurricane Isabel damaged and destroyed many of the waterfront homes along the coastal waters of the Chesapeake Bay, including my own. Going further with the techniques learned from Stewart, I placed the date of September 19 at my pineal gland to access further information. I found my answers utilizing the <u>Green Spiral Staircase:</u>

Taking the date of September 19, 2003 and placing it at my pineal, I began concentrating on this time period. With that specific date in mind, I immediately envisioned my self in medium green. Descending the spiral staircase, I began to access the memory from that reference point, and much to my surprise, I was at the Basilica of the Assumption in downtown Baltimore. Walking down the aisle of the cathedral, I was naked and dressed only in a gold ceremonial robe with a very long train attached (similar to that of a wedding dress). Flanked by attendants on either side, I walked towards the altar where Martin O'Malley the current mayor lie naked waiting for me. Behind the altar was a priest surrounded by people I could not identify, all of which were dressed in white robes similar to that of the Ku Klux Klan. Joining the mayor upon the altar, we began the sexual ritual. Shortly into the ceremony with knife in hand, I began cutting him (I found this a common theme in all such satanic ceremonies) during the sexual act.

I first made an incision horizontally across his stomach, cutting deep enough to draw blood. Above the first incision I proceeded to carve a large "X" into his chest, again drawing blood as before. During this part of the ceremony I took in the demonic entity, whereupon I descended from the altar to address the audience. In a voice not my own but of the demon entity I uttered, "I am the Light, I am the Power, all who come here kneel before me."

There were more words spoken, but after exiting the memory I could not remember what they were. Upon completion of the invocation I turned back towards the altar, and much to my surprise, there was the mayor suspended in mid-air. The altar however was not empty, and even more of a surprise awaited me. There was a German man I had dated almost three years ago, now ready to take his turn. That was all I was able to remember, so I ascended the staircase and merged the memory.

I couldn't believe what I had witnessed! Here I was in a satanic ritual ceremony with the mayor of Baltimore, and a man I had dated three years ago. Even more amazing, is that I had not seen nor heard from this man in all that time. A little over a week after the ritual he appeared at my home totally unannounced, under the guise of surveying the damage I had suffered from Hurricane Isabel. Stewart told me shortly after this, that the man's family had been involved in orchestrating satanic ceremonies in Germany. Well, that didn't surprise me one bit! He had a very cold and unemotional countenance when I had known him, and now I can see why.

The more cognizant I became of my abilities to deprogram, the faster the information flowed and the clearer I became. Quickly I came to the realization of my significance to the Illuminati, and my attainment of one of the highest levels within the ritual hierarchy. I was a "Goddess," a position very few obtain. Over the years the color of the robes I wore changed from the dark velvet colors of black and midnight blue, to that of gold, signifying my "Goddess" status. Knowing my importance did not make this process any easier. In fact it was the exact opposite.

To reach this level I knew the extent of the trauma and torture I endured must have been overwhelming. But how did I reach this point in my life? Who was responsible for creating this "me"? The "me" that was capable of partaking in, and even conducting such atrocities. I didn't know this person at all, so well hidden is the back Satanic alters of my matrix. They exist in the far recesses of my mind, just waiting for the opportunity to be called forward and perform whatever function is necessary to carry out the agenda for total control and enslavement of this planet.

I knew the key to my deprogramming was dependent upon uncovering the part my early years played in making me who I am today. That meant I would have to delve further into my past and identify those persons responsible for the installation of torture and trauma necessary to totally dissociate my consciousness into the 2,197 alters that comprise my programmed matrix.

As I began accessing these past memories of ritual abuse, the need to know who my programmer was became overwhelming. Using the <u>Green Spiral Staircase</u> to help me identify this person, I repeatedly accessed a computer control facility where a man wearing glasses appeared. Dressed in a white shirt and dark pants, he had medium to dark brown hair, and was between 30-40 years of age. I could not place a name to this man, yet I knew him as one of my programmers.

The first real clue I had to his identity was given to me by a close girlfriend while celebrating her birthday in March of 2003. During dinner, she mentioned that her father was a former employee of the NSA. A man of German descent, he was a retired programmer at the Fort Meade facility whose duties were never divulged to her family because of their secret nature. I didn't know the reason why, but as soon as she mentioned her father I became very upset. Shortly thereafter I had my suspicions confirmed.

The father of my close friend was one of my original program-mers, and the man I had seen in the computer control room. I knew I needed to do my deprogramming work to get more information and bring clarity into my life about this man and my past. It was necessary to unlock those deeply buried and painful memories, allowing me to move forward and attempt to gain control over my life.

What follows is beyond anything I could ever have imagined. Memories so horrific of my childhood began to surface, that I am still in a state of shock and disbelief. The memories of my trauma and torture by the hands of this man were unimaginable, and so calculatingly brutal, that I can barely speak of it to this day. Using the <u>Green Spiral Staircase</u>, I began to recall in detail what this man did to me at such a young age, totally splitting my mind and consciousness into one of complete dissociation:

I was seven years old when my mother took me to NSA in Fort Meade, Maryland. I remember being in a cage naked with another child who was slightly older than myself. In an adjacent cage my programmer was tending to the needs of several very young kit-tens. I remember him feeding the kittens and paying each a con-siderable amount of attention. I witnessed them playing with one another as kittens will do, without regard to the world or any other distraction around them. The little girl and I were both incredibly frightened. I was so terrified that all I could do was cry and reiter-ate repeatedly, "I want to go home. I want to go home." I kept this up over and over again, but my abuser totally ignored me. In fact the more I cried, the more attention my programmer seemed to pay the kittens. This only intensified the feelings of terror and horror I was already experiencing.

Becoming angry at our outbursts, he entered the cage and began to beat me. He then dragged me out of the cage into what appeared to be a chair used for dental patients, and attached electrodes from a generator over my naked little body. The area he concentrated on most was around my genitals. Turning the dial upwards on the machine, electricity soon began shooting through-out my whole body. Oh how excruciating the pain! It was all too vivid and clear, bringing up such feelings of hurt and despair within me that I could go on no longer. I stopped the memory immediately, and came out of the exercise.

I realized during this exercise that the other little girl tortured along with me was a close friend of mine. I will not reveal her identity as this is something she must explore on her own. Telling her would serve no real purpose unless she was ready to learn the truth. This unfortunately is not the case for she is shut down about her past, believing as I had that she has lived a charmed existence yet never knowing the real truth.

Shortly after accessing the above memory, I used the <u>Monarch Butterfly</u> exercise to delve further into the sexual part of my programming.

Concentrating on the wings of a Monarch butterfly, I envisioned a hand turning up a dial to increase the frequency, and elevating the hertz levels. As the needle moved forward with ever increasing intensity, I started to become more and more sexually stimulated. I saw this as the part of my programming that associated pleasure with pain. I felt that the electrical shocks I endured as a child were also part of my sexual programming, further splitting my consciousness into a total dissociative and mind-controlled state.

Delving further into the past using the <u>Green Spiral Staircase,</u> another memory surfaced with my programmer, even more appalling than the first:

I was five years old, and taken outside to a field somewhere in the Fort Meade area to play "Ring Around the Rosy" with a group of children, including my girlfriend I mentioned previously. It was a beautiful sunny day with clear blue skies and white billowy clouds. Walking hand in hand with the other children we formed a circle as we were instructed to do. My programmer was standing in the center of this circle wearing his white lab coat ordering us to begin the game. Dutifully obeying as children do, we started to chant, "Ring around the rosy, pocket full of posies, pussy cat, pussy cat, all fall down." Upon completion of the rhyme and with pistol in hand, he immediately aims the gun shooting the little dark-haired girl beside me in the head, killing her instantly. The blood of this little girl splattered all over me, and as it does my programmer tells me I would be next if I did not behave. Terrified, another little girl begins to flee and is also shot. I begin to vomit and quickly pass out after seeing the other child killed. Unable to go further into the memory I ascended the staircase and came out of the exercise. That was all I could handle.

It seems these poor girls were several of the expendable children used to further split and dissociate those of us who the Illuminati deem to be the more valuable candidate for programming and mind-control. Whatever it takes to cause this dissociation will be done to facilitate their agenda, at the expense and sacrifice of many others.

Knowing that programming is accomplished through sexual trauma as well as the torture I described above, I needed to go further into the process and access those memories that would allow me to find out how my sexual programming was put into place. I can thank my mother's side of the family for taking full responsibility for this part of my programming.

My maternal grandfather, a former Baltimore City Police Officer and Freemason, belonged to one of the "Committee of 300" families, and was the first relative I can thank him for initiating me into the sexual side of programming. Using the <u>Green Spiral Staircase</u>, I was able to access those distant memories that lay buried beneath the delusion of what I perceived to be my fairy tale childhood:

Going into the color of medium green and descending the staircase, I was able to visualize myself at the age of four being dragged by my mother into my grandparent's bedroom. Stripped naked, I was forced to lie in a butterfly position with my legs held up in the air by my grandfather as he raped me. I remembered screaming "Mommy, Mommy" for help as the pain was so great, but my mother did nothing to stop it. I could actually feel myself dissociate to escape the trauma I was experiencing, and reach a place utterly devoid of any semblance of emotion. My consciousness began to split and fragment looking for a sheltered haven where it would be safe and protected from the abuse I was suffering. I couldn't take any more of this memory so I immediately came out of the exercise.

The floodgates opened for me after this and the memories poured forth of the abuse I had suffered as a child. No longer did I view my childhood as I had previously. I was abused and betrayed by those closest to me and so brutally, that it may have stayed buried forever had I not met Stewart and begun the often torturous process of deprogramming. The pieces of the puzzle were finally beginning to fit, but this was only the beginning. There was more, so much more that was necessary to fully comprehend the magnitude of what my family had done to me in my youth.

The saying the "Apple doesn't fall far from the tree" would be most applicable to my grandfather's son. A Freemason like his father, he was the youngest and only boy of the family. My uncle was a computer programmer working for the government at Aberdeen Proving Grounds when he lived across the street from my family in the 1960's with his wife and three daughters. By living in such close proximity another phase of the programming process was easily put into place.

Suspecting he was also one of my programmers I again accessed the Green Spiral Staircase to find my answers:

The first memory I recall regarding the sexual abuse by my uncle was during my late teens. Taken to Aberdeen Proving Grounds, I entered into some type of torture chamber filled with Sado-Masochistic paraphernalia. There were chains, whips, and black leather masks everywhere in the room. I was stripped naked and tied with my hands over my head by a chain hanging from the ceiling. Upon securing me with the chain, he takes off his clothes, grabs hold of me, and begins to rape me anally. After he completed the rape, a woman dressed in black leather attire enters the room, and forces herself upon me, while my uncle watched. Completing this, I was compelled to get on my knees and perform oral sex on him.

The memories of abuse by this man only increased in their severity. Using the Monarch Butterfly exercise, I was taken back to an earlier age when I first recalled being brutalized by my uncle:

I was twelve or thirteen years old at the time I recalled visiting my relatives in the home they occupied across the street from my family. I was there frequently, many times spending the night with one of my cousins. I remember standing by the door to my aunt and uncle's bedroom watching transfixed as he raped his eldest daughter while her mother was holding her down on the bed by the shoulders. Her legs were held in a butterfly position over her head in a similar fashion to what I experienced during the rape by my grandfather. Afterwards, I was made to lie down on the bed to be raped anally by my uncle as his daughter, in tears, was made to watch.

More memories of abuse by my uncle surfaced, all of which were sexual and included anal rape. The degradation and pain I suffered only furthered my dissociation. There were other family members that took part in my abuse, most notably an older male cousin who has since become an ordained minister. Again using the <u>Monarch Butterfly</u> at my pineal, I accessed the following memory regarding my cousin:

I was ten years old at the time, while walking with my cousin and his friend (I believe his name was Ralph) in the marshy area behind our homes on State Park property. We entered the marsh from the end of the street onto a pathway far out of site. While walking on wooden planks placed upon the soft surface of the marsh, Ralph grabbed hold of my arms from behind, and pulled me down to the ground. Once down on the ground my cousin rapes me on the spot. I flushed the whole scene with violet, merged the event, and went to brown.

I was not surprised by that assault. My cousin had sexually molested me as far back as the third grade, however I could not recall the rape until I accessed the above memory. I was always cognizant of the many abuses involving sexual torture (especially with the use of knives) he inflicted upon me. They remain ever-present in my memory to this day. Deeply rooted feelings of shame and guilt kept me from telling my parents at the time. I was made to feel it was my fault for what was being done to me, knowing now it could not have been further from the truth. I was a young child, tormented and traumatized by those I should have been able to trust. Sadly, this was just another example of the abuse perpetrated upon me by my family to further splinter and fragment my conscious mind.

Still in the process of intense deprogramming, I have memories surfacing at a phenomenal rate. This however can be a double-edged sword. There are times I am thankful for the speed in which I am able to recall my past and integrate those fragmented pieces of my mind. However, there are other times where I want to retreat back to the safety of my own little programmed world, never having witnessed the depth of the horror that I have seen. By merging and releasing all the negativity and pain I have experienced up to my Oversoul, I am attempting to heal and nourish those mind-patterns that have held me back from utilizing the potential hidden from me throughout this and so many other lifetimes. It is a road fraught with many dangerous perils that I have embarked upon, but one I am willing to pursue in order to release myself from the victim mentality that has plagued me throughout my existence. I know in time, I will accomplish all that I have set out to do.

In conclusion, I would like to recognize and express my gratitude to Stewart and his wife Janet for all the help and support they have given my daughter and myself. Without them and the tireless amount of effort they put forth, we would not be on the path to recovery that we are today. I can never thank them enough.

Case #2 Analysis
Presidential Model Programming

This woman accurately described herself as a "Presidential Model" sex-slave. This is one of the highest levels of Monarch programming as these women are used in sexual ritual with the highest ranking government officials and religious leaders. This type of sex-slave usually performs with the "God" in ritual. Read my book, *True Reality of Sexuality* (*Expansions Publishing Company, Inc., 2005*) for details.

What she describes in her document is a participation in extremely high-level rituals of Sexual Magick that are designed to anchor the thought-forms projected out by the male participants into physical reality. Her strong proportion of Lyraen genetics allows for a lot more programming possibilities as these blonde-haired/blue-eyed characteristics are a programmers paradise. There is an enzyme in such genetic manifestations that enables programming to take hold easily. This is why such body types are promoted as being desirable by our society.

This woman shows a higher form of the Beta level Monarch programming that involves pure sexual energy and performances. For more details, please refer to the my *Mind-Control & Programming* DVDs and their accompanying Study Guides. Beta Monarchs are extremely sexual and dress accordingly.

Another type of programming that comes up for this woman is "Tinkerbelle Programming." In the past, this type of programming only occurred at Tinker Air Force Base in Oklahoma. Now it can be done at various locations as well as transmitted via satellite.

With Tinkerbelle Programming, the person stays youthful for an extended period of time and lives to an advanced age, always looking much younger than his/her chronological years. This happens because these persons have such powerful genetics, were born with established, inherited programming, and have the proper programming mind-patterns. These people become valuable assets in the Illuminati culture of ritual and ceremony, especially those involving sexuality.

Tinkerbelle-programmed people are sexually viable well into their advanced years. This type of person can be raised in the ritual hierarchy ranks all the way up to "Goddess" status. For a person to receive Tinkerbelle status, he/she must have quite a prized mixture of genetics and mind-patterns that makes him/her viable for prolonged sexual use.

Because this person is a Committee of 300 descendent, her programming is generational. Therefore, it is logical that her daughter and futurer grandchildren will become part of the ritual network. If this woman deprograms to the point where she is cognizant of her triggers, alters, switches, and codes, then she will become detached enough from the web of Illuminati control to assist her own daughter in her deprogramming. When a person's family is involved in working for the Illuminati, the programming eventually becomes genetically anchored and is usually passed on from one generation to the next.

In such cases, it is common for the mother and daughter to have "Twinning Programming" with each other. This means that they have identical functions, alters, and constructs in their pro-gramming matrix so that one can act as a back-up for the other, or as an enhancement for the other. This is given to "slaves" who have a high-level function or functions that cannot fail for the agenda of their programmer.

It is also quite probably that such a sex-slave would have other "twins" who have identical programming. They do not necessarily have to meet in person in conscious life, but their frequencies are intertwined for as long as both live. With the advent of satellites, "twins" can be programmed together without ever meeting physically. They may have dreams about one another or even have alters that are related to each other.

This woman also had a "psychic" alter created within her matrix. This is common amongst the people programmed before the New Age. These psychic alters are useful as mediums, connecting to other dimensional vibrations for the Illuminati during ritual. These people are able to "host" astral entities/demons for sexual interactions with the participants who are then able to download the energies of these beings via sexual union. This is a powerful and valuable procedure in Illuminati culture. Sometimes the psychic alter comes on suddenly due to time-sensitive events. Or, the alter may be programmed to activate on a certain date or when the slave reaches a particular age.

She also has aspects of "Porcelain Doll" programming which is an adjunct to Tinkerbelle programming. This type of programming keeps her emotionless at most times and presentable as a sex-slave as needed. She always remains in the proper "mode" for Sexual Magick Ritual. Her face never gives away her true feelings; she may not even be in touch with her true emotions. She is the stone-faced painted woman who always looks the same no matter what. Many wives of presidents have had this look, usually fortified via narcotics for a better and more constant public presentation.

Porcelain Dolls always wear more make-up than the average woman, and it is always applied to perfection. "Geisha Programming" and "Mannequin Programming" are closely related to Porcelain Doll Programming. There is even a sub-program that is connected to "Valley Girl" types, combining a lot of different techniques of sexual training.

A Presidential Model slave is always statuesque, appearing almost regal. Her figure is perfect and her clothing name brands that fit like a glove. They do not necessarily have large bosoms, but are nicely proportioned.

This slave usually has blonde or red hair. Sometimes they dye their hair back and forth between these two colors. Their nails are perfectly polished. You will never see them in sweats or ragged clothing.

A Presidential Model is either single, divorced, or between relationships. A married Presidential Model may be referred to as a "Stepford Wife," or more recently, a "Desperate Housewife," based upon a popular television show. These last two categories are newly developed. Movie and television programming is designed to maintain these programs and trigger slaves constantly. Often, the married version will have a husband who is open to "sharing" or swapping. He is most often a cheater, anyway.

The Presidential Model always wears eye make-up and uses a special brand of perfume. She can be identified by her diamond/ gold earrings and beautiful bracelets and rings. She never wears anything artificial or cheap. Her programming gives her an air of superiority. She can often be condescending to people in service positions and to those of lower financial means.

The Presidential Model's home is impeccable. The furniture seems as if it came from a museum. The house is spotless, like its owner. The home is in the finest neighborhood, most likely inherited or given to her by a family member.

The Presidential Model has a close relationship with her father, but probably a love-hate connection to her mother. If she has any children, there are deep emotional and psychological issues that need years of counseling and deprogramming.

Interestingly, the female child of a Presidential Model may not look as "pretty" as her mother. The child's beauty develops later on as she matures. It is rare for a Presidential Model to have or have custody of a male child. In the cases where a Presidential Model does give birth to a male, he often goes with the father after a divorce.

The Presidential Model usually has no career, or is supported by various males, from a family fund, or she is in a job that is considered to be powerful. Sometimes she runs her own business or is a fashion model. She often runs an employment agency or talent scout business. She knows people in the higher walks of life; usually they owe her favors.

As is often the case in deprogramming, some times a deeply programmed person falls back and does not continue. This is what happened with the person who wrote this story. Her daughter, who is a deeply emotionally disturbed person, continually runs away, as she has done for years. After working with this Presidential Model for years, she placed the blame for her daughter's behavior on deprogramming techniques, ceasing all communication me.

This is a sad event as the Presidential Model was doing so well and had made such great progress. Often, programmed people refuse to take responsibility for their own live, finding it so much easier to blame others, especially those closest to them.

It is my hope that this Presidential Model finds her way back to deprogramming, continuing the process. Sabotage, punishment, and low self-worth kick in so easily in these cases. The person must fight harder to overcome the urge/programming that stops all work at re-integration.

Case #3
The Seeding Program

A Butterfly's View

)(I was adopted when I was 4 days old. I was told that my birth parents were too young for marriage, and that they were both from Irish families. My folks couldn't have children, and through a Catholic hospital in northern Idaho that my Dad was auditing, he arranged my adoption through my birth mother's doctor, with the help of the Administrator of the hospital. Our family grew to include a sister and brother, two months apart, around my third birthday. They were from different birth parents, with their own histories. Our folks thought it would be a good idea to tell us that we were adopted and chosen to be in our family, and they did this as a bed time story during our early years.

In the beginning, Mom tried to be there for me whenever I so much as peeped until I was ten months old. Her friends practically sat on her one afternoon, and told her to let me cry. Within one month I was walking and shortly after that I was bathroom trained.

We moved across town when I was four to the surrounding hills. I learned how to ride a bike, slide on a big piece of cardboard down our hill in the summer, taste the juices of honeysuckles, and chew on the ends of pulled grass. It was all very typical of the early 60's, with doors that were never locked, and nearly all of my adventures were spent outdoors or playing in our basement.

Dad traveled a lot, and when in town, he'd usually take me on long drives after dinner. These started out when I was nearly four, the explanation being that Mom was very busy with the babies, and she needed time to put them to bed without anyone else in her way while this was accomplished. Until recently, I believed this, but in working through remembering the blank spots in my life, I've managed to recall a lot more of my story.

My father had a lot of influential friends. Many of them were involved in the government. Then there were those that were above that circle. These folks were part of an elite secret government that wasn't talked about at very many dinner tables. Dad worked for these people as a financial consultant, and also as what was known as a "Controller." He was fully aware that he was helping to further the New World Order's agenda through forms of mind control, programming, and rituals. All of these involved me to some degree, as well as many others that were a part of his world.

One of the interesting things about these nightly drives with Dad was that I'd see myself get into my father's car, but I wouldn't always remember where we went. On one occasion, I remember getting a glimpse of my reflection in the window, like there was a light on inside of the car, and I saw myself, and Dad's tan/orange jacket, with his favorite pipe in his mouth, puffing away while he drove with one hand.

When I was nearly 5, I remember coming out of what had felt like a complete blanket of darkness, with flashing lights blinking around me. I looked up, and saw that Dad was outside of his car, with me standing beside him. I was watching them tow the back of his car out of the mud. We were parked in front of what looked like a hotel with several cabins behind the main one where we stood. It wasn't unusual for Dad to meet with visiting clients at various hotels around the city. I didn't remember seeing this place before, not even during family drives that we took every Sunday. Years later, on my way out of town during college, I did see this place, in the outlying hills of central Idaho, and it was at least a two hour drive from the city, surrounded by trees, with the same "shooting star" neon sign above the Manager's cabin.

This was the place that my father took me to for the purposes of rituals or ceremonies that were below ground, gaining access to this chamber by way of one of the larger cabin's stairs to a large basement with yet another doorway set in one of the walls. I started out by observing these events. Then I began to participate in them during the summer of 1961. I would bring in hyperspace healing energy through being sexually stimulated to an "edge" like feeling, or pre-orgasmic, by those that would then "pervert" this conduit of energy for a particular manifestation. I was trained to keep it going, so that whatever needed to be done could be accomplished to everyone's satisfaction. Once released from this, through a blissful and draining orgasm, the energy would stop coming in, and Dad would take me home.

I had assigned "fluffers" that would get me stimulated before a "performance." Mostly these were young women, but I remember walking through a group of my father's friends before one ceremony, sitting on their laps, being touched and stroked, and I enjoyed the feeling of being wanted by all of them in this way. I didn't see it as good or bad, it merely felt wonderful, and I didn't want the attention to end.

At home, unaware of my other life, I'd try to recreate this with the neighborhood girls, seducing them in our basement, or in their homes. The resulting "edge" feeling must have been a beacon to both of my parents, as they seemed to catch me in nearly every case, even at a neighbor's home, under the pool table in the basement. Sure enough, I looked out of the basement window just as I'd removed my willing friend's clothing, and there would be my Dad, glaring in my direction from outside!

The summer before first grade, we went to Disneyland, staying at the hotel on site. This was my second visit, but one I'd always remember. Dad saw to it that I had a Disney Guide. Her name was Janet, and she took me everywhere. She was in her early twenties, with short brown hair in a page boy style and wide brown eyes. She looked like Natalie Wood, and I fell in love with her. We went on the train tour together, and she had me sit on her lap while another guide helped to fill me in on what was being seen. Upon returning home, I created an invisible friend. I called her Janet, and she was my companion for several months.

Catholic school in first and second grade had too many rules to absorb all at once. Always having something to say, even when the nun was talking, got my desk toted outside of the classroom on more than one occasion! Mingling with the boys when the playground was firmly divided by gender resulted in stern lectures about "those kinds of girls." I found it hard to focus on religion, and didn't see what the big deal was, but went with it because Dad seemed very serious about it. Thankfully Mom was NOT into religion at all, which was a great balance for me, even though it would get me into trouble. When given a religious drawing to color, I chose red for the Virgin Mary's veil. It seemed like a great idea at the time, however the resulting shame talk by our nun in front of the class explained what that color implied to others. I wasn't happy with religion, and it evidently wasn't very happy with me, either!

We moved to Hawaii in the summer of '65. Dad had been promoted to running the Honolulu branch of the accounting firm that he was also a partner of, and there were a lot of clients from the various countries in Southeast Asia that needed his personal attention. Dad and Mom did a lot of entertaining at home with Hawaii's elite in politics until the end of 1972. Dad would travel for up to two weeks at a time, to various Asian countries, South America, and the eastern United States.

Once we settled in to Island living, I picked up where I left off, and began the seduction game with several neighborhood girls. Whatever beacon my folks had during this time must have been set to low, I guess, because I wasn't caught nearly as often, however inevitably I'd go too far in a promiscuous game with friends, and be set back by being discovered. I learned how to talk swiftly and carefully, as the skill of verbal manipulation became as easy as breathing to me. I didn't know why I wanted to be in various stages of undress with others, and that only added to my confusion, as it didn't feel wrong when it felt so right! I then decided to direct myself further inward, and began to work with fantasy over reality.

We moved to another neighborhood shortly before I started 7th grade. I became addicted to a soap opera called "Dark Shadows," and the vampires and witches became my friends. I cut out pictures of eyes from the teen magazines I'd buy, placing them on the side of my closet door that could hide behind the other one, when opened. Family and friends would see my open closet, with the pictures of the Beatles, and other teen idols of my era, on the remaining closet panel. At night, when I was alone, I'd close the hidden door, and let the eyes watch me as I undressed. I liked it. I felt protected by having these cut out eyes watch me sleep, too.

Fascinated with witchcraft, I checked out books about the Salem witches at the school library, and began to think of myself as a witch, believing it was the only "fit" left for me. I began to keep stick matches for ceremonies that would take place over my bathroom sink. Sometimes I'd use pliant matches, twine them together, think of the boy I liked, and then let them burn as close to my fingers as I could manage. I kept a journal of drawn-by-hand vampires, mostly women with a lot of cleavage, blood drops dripping from their teeth, and inviting smiles. I watched any movie with a "Dracula" or witches theme. I was drawn in to all of the ceremony type scenes, fantasizing that I was participating in them, and I did a lot of daydreaming.

When Dad wasn't traveling, we'd go out to dinner every Sunday. One of my father's favorite restaurants was on the other side of the island. It had been an old homestead that looked almost like Tara in "Gone with the Wind." It still housed the family, but the front of the house had been converted into a restaurant. When going up the marble stairs we always admired the giant stone lions on either side of the entrance. Inside there were straw mats on the floor, heavy dark wood tables and chairs, with high ceilings and fans to stir the humid air. We always had the same waiter, a man that seemed ageless to look at, named Leo. This man later transferred to the main island country club, during the years that Dad was president of it, and he was always the waiter for our table.

Rituals and ceremonies were a large part of my life during my years on the Islands. These events never really stopped, only paused to re-group, kind of like being promoted to more responsibilities in the world of having a job. Ritual was explained to me as work by the other participants, regardless of it involving sexual acts that were enhanced through the illusion of being desired.

Love was never really a part of any of this, even though I had the heart of a romantic, and usually left it on my shirt sleeve. I was a performer, and the team I'd "dance" with would sometimes become friends as some combinations were used many times due to frequency matches. Akin to ballet, the movements were choreographed and exacting, using the sexual energy that is the most powerful force on this planet. There were other events that would occasionally take place simultaneously during some of the rituals, but I would be internally focused on what was in front of me as a part of my training to get the desired result.

During my 13th year, Dad would have me go out with him and his clients, whenever Mom was ill. This was fairly often in 1969. We'd go to dinner, then maybe a show, and go home. Usually there would be one young couple to entertain for these occasions. I knew not to talk too much, so I'd do my best to make my father proud by being what I felt was the perfect date. On one of these occasions, we were going to see the live performance of "The King and I" with Yul Brynner and Deborah Kerr. I remembered getting into the car after dinner, however the next memory was applauding as the show's stars came out on stage during the first act.

During all of my episodes of missing time, there was always something said or done that triggered me into a different "alter," and the "main me" would "go take a nap" in the back of my mind, while this adept person would come forward and take over to do whatever was expected. I now know that on this particular night, Dad drove everyone out to a stone circle that was on the other side of the island. The young woman with us sat next to me in the back seat, and brought out the "other me," through whatever trigger was used at the time. I knew her then, hugged her hello, and felt her hands move to find the private areas of my body that would get me instantly on the edge of orgasm. She worked my clothing off slowly, leaving some of it on, almost as an added stimulant. The mood would create the "edge" feeling, and I'd be good to go. Donning my robe in the car, I'd head to the changing tent while Dad and his companion walked towards the circle of stones.

Then the ritual would begin. I was the only one on the dais for several years, but after my first period, I began to perform different dances. Some of these were done with additional women, and others would include at least two young men. I was a virgin until I was 16, although that "title" loses a bit in translation, when I'd done pretty much everything else!

In the spring of my sophomore year I met and "planned to marry" a boy that I gave everything to, along with my virginity. Of course he didn't know that this was my agenda, and when that didn't pan out, I decided that I would use him as I'd been used. That's when he fell for me, and I walked away with my self-respect intact, not looking back. We left the Islands shortly after this event, as Dad had been transferred to Washington D.C., and our family moved to Bethesda, Maryland.

At 17, I was pleased with my long reddish-brown hair highlighted with gold streaks from 7 years of living in the Hawaiian sun. My hair had always been short, but I insisted on growing it to my waist after I turned 14. With hazel eyes that would change to complement whatever I wore, my body was freckled, thin, and pale. I towered at 5 feet 6 inches over the Islanders, but in Maryland, I was finally able to blend in with the crowd, and it was a welcome change!

During this time, I began to enjoy the company of those that already had someone to call their own. Not really wanting a boyfriend, I learned to listen, and be the "other half" of their other halves, giving more than their girlfriends usually did, and these boys would pour out their hearts to me. I found that I could appreciate these young men better if I wasn't looking for a relationship, and that helped to balance my "other world" of ritual. The talent of gaining confidences was easy for me, and I found myself caring in spite of my determination to remain aloof.

One Friday night in the middle of April in 1973, my best friend at the time, Sharon, was staying at my house for the night. She begged me to take her to her boyfriend's home, as his parents were traveling, and she wanted to be with him. I got permission to take Mom's car, however we needed to be back in two hours. In her determination to stay out as long as possible, Sharon created a chug-a-lug contest between us shortly after we arrived, supposedly all in fun. We were in her boyfriend's basement, with John and five other boys that were playing poker. Unbeknownst to me, I got most of the gin, and the least amount of ginger ale. Before I became too far gone, I was steered to a phone, and told to call my mother. I was able to express the desire to stay awhile longer, and cleared two more hours.

What I now refer to as "real time ritual" began. I was led into a bedroom with a boy I was dating named John. After he had his fun with me on the bedroom floor, John led me into another bedroom, leaving me with the rest of the boys. One watched while the other four of various ages indulged in every imaginable sexual fantasy that they could think of, and I looked like I was enjoying it, as I "viewed" it from the other side of the room. There wasn't a moment when everyone wasn't involved with the unfolding scene, as even the one watching took care of himself. Finally, they were done, and I was dressed by them. The youngest walked me back to the basement where Sharon was waiting. I was then bundled off into my Mom's car, and driven home.

Sharon didn't see anything dramatic about what had happened, and was pleased that she'd been able to stay with her boyfriend as long as she did. Shortly after this event, she was diagnosed as a schizophrenic, and she was sent away to an aunt in Virginia after pushing her mother down a flight of stairs (her mother broke an arm). We did meet one more time before I went to college, and she didn't remember anything about any of the events that had happened around that time.

The following month, in May, was the annual exchange trip to Long Island that our school choir made after housing their choir for a performance at our school earlier in the year. I was supposed to stay at an assigned home in Queens, however I wound up sleeping at the home of the man that taught their school choir. He was referred to as the Captain, and his home was near Islip.

One of the boys from my school band took me behind the Captain's home, and we started sampling his smuggled bottle of Johnny Walker Red. I didn't like the taste of it at all, but did my best to try to get past that feeling. I never touched scotch again! Bob saw that I was passing out, so he began to shake me, and at one point he slapped my face. Angry, I remember standing and wobbling out to the front yard. Bob had his arm keeping me up, and this other boy materialized with sandy blonde hair and hazel eyes that wasn't from our school, and he was holding my other hand and smiling as I tried to walk it off. Disgusted with the invasion of another person in the mix, Bob took off, and left me alone with this boy. He looked at me with eyes full of humor, smiling, but even with the liquor, I could feel he was also determined to finish his visit in the front yard quickly. He said a specific word to me then, triggering my response to fold up my "main" alter, while a more sober alter came out to talk to this boy that was suddenly not a stranger in this other world of mine.

He led me to a dark sedan, and I got in beside him in the back seat. I don't know where we went, however he explained that I'd had a lot to drink, and needed time to "sleep it off." When I arrived at an isolated two-story building, a wheel chair was brought out for me, as it was evident by then that I couldn't walk. I woke up the next morning, refreshed. Washing up quickly, this same boy was in my room when I returned, with a long robe in his hands. Shedding my clothing quickly, I donned the robe and followed him downstairs. There were four other boys in one of the main rooms, and I went in to get acquainted before getting down to business. They all had various shades of blonde hair, and blue, green, or hazel eyes. We were talking at once, laughing, and I began to feel more at ease. An older boy came into the room, and told us that it was time, and we filed out to go below to the stone chamber, where a lot of my rituals took place over the years.

All 5 of these boys were involved in this event. It was watched by fewer visitors than usual. One of them was my father. The dance was intense on the raised dais, all of them working to get the desired result in a multiple in and out, and round and round. At one point the heavy trance was briefly stepped around by me and the boy that had picked me up at the Captain's home. He whispered in my ear, asking me if I was all right, as I was starting to feel a bit overwhelmed. When I met his eyes and nodded, he quickly winked at me, and I relaxed.

Returning to the Captain's home the next day, I was especially surprised when I got out of the same dark sedan. It was morning when we left, and very little time had passed, and yet it was already night! Also, I felt drunk again, and I discovered recently that time had been folded to accommodate this event, and I was back to the point in time that I'd left, within minutes. Leaving the vehicle, along with my memories of what had transpired inside of it, I made my way to the back yard, where it was discovered that I was drunk. No scandal, no problems, and I boarded the private bus for the choir the next day. After a quick tour of New York City we headed home to Maryland.

The summer before my senior year, the rituals continued. Things would generally begin by Dad getting me up out of a deep sleep, tapping the top of my head, or brushing my forehead. He'd remove my nightgown, and place me within a long black cloak with a hood for my hair. We'd go down the stairs while I shook off my sleepy feelings, and he would let me outside, where the inevitable dark sedan would be waiting in our driveway. Sometimes the boy from Long Island would be at the door, and he'd talk to my father for a few minutes while I'd wait in the car. Once on our way it would all feel comfortable, and we'd talk a bit, like co-workers commuting to the workplace.

At the end of that summer, I found a job at a retail store that had a restaurant attached. One of the cooks attracted me. I started to go out with Steve after the restaurant side had closed, and we eventually became an item. He was made to order for the upcoming school events for my senior year, and I decided to trade the mistress hat for being a girlfriend.

Then came the spring of 1974, and my life chose to split in several directions, taking me years to sort it all out. Unbeknownst to me, my father was interested in furthering my genetic lineage. Steve had begun to date one of the waitresses at the restaurant, and I graciously told him to date the both of us, but inside I was crushed. Dad and his friends set up a "seeding" ritual, followed by a "twinning ceremony" within 24 hours of each other, unaware of the troubles that were brewing with my boyfriend.

Steve had been with me at the beginning of March, during a "parking date," as they were called. My period started the next day. Steve and I didn't have sex again until the end of April. The conception ritual took place almost two weeks later. Dad sent me in the car that night unaccompanied, and when I arrived I found my way to a special bed chamber that was set up to be very relaxing and romantic. It was nearly midnight, and I was a little nervous, knowing only that this wasn't standard for what I'd been doing so far in this other world.

Right away, I saw a boy seated on the circular bed with a black and gold bedspread with red satin sheets. His back was leaning up against several pillows at one end of the bed. His left leg was raised, right leg straight, head down. His left arm was draped over his left leg, with his hand curled except for his index finger, which was extended. His long sandy blonde hair had fallen forward over his face, and he seemed to be meditating. Candles were everywhere, along with filmy looking curtains that were pulled back away from the bed, giving the entire scene a very ancient appeal. I remember going forward, biting my lower lip, shedding my robe, and joining him on the bed. Then things warmed up as he looked up and smiled at me. A mixture of relief and lust took me over as I realized that he was my friend from Long Island. I was no longer nervous when he reached out for me.

All of what I'd been feeling and going through from deep inside of me came out to play, and I was incredibly wanting. This even surprised my friend, as he began to match my fervor, and everything became a dance of starting a life within a life. The name Baphomet was being chanted softly in the background, over and over, from all around us. Finally, I collapsed, happily exhausted. The scene faded as I fell asleep in this boy's arms, and when I awoke I was home, and it was the next morning. That night, I traveled alone again, to the same chamber below ground that was used when I'd been with the five boys nearly a year before. When I arrived, I saw that there weren't a lot of folks around, and next to the dais there was one girl and two boys. One was my friend from the night before, and the other I knew from different ceremonial occasions. I'd trained for this moment, and watched this young woman before, and I was inwardly thrilled with reaching this new level to finally be able to face her on the dais.

I began by circling my arm around her waist, reaching within her robe and pulling her towards me. She became warm and pliant to my touch, and as we embraced, we created a double energy field from hyperspace of enormous strength. Falling to our knees, still entwined, hands searching and soft, kisses light and unhurried, we removed each others robes, enjoying the feeling of being alone regardless of the eyes upon us. Then we were gently separated, and my seeding ritual partner had me first. Everything melted together after that, with an intensity that was felt by all of us, as well as by those that watched.

Within a few days of that weekend, I began to feel nauseous in the morning. I did graduate from high school, but I never made it to the stage to sing with the choir at Wolf Trapp, as I was too busy throwing up in their bathrooms. I barely managed to get my diploma. This was all explained away by saying that I was stressed out and worried about my future.

I went to Hawaii to visit my friends for two weeks in the middle of June. I was finally starting to feel better, and was very grateful to see Steve at the airport when I returned home. He was only picking me up to tell me that we were through, and he hoped I understood that he was finally in love, just not with me.

I went back to work, figuring he would tire of her eventually, and I'd be there whenever he was ready. Then I went back to the family doctor, in early August, with pains in my right side, and I was told that it was a 4 ½ month old fetus kicking me, and that I was due in December.

The doctor advised me to tell my ex-boyfriend that he was going to be a father, and I was too confused at the time to do the math. Steve, however was NOT confused at all, and denied being the father of my child from the very beginning. Without my memories to prove otherwise, this co-created event was going to happen, regardless of what Steve thought. My father was told, and he was only angry that I kept trying to include Steve in my life, NOT that I was pregnant!

During the next few months, I worked with Catholic Charities, my father's choice, for the adoption that would follow shortly after my baby's arrival. The night that I went into labor was a full moon in December, and I was the first woman to arrive. Thirteen others came into maternity shortly thereafter, and all of them had their babies before I did.

My daughter was born after 23 hours of labor on December 11, 1974. Dad looked at her once, satisfied that all was as it was supposed to be, and quickly walked away to see me. He was gentle with me, but adamant about my staying true to my pre-arranged course. I spent as much of those three days in the hospital visiting with my daughter as I could. Early in January, I tried to join the Navy, and the recruiter turned me away, saying that it wasn't going to work out for me in these circumstances. However I did take the tests, and I guess someone tipped off my father, as he'd been in the Navy during WWII. He came home one night, livid with me, and as I got more hysterical, his voice got calmer, and he signaled my mother to make a call to have me committed. I calmed then, and went to my room, petrified that even though I was over 18, I couldn't fight my father.

Dad came in to my room, shortly after this scene, calm as well, and told me he was leaving my mother. I didn't really hear his reasons, but somehow all of this was laid at my feet, and Dad left. The ploy worked, and I couldn't bear to see my mother so sad, moping around the house, her eyes not meeting mine. Finally, I went to see my daughter one last time at the orphanage. I cried till I slept, then cried each time I awoke. I could hardly see through my eyes the next morning! I went to Mom, told her I'd do as Dad had asked, and sign her over for adoption. I went to Catholic

Charities the next day, and I did it alone. Signing her over to the nuns took more courage than I thought I had, and I cried all the way home. I decided to move back to my home town in Idaho, and go to the local college. This was all accomplished in a whirlwind of calls and packing. I'd finally be on my own, or so I believed. Dad flew home the night before I left, telling me that I'd done the right thing, and that it would all work out for the best.

There were two rituals during this time. The first was with those I call the "Ancients," an old couple that can appear much younger, that are Reptilian hybrids. I know them as Dame Mother and Grande Pere. They've been in my life since I was training for my early rituals in Idaho, and they've always been kind and loving to me. Regardless of their agenda, I've never been afraid to talk to them straight out, about anything that was on my mind, regardless of being in ritual with them more than once. The private ceremony with them was over the last weekend that I spent in Maryland, and they told me where I'd fit in the future with them, as well as how it would all work out with my daughter. Many years would pass before I'd remember this conversation. The blood ritual sealing with only the three of us took place in the bed chamber that I'd been in for my seeding ritual. It was all very erotic, all of us at the same linear age, and the blood belonged only to me, and when it was done I knew I'd reached yet another level in this other world.

The second ritual was with the same folks as the twinning ceremony, and it was a night of many witnesses, happening mid-January of 1975. The following weekend I celebrated my 19th birthday on the 19th in Idaho with friends that I grew up with when last there, along with a man that would become my next boyfriend. Dad didn't like this man, not just because he was in the middle of a divorce, but because he didn't have a job of any kind. What Dad didn't know was that he was a dealer, and he made enough money for rent and food, which was all he really wanted out of life at the time.

Dad had business in the area several times a year, so we'd go out to lunch or dinner at least once a visit. I remember one occasion when I accidentally told the waitress to get something, prefacing that it was for my Dad. He got extremely quiet, and when she left, he glared at me, saying very softly, but each word like a physical slap, "Never call me your father when we are out together in public!" Smiling tightly, he went on to eat as if nothing had happened. It certainly makes sense now, but at the time, I was very confused. I never did it again, and the episode was dropped.

There was at least one ritual in August of 1977. I was in the process of moving to Seattle. The man involved was not from above ground, but from beneath it. This took place on an island that couldn't be reached except by ferry from Seattle. The man had a red tinge to his skin, was over 6 feet tall, and resembled a gargoyle. What was even more interesting was that when I saw the movie "Gargoyles" in the early 1980's, I was very attracted to the leader of these "Hollywood" creatures. I didn't realize it was because he resembled this man that I'd known since childhood in Idaho. He was a gentle giant, and very powerful, but I didn't fear him at all.

I moved to western Oregon at the end of '78 to find a job and settle down. My ex-boyfriend had moved to the area two years before I did, and his friends were high level dealers, involved in importing and exporting businesses that were used as a cover for the money they made in their trade. In a gesture to keep me out of trouble, one of them assigned his girlfriend to me. Kathy became my constant companion and best friend. However, I was talking too much, even to her, and it was decided to farm me out to Las Vegas or "lose" me in San Diego. Kathy knew what was happening, and intervened. Her boyfriend decided to turn me over to his brother, who was separated, and soon to be divorced.

This new man in my life took me out of my apartment, moved me into his home, and told me to quit my job. This done, I "disappeared" for three months. During that time I was gently "broken" spiritually and mentally. Finally, he took a Polaroid picture of me handcuffed to his bedpost wearing only a smile and a pair of black six inch heels. As soon as he showed this to his brother, it was decided that I was no longer a problem.

He referred to himself as a hedonist, and enjoyed every possible sexual fantasy with me. My "job" was to seduce the woman or couple that he would choose for us. He called it "handling school." I learned to drink a lot of alcohol and remain reasonably sober. I mixed it with an array of mind bending-drugs. This behavior continued through our wedding day, and into the early '80s. The verbal abuse from him became more physical, especially if I tried to stand up for myself. I was told I was a battered wife, but I wasn't listening.

We moved to California to be closer to my mom and dad. I was blacking out more often when I drank, and growing tired of the constant party atmosphere. I began to fight back by saying no, getting hit in the process. We decided to visit his brother and girlfriend during the summer of '83. She became my lifeboat in a sea of sexual misery. She began to seduce me, and I let her. We'd allow my brother-in-law to watch our enjoyment of each other, mostly because she wanted his permission to continue the affair. During this time my rituals were further apart, mostly due to tapping the energy from me that was easy to glean from my intense lesbian affairs. Being with women was the safest escape from what was already a prison-like existence with my husband. I returned to California in August, and we decided to move to an apartment across town.

There was a ritual in December of that year, when I was 27. I remember it now as being with the "Ancients" and the same boy that fathered my daughter from my core ritual team while I was in Maryland. This was through time-folding, as I found myself in an underground chamber that resembled the one I'd been in during my years back east, but I'm not entirely certain. Dame Mother and Grande Pere became the same age as we were for this ceremony, and it furthered their agenda. This particular ceremony was without anyone around to watch us, like the one that involved them in 1975. As usual, I awoke in my apartment, clueless to all that had happened!

I was told by my husband that I'd need to find work, and I expressed a desire to sing with a band. I found a local group that would let me sing a few songs during every gig. Finally, my husband began to disappear for days at a time. I found out later that he'd established a new identity in the area. He had girlfriends, places to stay, and I was no longer included in his world. Because he was less and less sober, I'd learned to sleep perfectly still for the entire night when he'd come home. If I made any kind of movement, he'd force himself on me. After a particular unwilling episode on our bedroom carpet, he stood up and passed out on the bed. I took out our gun and pointed it at his head. My plan was to kill him and then turn the gun on myself. I stopped before firing, sank to the floor in the fetal position, hugged myself and asked why God had abandoned me. A few minutes passed, and I decided to put the gun away and take a shower! It saved me a prison sentence, and for that I'm grateful.

Finally, he moved up to Oregon for an extended stay. He became clean and sober at the end of 1986. My mother died in the middle of 1987, and it hit me hard. I began to drink to blackout as often as possible. Dad told me to file for a divorce in December of 1988, find a job, and move to a place of my own. I did all of this, but couldn't stay sober. Then my brother died in January of 1990, and I not only lost my job, but the next three assignments through an agency.

I'd alienated my family, my friends, and was dangerously close to losing my latest job that I happened to like, but not quite enough to keep going. On November 6, 1991, I took four over the counter sleeping pills, and drank a lot of vodka. I managed to call my family to tell them it was over for me. There was a knock on my apartment door. An ambulance had been called, and I was taken to County by the police to have my stomach pumped. Although it may have been the drugs and alcohol, I left my body for awhile, watching my family crying behind me. I was finally ready for sobriety, and checked into a center for recovery that weekend.

Clean and sober at last, I was welcomed back to my job, and have remained at the same company for 13 years, learning a variety of new responsibilities over time. The man I sang with lost his wife to another man a year after I got sober, and we began to date. In 1995 I found out I was pregnant at the age of 39, and that I was going to have a son. I waddled down the aisle with my father ten days before my son was born, but he truly didn't seem to care whether I got married or not! Apparently my son was also "planned" with the help of my father, but I carried out the marriage because I felt it was important to do it in this way.

Dad was always around after the birth of my son. He visited constantly, and spent his last Christmas at our home, when my son was 10 months old. We were told the following April that he had ALS, and I begged him to write a biography of his life. He did this through August of 1997, then by October he was in a nursing home, and he passed away in December, on my daughter's 23rd birthday, four days before he would have turned 79. Interestingly enough, Dad's story of his life was all about his Navy and financial consulting years, with very little reference to his family.

There were two rituals in 1993. Again, I was "removed" from my area, and returned without the loss of time. One was in August, and the last one was in mid-December. As I write this in the spring of 2004, I'll admit that I've only been gathering my memories for a year, with most of my rituals coming to light for me last fall. It was a shaky journey, but one with a recently found support group that have helped me to heal myself, as well as heal others in the process. Things fell into place, and my daughter came back into my life one week after her 29th birthday. I was eventually able to share with her how she'd come into existence, and she's been a fabulous set of eyes reading my masked memories as they have continued to tumble out to be healed and settled within me. I feel incredibly fortunate, and have worked hard to deprogram and heal my past.

The journey continues, and I'm ready to move forward to wherever it takes me.

Case #3 Analysis
The Seeding Programming

This story provides an extremely insightful view into what is termed by the Illuminati as "The Seeding Program." This type of programming began in the Nazi era and continued after the end of World War II. It was designed to perpetuate the German concept of the Aryan Superior race.

The Seeding Program was conducted by finding a male and female with genetics that closely resembled, or was identical to, the original Human-Lyraen ideal. These genetics include blonde hair and blue eyes, red hair and green eyes, or any combination thereof. Very often, these genetics are found in the Celtic or Germanic peoples. Sometimes, Russian and other Eastern Europeans are used for this breeding purpose. Usually the ancestries of these peoples can be traced to ancient Viking origins.

The Nazi "matchmakers" mated males and females of these desirable genetics to produce offspring with similar genetics. The infants were preliminarily programmed, then either placed into an adoption agency that worked with the international Nazi network, or placed directly with a family trained to raise the child in a specific manner. The adoptive parents then become the handlers of the child.

In the US, many of these children of the Seeding Program were placed in the northern Midwest, the Rocky Mountain States, parts of Appalachia, and in many rural areas of California, Texas, and the Pacific Northwest. They were monitored frequently. Their progress and further programming were closely analyzed. They were part of a system created in the 1930s to create "super-children" that would be the next phase of humanity.

Many of these children, as in this case, were used in sexual ritual because their mind-power and physical bodies could take so much. Most "normal" children would have died from the experiences these superkids were put through. Blonde-haired, blue-eyed people are more easily programmed due to an enzyme in their DNA that allows for an overlay of instructions. This could be an indication of genetic manipulation going back millions of years.

Many of these seeded children were themselves made to reproduce, in turn placing their offspring up for adoption so that a new phase, or level, of the Seeding Program could be observed and solidified. The offspring also inherit ancient programming, becoming very valuable and prized by the elite families that "own" them.

It was from this program that genetic combinations and sequences were created that were then seeded into the standard population, inclusive of genetic programming. These are now known as the "indigo children" or "star children." These are Illuminati terms given to the new crop of genetically-altered children who are specifically programmed to perform certain functions for their NWO masters.

This woman has many memories of ritual ceremonies where she is used in many ways for creating in physical reality. Her genetics are perfect for programming and Monarch functions. Her adoptive father was an excellent and strict handler for her. She needed to do a lot of release work on him to remove negative mind-patterns before she could successfully begin to unhook the attached programming.

Her protocols are heavily involved with Monarch Butterfly deprogramming procedures. White Rabbit deprogramming is also necessary because of it is highly likely that her energy is used for inter-dimensional uses.

She was moved all around the country to where her handler and her father's controllers could use her energies and programming for Sexual Magick Rituals in the various locales. In her case, many country clubs were used to provide easy access to high-ranking government leaders. Of course, she is denied access to her birth parents as contact with them may activate her true self-identity and open up genetic sequences that would become a problem for the programming in her matrix. This is a common scenario in the Seeding Program.

These Monarchs, both male and female, are able to handle a lot of abuse. What would damage or even kill another genetic mix, is taken in stride by this group. They pervade all levels of Monarch programs, but there is a heavy concentration in the mainly sexual Beta Monarch category.

There are many characteristics that are common to this group. They tend to be taller than most people. They stand out in a crowd. When they walk in a room, everyone knows that they are present.

They tend to have lighter color hair that they make extra light through dyes or sunlight. The women tend to be voluptuous and the men tend to be muscular and hairy. They all have good bone density and always look younger than their chronological age.

Both the males and the females have bisexual abilities and desires. This is necessary due to ritualistic requirements where they may have to participate in sexual activity with both sexes—sometimes at once. However, in their personal relationships that are permanent, they generally choose opposite sex mates.

Both sexes in this category are groomed to take high-level positions in ritual. This means that they apprentice under high-ranking ritual teachers. The teacher changes as the Monarch ages, with new instructors for different types of rituals.

Often, this category of slave is trained to become a "god" or "goddess" in ritual as they progress up the ranks. Refer to my book, ***True Reality of Sexuality***, (*Expansions Publishing Company, Inc, 2005*) for details.

Another trend here is that there are usually children born to these Monarchs that do not grow up with them. This is true for both the males and females. Often, a fetus is extracted and used as a sacrifice. However, many report an actual birth and the child is removed from them. Then, years later, there is a reuniting of the parent and child, which can act as a trigger or activation for all involved.

As these people age, a lot of memory bleeds through and manifests in flashes or visions. Sometimes dreams or nightmares evolve. Often, they abuse alcohol or take drugs to avoid or block these memories from coming through to the conscious mind. In addition, they may smoke cigarettes and/or marijuana in an effort to ground themselves so that they can deal with the enveloping emotional waves.

Many have to deal with frequent suicide alters. It is likely that they will not succeed, but a close eye must be kept on them when in such a mental state. During the deprogramming process, this group has a tendency to flee or alter their consciousness with drugs and alcohol.

This category of slave tends to be scattered or flighty. They are insecure in their interactions with others. Their relationships are precarious at best. It is also difficult to maintain a job and even to take care of the home environment.

The good news is that when this genre of Monarch seriously makes efforts to deprogram, the results are fast and furious. They make great strides in re-integration of the whole personality, easily developing an awareness of their specific triggers. They have the ability to easily self-correct. This attribute makes them some-what of a liability to the Illuminati as these slaves need constant reprogramming. This means the Monarch must be ever-vigilant, constantly working on deprogramming techniques. They have a great success rate which enhances their natural sense of humor!

Case #4
Experimental Monarch Programming

Stewart entered my life suddenly in May of 2006. He consulted with a friend of a friend who suggested that my son-in-law Matthew speak with Stewart since Matthew was in a time of career transition. I remember saying to Matthew that if he felt the consultation was worthwhile I would call and make an appointment for myself.

Matthew was impressed by the accuracy and helpful insights expressed by Stewart so I made the call. One call, one moment, one seemingly small decision to get some advice regarding my health!! That first call began a process in which I am still engaged. A process of self-discovery on levels so deep I often do not understand it, cannot control it, and at the same time a process that holds the potential to integrate many parts of myself, to help me understand what has driven my fractured life, and to free me from some of its violent upheavals and self-destructive actions.

Even as I am involved in long-term consulting with Stewart, he has already given me my life and health back. There is no way to repay him except to "pay all I can forward," as the saying goes! Now as my own work benefits others, Stewart's help ripples out into this world.

I injured my lower back ten years ago and suffered severe back pain with recurring episodes until Stewart! The intense pain of two ruptured disks left me flat on my back for weeks on end. Two MRI's clearly showed the damage. I injured it again and again, gradually losing all confidence in any hope of recovery, in myself, and in any sense that healthy possibilities lay ahead for me. With Stewart's help I am completely free of pain and can sit, exercise, drive, work, and do everything that healthy people do. Before the injury, I always had a tremendous amount of energy and now it is mine again! Stewart awakened me from a coma of sorts and then I began remembering.

My life is marked by sudden violent changes. Each was precipitated by a meeting with a particular individual. The similarities in each episode exist in their sudden beginnings, intensity, duration, and the severing endings. Each segment has its own cast of characters.

I have a photograph of myself at five years old. For years at a time I could not bare to look at it. I look out of that photograph with such solemn eyes, from a face too serious and sad for one so young. I never threw the photo away but kept it hidden in a drawer in every place I've lived until now. Only now am I facing that child with Stewart's support. I am slowly uncovering masked memories, ones camouflaged deeply underneath layer upon layer of stories.

My childhood memories are disjointed, incomplete; suddenly appearing in my mind as if from nowhere, then leaving me wondering, filled with doubts about what happened, distrustful of myself and my own memory. These memories may even be out of order as I write now because I am unsure and I am aware of an energy that is trying to stop me from going further. I get ice cold, feel sick to my stomach, and lately there is a sound in my head. Only Stewart knows about any of this.

There were the nightmares as a very small child. Someone or something came in through the window and tried to hold me down in bed, choke me with my own sheets and blankets, smother me, put something inside my vagina while I screamed for my mother. She told me to stop crying but would not listen to what I was screaming about. I begged her to pin down the sheets and blankets to hold them away from my throat. What I am saying is not reasonable and I cannot help that. I do not understand it either.

There is a scar on the back of my neck. My parents' story was that I needed radium treatments a few times to stop something that began growing there. I think I was only two or three years old. Maybe I was younger. I cannot remember those treatments. They were done in Rome, New York. Only the strange scar exists today.

A memory surfaced about a cat. I think I was five; I'm not sure. I was playing with a cat near a fire hydrant and choked it to death. I have no feelings associated with that incident, no feelings at all. That is what is so strange. I loved animals and still do. The story told was that I did not mean to choke it. I had somehow wound a fire hydrant chain around its neck. That does not seem possible. I remember my mother just smiled and life went on.

Meanwhile my father was always frightening. One moment pacing in the kitchen, the next raising an angry voice. He was so unpredictable, we all tip-toed around him. I loved and hated him. It seemed like he was always watching me, preoccupied by how I looked alone. All else about me was irritating or unimportant to him. In fact, he criticized, and belittled me often. One day he threw me onto his bed when I was little, maybe eight or nine? I'm not sure of my age. Then he lay over me, on top of me, while I screamed for him to stop. Then I stopped screaming. His anger was always sudden, intense, and terrifying. There were no ordinary conversations, no softness, no affection. His handling taught me that the hand that strikes you touches you sexually, then buys you beautiful things, hates you, and loves you without tenderness.

All holidays were nightmares. Something would set him off and I would eventually escape upstairs to lie on my bed sobbing. That is just the way it was. During my teenage years I began to yell back at him, slam doors, and return his anger to him. I was always physically healthy except I often vomited, was sick to my stomach, then fine.

The dentist remained a dreaded experience. My mother would trick me by saying we were going shopping downtown and then as we passed Dr. Rowlson's door she would suddenly take me in. That fear lives throughout my body even today.

We lived in a dismal town south of the Canadian border called Plattsburgh. It had a big SAC (Strategic Air Command) base. My father moved there as a boy from New York City with his five brothers and sisters, and mother and father. His father was mysteriously killed in Canada when he was very young. No one ever said how his father was killed. My father's friends were mostly lawyers, judges, military officers. His closes friend was George Fagan , a colonel who became second in command at the Air Force Academy in Colorado Springs when I was in high school.

I was taken to McGill University in Montreal, Canada for an operation to remove a cyst on my jaw when I was maybe seven years old. I was in the hospital for weeks. My memory is faulty here. I can see the huge room my bed was in, long halls, a metal table I was strapped down to and the buildings outside where I think I was. My parents told me the doctor was a famous plastic surgeon, one used by British royalty. His name was Dr. John Gerrie. His face looks so much like Dr. Ewen Cameron. What was done to me there? Does it connect to my nightmares earlier on? My mind just stops. No answers come. As I write this now I feel sick to my stomach, anxious, and shaky inside. The sound in my head is blaring right now.

School went on and as I learned about the Holocaust and saw films of the victims I lost hope. I immersed myself in existential literature and any belief in a Christian God or in ultimate goodness in this world left me. Western religion seemed woefully inadequate when faced with the problem of evil. Life, I decided was essentially meaningless, absurd. I trusted no one. That refrain haunts me to this day.

Home life in Plattsburgh continued. My younger brother Robert retreated into his room as I became more volatile and openly confronted our father. I hated my mother's lack of courage in staying with this man with the strength and judgment only an inexperienced fifteen-year-old can muster. As I became more disillusioned with upper middle class living, Robert dealt with our father by trying to please him. It was impossible. Rob just kept trying. My father's plan was for me to be "watched over" by George and Ernestine at the Air Force Academy so they sent me to Colorado College.

I escaped; first to Chicago, then to New York City where I lived with Bob Dylan's McDougal Street crowd, taking mescaline and watching energy run through the veins of everything, at times feeling very alive. I was even a little hopeful when looking at art. Great art became my proof that man could create something other than destruction, other than the Holocaust. Rob went on to Middlebury and then Dartmouth for his graduate degree in Business Administration to please Dad. He married a very ambitious woman who hated me on sight – an experience later repeated by my son's wife.

A recurring nightmare began when I was about seventeen: I am in a house with many rooms, windows, and doors. Some men, military Nazi-like men, are trying to get in. They want me, to kill me I fear, or something much worse. I feel only terror so I frantically try and try again to tell my mother, tell my father, and all the others in the house what is happening but no one will listen. No matter how hard I try. They do not see the men coming after me. I run to lock all the doors and windows. They somehow get in. One man grabs me holding me and pulling me toward him. As I look into his face, his face changes into my father's face. I keep screaming and another man holds me and his face becomes my mother's. I realize there is no one who will ever help me, no one! That's when I wake up. Every time.

In my waking hours I daydreamed about becoming a lawyer in hope of saving the world from corruption, a poet because only a poet's music can open the heart and mind, and a psychiatrist in hope of saving my friends in Plattsburgh who were suicidal, hospitalized, and given shock treatments. I had no idea how to accomplish any of these goals, so my life drifted along.

One very positive and consistent trait I have is this: I have a gift for making close friends. My friendships have rarely been difficult. They were and are a source of deep delight and mutual understanding. During each of my "different" lives within this one life, I always had friends around me who helped me through the roughest times as I did the same for them.

My first lover ever was a German bass player with the great jazz pianist Cecil Taylor. Buell was a brilliant musician, a cold, crazy guy who became a heroine addict before my eyes. Why didn't I join him? My mysterious good fortune and phobia of needles is the only answer I know. My drug of choice was always speed. I craved control before oblivion! From seventeen on I sought wild experience. Sex happened but it was essentially work not pleasure for me. It never occurred to me that sexual pleasure could be connected to tenderness, to loving intimacy.

I think deep down I felt that no one wanted to really know me and that if he did he would not love me so I created a persona designed to please. Over time I could not keep the façade going. So violence and the end of each relationship was always close by. Sex became giving a performance accompanied by sudden anxiety and fear. My feelings were ambivalent: excitement, distrust, hurt, the desire to give a good performance. I always felt very, very alone. I kept hidden deep inside myself, with a sense of meaninglessness and despair always with me. Thoughts of suicide became my constant companion. At the same time I began to race after life's experiences, wanting to experience everything. What that "everything" was I didn't really know. With Buell I was in the center of the New York City jazz scene, at clubs until dawn, feeling cool, and scared at the same time. As would be my pattern lifelong, I was rarely attracted to anyone and when it happened it was intense and all consuming.

The first gay bar I went to blew my mind. There were so many men, and none of them wanted me to perform for them and none of them wanted to hurt me. It was heaven!!! I loved it. And I loved them, immediately. The most courageous men I have known have been gay. From that time on I began to have homosexual men friends. I left Buell. Heroine addiction is all consuming. There is either recovery or complete addiction with nothing in between.

Viscerally I know addiction versus recovery as a state of mind. It is how I have lived most of the time, only without the drugs. I cannot find middle ground, balance. I think in extremes, am at home only in them no matter how hard I try.

Then I met Michael Mott, an artist who lived in Manhattan. I was designing costumes for a summer theater program and one spring day Paul Gray, the director, and I interviewed Michael. We were looking for a costume designer. It was instant. That instant attraction followed by my immediately changing my life completely would be a pattern that only now I see. I left my other connections effortlessly, as if I had never known them. No conscience, no regrets.

Michael was a very talented artist, a bisexual with an addict's problems. I feel sad for him now but that is another story. We were so young. Not yet twenty. We worked together creating cutting-edge fashions in the middle sixties. He was a brilliant designer and I was his model and sales representative. We were a winning combination except for his raging alcoholism! He could be kind, even worshipful of me. He painted my portrait in oils, made sculptures of me, designed all his amazing clothes for and on me. Then when he drank he was violent, cruel, impossible to reason with. In fact when we first worked together on a theater project a few days after meeting, Michael got drunk and tried to choke me to death. My friend Vic pulled him off. Yet I felt compelled to be with him. I called it love!

I married him, had a son with him and suffered through his addiction for another five years before running away with Anthony. What was all that about? It is as if I had no sense, no intelligence, no will of my own. It has always been the same. I see the person, a sudden rush, and then I become obsessed with creating a self they will love, at any cost to myself. As I remember and write this I realize how Michael's punishing side resembled my father's. I never knew when he was going to drink, when the irrational anger would strike. Just like Dad. The cruel and the loving hand are the same hand!

One time we were visiting my mother and father in Plattsburgh. My mother offered Michael a drink and it began. I stayed with them for a while growing more anxious by the minute. Finally I went upstairs to try to go to sleep. It was impossible. How many hours went by I'll never know but finally Michael came to bed and grabbed me, shaking me harder and harder, then telling me that my mother hated me, that she always had and always would. It was true. I already knew that. Later with Anthony it was much more frightening.

With each of the people I have lived with in my life I was only to be able to leave when I had exhausted every experience; when life with them had been wrung dry through harsh times; when I could look at each one and the obsessive feelings were gone. Then when each life was over, it was completely over. I had no feelings for them, no ties to them.

Michael and I lived an exciting New York City creative life. We worked for Paul Young and designed clothes for the iconic clothing store Paraphernalia. We did live shows at Filmore East and television shows. We lived in extremes. We visited Hugh Hefner's mansion in Chicago because he wanted us to redesign the "bunny" costume. I was interviewed on television there. Inside I was unable to relax, always worried and frightened, waiting for Michael's inevitable drinking. Fame was so close!

One night Michael introduced me to a new, very cool Italian New Yorker named Anthony Musachio. We looked at one another, that huge rush consumed me. Michael and I brought him home with us that first night. We were drinking, taking speed, and Michael wanted to take both of us to bed. I began to feel a terrible trepidation because I knew Michael could get angry at any moment and with all that speed racing through our systems it could be a long, long night. Anthony and I were held together with an inexplicable force so into the bedroom we all went.

Within minutes Michael saw the attraction between Anthony and me. He began to yell at Anthony, telling him to leave our apartment. Both Anthony and I scrambled to get some clothes on and somehow we got out the door slamming it behind us. I loved that adrenalin rush plus amphetamine with its illusion of power and control! Anyway, my addiction was to destruction which became easy then because I saw life as meaningless with despair living at the center of all the highs!

Anthony and I slept at an Italian friend's place that night, at the writer Ronnie Miglionico's, and my Italian period began. I loved Anthony. He was so strong physically, had shining black eyes and hair, behaved the same way drunk or sober, loved art, loved me, and loved destruction. We hung out at the famous Max's Kansas City frequented by artists of that time: Andy Warhol, Robert Rauschenberg, Janis Joplin, etc. Closing the bar, we'd walk around the city or ride the Staten Island Ferry back and forth, watch dawn come to our beloved New York City and end up at a café for breakfast. Bob Dylan's words belonged to us: "How does it feel? Oh, how does it feel...to be on your own, with no direction home, a complete unknown...like a rolling stone".

We loved the film Bonnie & Clyde. Very literally, we began to live our own version. I saw the law as a corrupt construct serving the rich; the government as beastly corrupt; the military industrial complex as insane. From this perspective, what ordinary people call crime, I thought was a fair enough idea! No cheating friends, though. That was my only rule. I will not write about our crimes. Suffice it to say that we would have spent most of our lives in jail had we been caught.

Anthony grew up in Red Hook, Brooklyn. His friends were either artists like Peter Max and Tom Daly, or mafia. On several occasions Anthony saved my life by keeping me safe from his friends. One time we were walking down St. Mark's Place toward Second Avenue, when I was pulled from behind up against Bobbie D. He just held me and said to Anthony, "How about the money you owe me, or we'll take her for a few hours." Luckily Anthony gave him the money. Unless you have been near these men you have no idea what they are like; what they routinely do to women.

I became pregnant and felt overwhelmed with the prospect of a baby. I found a truly humane doctor to help me, Dr. Nathan Rappaport. His daughter had died trying to abort an unwanted baby and he had refused to help her. From then on he helped women both by delivering babies and giving abortions. Anthony said he didn't care what I did so my friend Myrna went with me. Always my dear friends helped me! I'll never forget going home from that experience. Anthony greeted me at the door and said, "You should not have done that." I slapped his face and sobbed for a long time. He did not raise a hand to me...that time.

We took off from New York for Mexico driving a big Caddy with just the clothes on our backs. We lived on pills(speed), coffee, Johnny Walker Black, and our dreams of crimes that would make us rich. We barely escaped death in Matzatlan at the hands of some coke dealers. By the time we got to Los Angeles, the tension involved in living underground was too much for me. One evening at an Italian restaurant I started to hemorrhage. My friend Kay took me to a hospital emergency room. I began to realize that what goes around comes around. That is really Anthony's biggest gift to me. I found I could no longer pretend that black was white, and that my actions had no consequences.

Six months later back in New York, I was pregnant again. I fantasized about having a "little Anthony" of my own because by this time Anthony was often out with other women. Everyone knew I belonged to Anthony so no one ever dared to come near me. My heart was broken, and he couldn't understand why. "After all," he would say, "I love only you."

Anthony's father often visited us unannounced, sometimes pace the floor, make a few calls, brew espresso, cook some gravy(red pasta sauce) and then walk out into the night. I met him for the first time while in the hospital having Colette. He just came through the door of my room toward me. His face was hard and so tough that I yelled, "Get out of here. You must be in the wrong room." He kept coming toward me. "I'm Anthony's father, for Christ's sake," he said.

I was overwhelmed and bored with our criminal life. Anthony began to make mistakes and I could not stop him. I needed to do something else. Fashion had been wonderful but too superficial in the end to sustain me. I decided to go back to college and become an art historian. My dream was to be a curator at the Metropolitan Museum or at least work at a top gallery in New York City.

In the meantime, it was obvious that my parents approved of my brother, Rob's efforts so they bought him a beautiful French restaurant on the Cape. Nothing was available for me. It always seemed that I ought to just have money. I never considered doing anything for it! Colette was a baby and childcare was too expensive in the city so I decided to go back to Plattsburgh. There, my mother could take care of Colette and I could go to New York State University there.

Going back to school was fabulous for me. I loved every text, devoured every lecture, and memorized hundreds of slides of the world's great art. Meanwhile, Anthony and I grew farther and farther apart. He grew sullen and angry. My growing independence threatened his hold over me. He became increasing abusive. One evening as we drove back to our apartment in the convertible my mother gave us, it began to rain. I asked him to stop and put up the top. He swore and continued driving. Again I asked him to put up the top. We were all getting wet. He swerved the car, slammed on the brakes and began screaming obscenities at me.

I realized that if I wanted to get home alive I had to become silent, invisible, and wait for the tirade to stop. At home I carried the baby into her room and stood by the crib praying that he would go out. Finally he did. I lay in bed hoping he would be hit by a car and I would not have to face him when he got home. He came home and by morning he was still violent. I escaped barefoot pushing Colette in her stroller walking a few miles to my mother's home. From there I called Anthony and told him to get out, it was over. He stole the car and headed for New York City. I felt such relief.

Relief was short-lived though, because Anthony threatened my life for the next five years. Five years! His obsession with me nearly made me doubt my own sanity. Many times I did not think I had the strength to survive. It had been so hard living with him only to find the further irony that after leaving him, his violent feelings for me grew, rather than lessen. He began calling at all hours with obscene threats, broke into my apartments, and once kidnapped

Colette. The police were useless, one officer asking me what I had done to make Anthony so angry! I felt safe only when driving a car.

In my experience, brutality awakened many emotions and as it continued my heart shut down so completely that it is hard for me to open it. Eventually, I kept a .38 under my pillow knowing I was ready to shoot him if he broke in again. Anthony did not give me the opportunity.

A woman friend introduced me to feminist literature. I read and read and read, devouring and digesting all the truth that I was reading. This was a perspective that partly explained my father and all the other men in my life. How could I ever be with a man again? Ever? My answer was that I would never know a man again.

Then Connie appeared in my life. The irony is she was actually more like a man than a woman, yet at first her lack of involvement with men impressed and intrigued me. How was it possible for a woman to not want a man? This woman did not need a man. She lived in a world of only women. The gestures, the costumes, interested me, too. Always I saw all of life as theater and this was one theater I had not been involved with yet! I did not mind the sex. I never had to be afraid…this was a woman who did not throw me face down on the bed and fuck me in the ass until I bled. None of that. So I managed. I was so used to faking it I just continued and she didn't know the difference anymore than the men had.

I am aware that my feelings for each of these people in my life were similar! The situations were different, my reactions, obsession, and lonely dissatisfaction, the same. It was as if something within me ran and repeated the same tape, the same movie, again and again. Each time there were different characters but my role remained the same: first the sudden, overwhelming attraction, then the complete lifestyle change, more dark explorations, a slave-like attachment to each person, then rebellion, my intelligence would kick in, and I'd leave the whole scene, that whole life.

After some time with Connie I grew very unhappy and found I didn't really fit into the gay scene. I simply was not gay. I loved women as allies and friends. I loved my close gay men friends so much but I became irritated and impatient with these women who were either acting like men or pretending to be feminine counterparts to what I saw increasingly as counterfeit men! Drag shows were fun theater with great costumes. I appreciated the humor, style, and courage of some very strong men in crazy costumes! But the life was not mine.

My next life began in Salt Lake City, Utah. A long way from New York! After I graduated from New York State University in Plattsburgh I also got my Master's degree in Education and began teaching mentally-challenged children. Often violent, caught within alternate realities, abused at home, I found I naturally loved and understood these children. All my difficult experiences enabled me to reach these kids and help them a little and actually often a great deal! This was not the career in art history I longed for, but it was in front of me. I learned how to accept what is and I also knew that the only way to work with people was to receive them as they are, love them, and believe they could gain agency over their lives. I worked in this rural ghetto for four long years before moving to the Poughkeepsie Day School at Vassar.

Next was life in Salt Lake City. I worked in a beautiful private school with privileged and gifted people. I learned so much there, found myself looked to as a mentor, a master teacher who developed programs, supported teachers, parents, and the children. My work was a bright light in my life from then on. I don't feel like I chose my work. It happened in spite of me; was simply my destiny.

Paul was my last husband! We met in Salt Lake City and began an animated, intense dialogue that lasted for years. We were natural best friends. For three years I refused to be anything other than friends with him. Then one evening, everything changed. The rest is a wild ride with big highs, terrible loss, and the old severing way of ending. I followed him to California, joined a spiritual community called Ananda that is dedicated to the ideas of Paramahansa Yogananda.

I began an elementary school based on universal spiritual principles. I was always very skeptical of organizations, any formalized structure, being at heart an anarchist. I hated small towns and loved the anonymity of big cities. Now I was living in a yogic community. How could this have happened? A small town where everyone knew too much about everyone else. I did not know the first thing about where I was and what was going on. Yet immediately I was at the center of it all. Like usual!

Paul mistook the attention of the leaders of the organization personally and felt he was going to be a leader somewhere at last. That was a ridiculous misperception. I always knew better even before I understood the ideas behind the behavior of Asha and David. I got knots in my stomach and knew that the destruction of the ego was not going to be the fun he so misunderstood.

Ananda is deeply rooted in Paramahansa Yogananda's ancient wisdom tradition of kriya yoga meditation. Ananda communities exist as places where devotees of Paramahansa Yogananda can live near one another, meditate together, do service to the community, and otherwise live as privately as each person chooses. Ananda is not a corrupt cult. However its leaders are a small group that has isolated itself. The ministers want to build the organization, so truth gets distorted because of their priority of increasing the organization's size and their need for money to accomplish this!! So, what's new in organizations? Same old story but with the added language of spiritual ideas.

I choose my own way, my own inner guidance and freedom, and will not join another organization that claims to be selling The Truth. What a relief to know that now!!

Beginning a school in this context provided me with an opportunity for an astonishing amount of learning. I have been able to bring into practical form some Eastern philosophical ideas. Every rough experience in my life enabled me to work with people in a way that built this school. Again I am reminded that my way of dealing with harsh experience is: "Do for another what was not done for me." Contribute to another's life in a positive way. This brings personal pleasure and on a deeper level supports my own healing as well as someone else's.

By spring of the first year Paul left and I was on my own to carry on the work of the school. We began with 13 students.

The life experiences that brought me the understanding that what goes around comes around grew into an understanding of the universal Law of Cause and Effect, or Karma. The problem of evil that I found insufficiently answered by western theology was placed in the larger context of reincarnation and duality. The western psychological understanding of responsibility expanded into a sense of ultimate responsibility far exceeding the idea of personal responsibility for one life alone.

Here at Ananda, I have had the chance to learn the difference between an organization's needs determined by personalities and ancient truth. It has taken me these fifteen years to learn how to not "throw the baby out with the bath water" as the saying goes. I have learned to be patient, sometimes! I am learning how to express ideas calmly when disagreeing in my school instead of being so attached to my way that my energy is not clear.

Living Wisdom School is an extraordinary place where children thrive because they are each appreciated, accepted, loved for who they are and given a cutting-edge, integrated, imaginative cur- riculum. By now we have kids in high schools who speak about their school experience and what it has given them. I live with the understanding now of the benefit of staying somewhere and working things through instead of always leaving. I see how long it takes to really accept people who do not think as I do and how valuable that is.

I needed to free myself from involvement in Ananda's organiza- tion. Having done that, I can freely reflect on my life here, choos- ing in what I wish to participate. I am finding right relationship to those around me and feeling some equanimity inside myself.

I do not yet have a new direction for the future. My old pattern would be to simply take off. Now I am not willing to do that. Where shall I go from here? Here after fifteen years I have loved friends. My work has meant a great deal to me and many others. I'm not sure it's wise to just leave it. I have lived so many places, left so many people. Yet at the same time I am open to new possibilities.

Is it time to face that there is nowhere to go but inside? Reason tells me it is too late in this life to find another love, another distraction from the inner work that eventually holds the only hope for true freedom.

Case #4 Analysis
Experimental Monarch Programming

Here is a perfect example of a woman who was at the incipient time period for Monarch Programming in the United States and Canada. This happened in the late 1940s through the early 1960s. During that approximately fifteen years, the Illuminati experimented and refined various versions of the programming.

They looked for certain types of females, young and a clean slate, who could then be downloaded with all sorts of functions and alters. Then, they were watched over a few years to see how the programming meshed with their mind-patterns.

In those days, medical doctors were employed to watch the females as they developed. Places like the one mentioned in Montreal were used as centers for the programming, as well as Air Force bases in remote locations, like the one in Plattsburgh, New York.

When the programmers or controllers determined that a function or alter groups were not viable, in those days, they simply either added more programming, or attempted to "write over" the old or "bad" programming function.

This caused many mental and physical conditions to develop, especially later in life to these "slaves." They often developed back pain, immune disorders, nervous conditions and weight issues—going to extremes one direction or the other. None of them had easy lives.

Most of these women were sent into different life scenarios to see how they reacted. Almost all of them were the daughters of military, police, government workers, or descendents of elite families from Europe.

In many cases, the fathers were the handlers. The mothers were often treated like non-people or were very weak in the family structure. The programmed females often disliked or despised their mothers. They usually had a love-hate relationship with their fathers and/or grandfathers that at times was sexual. This altered their outlook on men permanently.

All of these females who were part of the early Monarch experiment have relationship issues, not only with their mates, but with people in general. These women tend to be quite adventurous and take many chances in business, sexual partners, and in general lifestyles.

In this example, there is a Bonnie and Clyde scenario. The "life of crime" played out as part of this particular programming function determines survival skills and endurance for being on the run. This proved to be valuable in subsequent Vigilante Programming inputs that were developed in the late 1950s through today.

Many of the early Monarchs were trained to surmount obstacles and blocks placed in their way. Just as scientists use lab rats in a maze to see if they can find their way out, so did the early programmers watch how their subjects maneuvered through difficult and dangerous situations.

There were many who did not survive. Those programming functions were then deemed to be failures and any Monarch with those functions wass eliminated in some way—perhaps in an accident or sudden illness, but usually in a suicide made to look like an accident.

These prototype Monarchs were matched with different males to produce offspring with a genetic blend. Their progeny was used either to begin a new phase of programming or to implement some change within the collective unconsciousness to create a new humanity. The children produced were often extremely intelligent with unique ways of looking at the world. They also had to be monitored carefully as they tended to be highly psychic and could manipulate time and space. Such progeny were used in the secret psi-corps that continues even today.

Another part of the experiment which is evident from this case is the use of varied sexual experiences and lifestyles. This was important back then as it is now for the purpose of establishing a New World Religion where sexual ritual with males and females in all sorts of combinations would be viable. This means that it was important to install alters physically able to deal with same-sex partners, then monitor reactions, psychological damage, and repair options.

Many of these women from the early stages of Monarch programming had bisexual tendencies, or at least had a same-sex relationship at some time in their lives. This allowed the women to be versatile in ritual settings and desensitized them to interact sexually with anyone.*

Physically, these women tend to be fair-skinned with light-colored hair and eyes. Many trace their ancestry to Central or Eastern Europe with connections to Viking or even Mongol genetics from over a thousand years ago.

The Viking-Mongol-Mayan connection must be looked at closely. These three civilizations were extremely powerful and aggressive. They all practiced sacrifice ritual with sexual overtones. The people with these genetics are considered quite valuable for programming as their mind-patterns allow a multitude of different inputs and functions not normally found in the general population.

Eastern European ancestry, especially Polish, Ukrainian, and Russian are commonly found in early Monarchs. This is because

*Refer to my story about Rosie 2 in *Blue Blood, True Blood: Conflict & Creation*, Expansions Publishing Company, Inc., 2002

in 90% of these genetics there can be found Viking and Mongol DNA. These two groups traipsed across Northern and Eastern Europe, mixing with locals and leaving their genetic markers to be found in the twentieth century and beyond.

Another popular genetic mix in the early and current Monarchs is Celtic-Native American-Teutonic. This is perhaps the most favored combination because this group tends to be extremely psychic and mentally powerful, whereas the first group is more physically powerful.

On occasion, they would find a female who had both sets of groups in her background. Such a woman would be filled beyond capacity with programming because she could mentally and physically withstand the input.

Many of these women would also be loaded with Tinkerbelle Programming because they were too valuable to last only a normal lifetime. They would have to be used for an extended period of time to get the most use out of them. Unfortunately, they would be overused and many died suddenly of a stroke or heart-attack. Many of these women also became alcoholics or drug addicts to help them cope with the emotional strain of their functions.

It is very important to analyze the dreams of the early Monarch versions. Their programming, being so preliminary as compared to today, often breaks through mental barriers and manifests in the dream state.

As these women are aging now, much of their programming enters into their waking life and creates disturbances which others may perceive as mental and emotional illnesses. They need to deprogram as soon as possible before the virtual scattered world of experimental programming becomes their normal function.

Yet another factor common to this group is that they move a lot. Not to just a local area, but across the country and even to other continents. Part of the Monarch programming in the beginning, as it remains now, is for mobility to travel from one place to another easily. This makes access to target male figures easier. A side-effect of this programming is that these women do not stay in any one place very long. If you ask their residential history, you will probably get a long list of venues in which they lived and worked.

As they become senior citizens, they again are confronted with ideas of where they should be living and who they should be with. They have doubts on all fronts, yet they feel motivated to keep going. Even in their 60s, these women live and act as if they were 30 years younger.

Deprogramming becomes a challenge for these women. Because they are filled with so much doubt and because their programming is often scattered, incomplete, and experimental, it can be difficult for the untrained counselor to know how to proceed. It must be handled even more gently than any other situation, including a child.

The other difficulty is that since these women are near or just past retirement age, they find little to look forward to after achieving a decent level of deprogramming. Many of them feel that their lives are almost over anyway, so what is the point?

The answer is that life is eternal and any semblance of cohesive personality that can be achieved now will carry forward into any other lifetime. Plus, the Oversoul holds the information beyond time and space, so at any point, any of their lifestreams can access the information and be helped.

The original Monarchs are unique now. There will come a time when they are no longer around. They are the Model Ts of programming in the modern era. Working with them has been a tremendous privilege and learning experience. So much insight into the minds of the original programmers has been gained.

As is the case with so many older versions of anything, we find that they are built well and simply. The same holds true for the first Monarchs' programming. The deprogramming techniques should be simple, but the input was strong. The good news is that the older Monarchs are not part of the reprogramming process.

Therefore, there is little concern that their programming will be reconstituted during the deprogramming process. That is a problem for modern Monarchs.

These older gals have mostly been "put out to pasture", as they say in programming terminology. They are considered harmless; not a liability. Of course, there are exceptions. The ones who are connected to very elite families and who have worked their way up to high levels in ritual are still viable, even on an astral level.

Each case must be viewed individually. There is no standard original Monarch programming. Each programmer took liberties and treated his subjects like laboratory rats. Each test was a curiosity.

These women paved the way for what came later. They can now become examples and role models of how to fix it all.

Case #5
Male Monarch Programming

My name is Daniel and I am the youngest of three kids. Elaine is the eldest and Julia the middle child. I am now in my 40s and my still-married parents are in their 60s and 70s. I'm told I look a bit like the magician David Copperfield, and a younger version of the actor Peter Gallagher. I travel a lot and when in France people think I'm French…the same is true when in Greece, Spain, Italy, and the Middle East.

Conversations inevitably turn to my heritage and I am frequently asked the question "What's your background?" to which I reply "4 years of college with numerous thrills and spills with the famous and infamous alike!" The cause of this confusion and curiosity is probably due to my mixed genetic heritage. My Mom's side of the family is originally of Jewish descent with some sprinklings and dashes of different races.

But to put it all more bluntly, my great, great grandmother Sophia married a Creole man (French/Black) and was disowned. Her daughter, my great-grandmother Christine, was born with very light red kinky hair, fair skin with green eyes. She led a scandalous life, no doubt from having been ostracized by the immediate family, but eventually ended up in Chicago where she married a Hispanic man.

They had several children one of whom is my now deceased Grandma Gina. Gina was also of fair complexion with wavy brown hair and hazel eyes. Gina married my Grandfather Alonzo who was from a Indian tribe in northern Mexico.

Dad's side of the family, while equally colorful in the things they've done, are of indigenous Indian tribes from Mexico. So in an "Earth's population" sense, almost everyone is represented in my genes. . .and as many people have often said, "with your background you are every politician's dream" – little did I know every black magician's dream, too.

What I offer to you is a very brief telling of some of the situations I have encountered from my childhood, teen, young adult, and adult life. Due to space, much of what I relate to you is in no way complete and many, but not all of the names and a few locations have been changed.

Redwood City, California - the beginning of the end...a childhood battered by ghosts, demons, and aliens. By day I would catch the shadowy glimpses of figures in the hallway and by night I would pray with everything I had for peace and for some sort of help, but it didn't come. Somehow writing this description seems so typical. A child who thinks there's a ghost in the room with them is told to go to sleep, but this happened night after night. It was a living hell. Sleep, or should I say the lack of sleep, was something to which I grew accustomed.

I can't remember how the evil presences first made themselves known, but indeed they did despite my nightly prayers. I have some really fond memories of kneeling beside my bed saying my bedtime prayers with my Mom and Dad. Above my bed was a small picture of St. Anthony. With a gentle tucking in by my Mom and Dad a peaceful sleep was supposed to be in store for me. My Mom and Dad always asked if I wanted the night light on and I always said "yes." They left my room with a sweet "good night." Then, as late night crept in the creatures emerged.

They announced their arrival with very loud echoes filled with dragging footsteps. It is important to realize that this is not the normal sound of any person dragging his or her feet. This dragging sound was LOUD and became louder still as it came down the hall towards our bedrooms. Pounding and thunderous booms also occurred as was the sound of what I can only describe as someone wiggling a large metal saw so hard that the reverberation from it seemed to split my head.

I hid under my bed covers pulling them tightly around me, praying to Jesus for help. But there was only an evil and mocking laughter in return. I prayed to Saint Anthony "help me!" Then, as quickly as all the noises started they suddenly stopped. I breathed a hot and stifled sigh of relief and loosened the covers that I drawn so tightly around myself, deciding that I was safe I slowly pulled the covers away from my face to be even more shocked by what happened next.

A man in a trench coat stood next to my bed. I clutched the covers hard and closed my eyes. I would tell myself "he's not there" but as I peered through my squinting eyes I could see the beige color of his coat. I was now scared beyond belief. My heart was pounding and I pulled the covers back over my face. Horror filled and unable to think of anything else to do I threw the blankets off and ran panic-stricken to my Mom and Dad's bedroom.

The man was gone, of course. I was left to struggle, explain, and understand then, as I still do now. What was happening, how this was happening, and why events similar and worse than this continued to happen. As time and more horrible experiences came and went it became more and more important for me to do one thing - not cry.

The haunted days and nights continued. My sisters and my mom all heard and saw spirits. Only my Dad did not experience anything in this house - he snored through everything. Finally, we moved to sunny San Jose where things promised to be very different and indeed they were...

I thought San Jose would bring relief from the hauntings and in some ways it did. The house we moved to was a newly constructed home in a beautiful area. There was a barley farm behind our

house that in the spring turned into a huge expanse of tall bloom-
ing stalks of yellow flowering mustard plants. The area was not
entirely built up as San Jose is now so there were dirt bike paths
to race around on and plenty of other kids my age to play with,
too. The dragging footsteps and other sounds were gone, but now
something else entirely unexpected occurred. Entities were now
making themselves known and were attacking. One afternoon my
Mom and eldest sister Elaine were sitting by the swimming pool
enjoying the sun and water when they heard footsteps walk across
the roof of the house.

The wood shake shingles creaked under the weight of the visitor. My Mom and sister looked, but there was nobody there. My
other sister Julia felt a presence sit at the end of her bed which
then tried to suffocate her, but the ongoing brunt of it all seemed
directed toward me.

I was not quite a teenager when I discovered that night time
exploring in the barley field was a fun way to have adventures. In
the silence of night, the wind made soft wave-like sounds across
the tops of the reeds of barley. This quiet night I decided that I
was going to walk all the way across the ten acres to the farmer's
house. The farmer was not a nice man in the least. By day he chased
anyone out of the field with his shotgun if he saw you trampling
around on his barley.

The barley at this time was probably three feet tall. I remember
being really excited about the possibility of seeing the farmer's
house at night. I ventured out but hadn't made it very far when
up ahead in the distance I saw the outline of a man. It was a total
surprise to see him. I didn't hear him driving in the field with his
truck, but there he was up ahead of me. We were only twenty feet
apart and I struggled to see him clearly. He seemed to be about six
feet tall. From his silhouette he appeared to be wearing a jacket,
trousers, and most distinctly a brimmed hat. There was something
very strange about him; his lack of movement and visible features.
Yet as I stood there I kept thinking to myself that there was also
something very normal about this situation; a farmer protecting
his field.

Still, I couldn't explain how he found me in the dark. As I continued to think about this fact the more and more frightening the whole situation became. I stood there with my heart pounding, deciding that he still does not see me so I took a step toward him. He still didn't move. I remember looking behind him, noticing his truck behind him, but I couldn't remember hearing a truck approach. At this point, enough was enough. I turned to leave, but his eyes suddenly lit up in a bright green color, illuminating eyes that were a multi-pointed star shape. I stood there transfixed and before I could run away a green beam of light shot out of his eyes and hit me hard in the chest. I fell backwards unconscious into the field. I came to sometime afterward, but don't remember anything about getting home or even being troubled by what happened.

It was also during this time that I had dreams of spaceships, often waking up with nose bleeds. I recalled several times waking in the middle of the night with the room being filled with bright white light. I remember quite vividly being taken into the bathroom by a group of short gray aliens. I remember being very upset and asked them why they were taking me. They turned me toward the mirror and when I heard in my head "you are one of us" - I screamed.

The twists and turns of life zoomed forward, hurtling me down its science fiction pathways. My graduation from high school brought about many opportunities and with it the opportunity to explore my suppressed desire for men. From the age of 5 or 6 I was having physical contact with other boys my age, yet I still found that I was having a great deal of problems with my sexual identity. I decided that getting away from the small town of San Jose was probably the best idea.

I left for New York with $500 in my pocket and a one-way airline ticket on a now defunct air carrier called Peoples Express. Life would never be the same.

During my years in New York City, I entered into a relationship with Chad, a well-known record executive for Atlantic records. We lived in Manhattan and East Hampton, attended the Grammy Awards, and partied in London, Austria, and Los Angeles. Everything seemed to be going well on the outside, but inside whoever or whatever was behind my life's direction was firmly and steadily heading my life towards even stranger encounters than I had already experienced.

During this period, I was struggling desperately to maintain my sanity. I knew I was being visited by creatures, but didn't have anyone to talk to about it. My psychic abilities were taking on an uncontrollable life of their own. I frequently saw spirits or colors around people while walking down the street. I also had the feeling that someone or something was watching me. It felt evil and menacing, making it impossible to sleep at night. All this was in direct contrast to the serene, peaceful environment that East Hampton offered.

Chad loved to visit our house in the Hamptons any and every chance he could but my fear and extreme difficulty sleeping at night put a strain on our relationship. In addition, I was also extremely sexually charged and couldn't keep my sex drive under control whatsoever. I was having huge amounts of casual sex in as many different places as there are people in the world. Yet my sex life with my partner was cold and frigid. I struggled to understand why I would want to have as much sex with people I do not love, but very little sex with someone I do love. I was frequenting sex clubs, movie houses, and bath houses.

The general atmosphere in these places is dark. Many are decorated with red light bulbs and lots and lots of maze-like-hallways leading off to more dark hallways. Many of these dark mazes are walled with mirrors, chain link fences, bizarre artwork, and pornography. The music is dark, dreamy, pounding techno. A few bath houses have a more homey feel to them, but there are always halls and rooms to wander around for hours and hours, and that is just what I did. Oftentimes, I frequently found myself in these places not quite knowing what I was doing there. Sometimes, I just found myself standing in a dark hallway, not necessarily feeling sexual, but finding some sort of relief from being in the environment and walking around in circles.

This was the environment the relationship operated under. I prayed for help, looking for some way to save this sinking ship. I now believe that prayer is answered, but I think we must still be careful as to from where the answer comes from. Perhaps there are others with their own agenda who are eavesdropping, waiting for the opportunity to offer aid. In any event, my prayer was answered in the form of a "coincidence."

Coincidences in my life happen with unusual frequency. In an effort to keep my relationship going and my sanity intact I decided to seek out the help of a therapist. I told her about the psychic stuff that was happening She said she happened to know of a person who could help me. This person was UFO researcher Bud Hopkins, who also happened to live a couple of blocks away from where Chad and I lived at that time.

Chad and I went to Bud. I was put into a hypnotic trance. While under this trance I recalled being floated out of my bedroom window and various other memories surfaced, too. I was relieved that things would finally be getting better, but they didn't. I started to awaken with the feeling and message that if I didn't leave Chad these aliens were going to kill him. I pushed these messages away time after time until one morning Chad woke up screaming.

Chad is a very logical, kind-hearted rational man. He is not the kind of guy that ever awoke screaming from a nightmare. But one morning we awoke to his screams. He sat up in bed visibly upset. I reached over, held him, and asked, "What happened? What happened?" He said that he dreamt we were in our bedroom in the country house. He went on to say, "I looked over at the closet door and it started to slide open. There was a man inside. He was wearing some sort of dark suit. He had a brimmed hat on his head. I couldn't see what he looked like too clearly, but he reached down and pulled out a gun. He pointed it toward me and shot me in the chest."

I was dumbfounded, scared, and sad. I knew then that these creatures were not joking around. I calmed Chad down until he seemed to be pretty well resolved that he just had a bad dream for some reason. But I knew then and there that I had to leave him before anything else happened. I thought by cooperating things would get better, they didn't.

The week of the beings' next visit started ordinarily enough with Chad back to running the various record labels. I finished up my degree at the New School for Social Research. School was exhausting, but even more was the way in which I was leading my life as two different people. I told people one thing, then did something else. For example, I told people that I was going to lunch, but instead met someone else for some quick sex. I would tell myself that I would stop this behavior and that I'm bad, but I kept doing it with reckless abandonment and felt good about doing it.

I was both Saint and Sinner, but never an entire person; a whole person. I remember how one such dream seemed to reinforce this observation. The dream took place in a boxing ring. I saw the "good me" being walked away from the "bad me" by some large hands. I watched the peaceful, loving part of me look back over his shoulder as these large hands pushed him toward some unknown place while my negative personality sat on the mat yelling, "Come back here and fight!"

In addition to doing one thing and saying another, I found that I was frequently double-checking myself, or had to do things twice to feel okay. Anyway, it happened in the fall on an ordinary late afternoon. I decided to take a nap before Chad arrived home from work. I slept for a few moments, but then awoke sometime later feeling very groggy. I heard voices in the bedroom. I opened my eyes to see a huge struggle. I was able to see a soft glow, but I didn't recall leaving a light on before I went to sleep. I rubbed my eyes, then sat up bolt awake.

There was a handsome young man standing by the dresser. He was glowing in a yellowish-gold color. He had spokes of lighted rods emanating from his glowing aura. He was just amazing, and looked ageless. He probably stood about 5'9" and was of medium build. His straight dark brown hair flowed nicely around his head. His clean-shaven face was accented by gentle deep, dark brown eyes. A large welcoming smile with perfect teeth added to his stunning presence. I reached out my hand to get him to notice me, but he was more interested in the picture that Chad had of me on our dresser.

He picked it up, smiling at it. I wasn't able to see who he had been speaking with, but I kept my hand outstretched to him. There was however, one huge problem - I felt my energy draining from my body. It felt like I was going to have a heart-attack or perhaps like there was a large energy stone in the center of my chest that was slowly draining of its power. I kept my eyes on him, placing my other hand over my heart. I felt myself becoming weaker and weaker. I knew my life was slipping away, yet I couldn't take my eyes off of him.

Since I couldn't gaze upon his face I focused on the back of his vest that he wore as well as his butt. He wore jeans and I felt a little odd about focusing on his butt, but I did so despite my confusion of what was taking place. I thought, "I'm dying!" Then, my eyes were drawn toward a motion at the end of the bed. I looked down to see one of our cats sitting there staring at me. The cat sat at the foot of the bed, its eyes aglow with a bright penetrating green color. It didn't move until we locked eyes for a while. This broke my stare from the young man.

The cat slowly moved up the mattress, curling up next to me by my underarm. I gave the cat a couple of pets, then passed out. I came to consciousness some moments later. The glow was gone, the cat was gone, but now standing at the foot of my bed was a very tall black-hooded figure. That's all I remember as I think I fainted.

I awoke yet again. The room was still glowing. This time I found myself under what I can only describe as an extremely large glowing butterfly wing or some sort of white-colored Frank Lloyd Wright designed glowing transparent form. I was still on my back from fainting and observed the geometric shapes of this object. I never felt in danger, no energy drain, or any other negative reaction. It felt friendly, kind, and nurturing.

Turning my head to the left to look around the room, I found myself looking into two very large black circular eyes that were surrounded by a white rectangular type of head. This rectangular head was attached to a long neck. This being or object looked like some sort of living periscope with wings. it stayed for a few moments, then rose straight up and left. After this, I decided I better do something immediately.

I left Chad, New York City, and stopped using my first name. I set my sights on some place warm; a place where I could start over, swim in the ocean by day, party by night and forget all the unexplainable weirdness. So off I went to Miami Beach firmly believing that things would be better there.

It didn't take long for something to happen. I lasted eight months when I left there a shattered, broken man. The feelings of terror, intense sexual arousal, and psychic activity didn't stop as I so foolishly thought, but instead increased at least 100%. I rented an apartment directly off of Lincoln Road Mall. From there I could easily walk the strip at all hours looking for sex, looking for peace from the evil presence I felt watching and following me. I somehow maintained a day job, but during the work day I typically found a stall in the men's room to take quick fifteen minute naps to counteract my drowsiness.

Lunchtime was a perfect excuse to sleep for an hour, not that I ate much because during this time I decided to take up a raw foods diet. I'm already slim, so a raw foods diet had obvious physical results. I also started going by my middle name Anthony in hopes that I would have some safety from my haunted life just as I did when I was a child. And in a further effort to get away from the old me, I straightened my hair, died it blonde and then later red.

My hair color finally settled out on a light brown when I met Darrin, a fashion photographer and photojournalist. We had an intense first meeting. I used to think it was because he was so largely endowed, but sex with him was very tingly and energizing. The more I saw Darrin, the more afraid I became for myself. I never felt any sort of physical sort of impending harm, but I also couldn't figure out why I was so worried about something that I couldn't put my finger on. He treated me well and was very nice, but some voice kept telling me to stay away from him.

It was early November when Darrin called to ask if I was free. I said, "Yes, but I kept getting this strong feeling to tell him "no."

I kept hearing a voice inside my head saying, "Tell him no," but I ignored it. He asked me to come over, but I declined, instead inviting him over for dinner at my place. The voice surfaced again and said, "Don't let him stay over." I brushed the voice out of my mind.

When Darrin came over we ate. After dinner we became sexually aroused. The voice started up again telling me, "Do not have sex with him; stay out of the bedroom." I became a little afraid, so I led Darrin to a foldout couch in the living room. As I started to pull the bed out, Darrin protested, asking incredulously "What are you doing?!"

My best answer was "I thought we would try it someplace different." He just chuckled, grabbed my hand, and led me into my bedroom. The voice was going crazy saying "No, Danny, don't do it; leave a light on, leave a light on!" over and over. We were already naked and erect, but I pulled away from Darrin to light a candle on a table that was just outside my darkened bedroom. I went back to the bedroom, back to Darrin and his huge cock, and the most intensely amazing sex. We both came and as we lay in bed dripping with sweat and semen we both started to fall asleep. I heard that voice again, "Stay awake, don't fall asleep; stay awake, Danny, stay awake!" The next thing I knew, I fell into an evil dream.

I found myself outside my apartment building with my friend Martin. I was outside at the entry gate. He was warning me to stay out of the building. He was pleading, but I told him that I had to go in, that I had to confront Bud Hopkins to find out why he was working for the C.I.A. Martin said, "I'm coming with you!" We went up the stairs to my door. I knocked. Bud answered. He led me into my living room, offering me a seat on my couch. As I entered the apartment, Martin made an odd muffled sound. I sat down. Still standing, Bud leaned over me, asking, "What's wrong?" I started crying, telling Bud "I don't understand what's happening! People are telling me you work for the C.I.A. is this true?"

He smiled as he said "There, there it's just the Reptilians fucking with you Dan!" I was shocked, stood up to run out of the apartment, but before I could, Bud grabbed me from the back of

my neck, slamming me down on the floor. I cried and yelled for
Martin to help me. I looked across the room to see that he was tied
and gagged. A small creature in a black robe stood next to him as
he struggled to get free.

Bud was now standing over me yelling obscenities and kicking
me with all his might. He was saying "You're supposed to be…" He
was dragging me across the floor to the changing room. The room
was entirely black. I knew that if he dragged me into it I would die.
As he dragged me across the wood floor, I reached out, grabbing
onto the legs of a nearby table. I was crying hysterically and looked
over at Martin with a great sense of sorrow for having dragged him
into this. But Martin had now struggled free of his ropes and ran
out of the apartment. The cloaked thing chased him and government agents ran up to the front gate to stop him. Martin started
to climb over the fence between my apartment building and the
building next door. I saw his feet clambered over the fence as
multitude of hands reached and reached for his scrambling feet.
Then I woke up.

I sat up with a gasp, looking at myself in the mirror opposite my
bed. I looked alright. The candle was still lit. I sat there for a moment silently composing myself. I then remembered that Darrin
was with me. I quickly turned to see if I had woken him. It was laying
there quietly, its snake eyes staring straight up at the ceiling…its
skin white and its mouth parted slightly. My mouth dropped and
I looked away. I looked again. It was still there, its reptile eyes un-
blinking, its white skin pulled tight around its muscled body; then
it moved. The eyes turned completely brown and as I watched, this
creature changed back into Darrin.

His eyes remained open for a moment and then closed. After
it changed into a human, I jumped out of bed. The second my
feet hit the floor Darrin asked, "Where are you going?" I didn't
turn around. I stopped for a second to say that I was going to
the kitchen to have some pumpkin pie. I raced away from the
bedroom, heading into the kitchen where I gripped the kitchen
counter, holding it tight.

The voice came back, saying, "Whatever you do, don't cry. DO NOT CRY, don't cry, don't cry." I said "Okay" in my head and stood there. I wanted to run, but my clothes were in the bedroom. I was naked, covered with dry semen. The air in the apartment felt thick and electric. As I stood there wondering what I was going to do I heard Darrin get out of bed. I'll spare the details of what happened next, but I left that apartment fully furnished, clothes still on the hangers, dishes in the cabinets, food in the refrigerator.

I prayed for help and he came just prior to my leaving Miami Beach. His name is Richard Servant. He is a famous jewelry designer who happened to design costume jewelry for Diana, Princess of Wales. He is a very socially connected person. At the time was on the chairing committee for a benefit for Princess Margaret. He said that he wanted me to go to this event and that perhaps I could meet Her Royal Highness. The relationship quickly became sexual and romantic.

I explained to Richard what happened with Darrin. He said he believed me and that he had a friend that could perhaps help me. He also said that he wanted me to go to New Mexico with him to celebrate his birthday at his best friend's house, a well known retired actress. I was making plans to go, but the voice returned to warn me that if I went there that I would die or be sacrificed. I didn't understand and tried to push the voice and feeling out of my head, but I couldn't. I ended up not going with Richard who became totally furious with me for not showing up and making him look bad. I had no other reasonable excuse except for a voice in my head and a feeling said, "Don't go." So it was goodbye Richard Servant, goodbye Miami Beach, hello Hollywood.

I found myself in Hollywood doomed to walk the same bath house hallways as I had in my prior residences. This time, I decided to try anything to fight back against whatever was happening. I went to see psychics most of whom said that I should be reading them. Still another cried, saying it was an honor to meet me after I drew the Queen of Spades card from her deck, adding, "You are THE Queen of Spades!!" Very flattering I suppose, but I had no idea and still to this day still do not have any idea of what it is these people are seeing and feeling that emanates. Psychic Sylvia Brown told me that I would be the one to take things much further than she has been able to take them. Others have described me as the "Rolls Royce of psychics." And here I sit, not understanding who I am, what I am, or what to do with this gift.

In an effort to understand myself, I started to record my dreams. I recorded dreams in which I met Gods and Goddesses. They flew me through environments with red skies. I found myself in dreams with the British Royal family. In one dream, Queen Elizabeth said to me, "I have come to marry you."

I was having the usual difficulties sleeping but now I was also fighting off shadow figures from trying to jump into my body. I often woke nauseated to see black silhouette figures from the Victorian era in my home. Once I awoke to find a naked man in my apartment wearing a wolf's head over his head. He quickly jumped on top of me, holding me down by my forearms. When I struggled to get free, he quickly vanished.

By day, I sought out the peace of nature, but only found myself drawn to a hidden area in the Hollywood hills where black magic rituals were held. I watched black-hooded figures float through the trees and boyish naked transparent elves scamper around the bushes. Sex clubs, my only source of sanctuary, also became alive with evil and danger. As I sat in the steam room, I watched as a well-built, buffed naked male body formed in front of me out of the steam, his head ripped off at the neck. As I walked down a different hallway, a skull appeared. Still another time at the bath house, as I sat in my small room with the door open, a man in his 30s entered my room.

He came in, closed the door, sat at the end of my bed, and said, "The Queen wants you to know that she is taking very good care of you." I just looked down. As he got up to leave, I stopped him. I tried to get him to have sex with me, but he wouldn't. He said he had to go. I stopped him again. I asked, "What are you doing here?" He said that he came to deliver this message to me. I then asked him what else he did and he said he couldn't say exactly, but it had to do with computers. He left my room, passed by a couple more times, and I never saw him again.

Driving through the streets of Los Angeles also had its share of strangeness. On more than a few times the city vanished. I found myself sitting in my car looking out the windshield onto a giant grid with a black background delineated with white lines. Still another time as I drove along the highway, I looked out of my window and saw a huge tree. Floating above the tree making up the points of a square were four very large black-hooded smoky figures. In fact, what drew me to look at the tree is that I thought it was on fire.

Loneliness set in as I struggled to find someone who could understand me. I prayed again and met Jackson "Alleycat" Mcgee. I have been with Jackson for just over two years. He, like my other boyfriends, is well-known, rich, and successful. He is known for starting the world's premiere gay men's fashion monthly magazine which he owned for 13 years until he recently sold it to a media conglomerate.

Being with Jackson is not the easiest thing in the world which is quite sad really. He is a really genuine loving, man with a big heart. He loves me deeply, but I find that there are many times I just want to leave him for no reason. I have to use the merger symbol at the pineal to settle out the feeling. I am also terribly afraid of feeling deeply for him because sometimes I wonder if I'm able to feel anything at all.

Yet I do love him, but because of the past I have many times in the night looked over at Jackson, expecting to see a Reptile in bed with me. I'm afraid I made another mistake, but so far so good. If anything, I have had to instruct Jackson as to how to protect himself. Many, many times he has awoken screaming and a few times was unable to get to sleep. The first experience he reported to me was that a glowing red form was trying to pull him out of his bed. He is dealing with the situation by using a little bit of denial, plain old fighting spirit, and a strong commitment to stay together.

I am grateful and lucky to be with him. I love him dearly, but I am afraid of what loving a person such as myself will ultimately bring to him. How do I reconcile that the love I can offer someone is good when being with me means my partner will have to fight the demonic? It is a terrible thing to wake up night after night to the screams of the one you love, knowing that they are being terrorized while they sleep to be asked, "Why is this happening?" and to know the answer is because of you. Jackson has already had to confront the astral, what next?

Up until recently, things seemed to be under control and quiet...then I found myself in a tiny town in Montana on a work trip. A colleague dragged me out for a drink. While at this bar I saw a guy that I just felt I had to meet. I was amazed at the similarity of our lives. He talked about wanting to move to Palm Springs as I have from time to time but things like this aside, there was something very familiar to him, and me to him, that we both recognized. I spoke to him about my dreams, and he told me that he was a heavy dreamer, too. I told him about my memories and dreams of the British Royal Family. His response was a completely unfazed reply of: "I'm dating someone from a royal family."

Well, this is what my life is like. By night during my sleep, demons come to me, asking to have sex with me and still other demonic entities try to jump into my body to take it over. Sometimes sex with the demonic is fantastic and energizing and I want more, but other times I wake up and feel like vomiting. By day, it is coincidence after coincidence of a deliberate nature. I'm a man of direct opposites and I often feel like I'm two different people. On the one hand I'm told I'm very psychic, but I have a difficult time producing anything. I appear quiet and fairly nondescript, but my life is anything but quiet and actually defies description.

Despite the time I've spent out in bars and clubs, I consume very little alcohol and do not use recreational drugs. I know what I want, but do the opposite to achieve my goals. Completing any project including writing this for this book is a huge effort. I used to seek out therapists for help, but found that psychologists and psychiatrists do not have the understanding, skill, or frame of reference to handle my reality. Most want to offer help in the form of tranquilizers.

Anyway, it is my sincere desire that the telling of my story will help humanity in some way and help others who are having similar difficulties to hang on another day. I'm using the merger symbol and even made pillow cases with royal blue and violet which has helped Jackson and I tremendously. I've made a lot of mistakes and taken many wrong roads, but I've never given up on finding out who I am and taking a stand against the deliberate manipulation that the Earth's population is currently under.

Case #5 Analysis
Male Monarch Programming

This amazing story is a complex programming combination. We can see that he is absolutely a male Monarch. Only 15% of Monarchs are male. His story is further complicated by his incredible mix of DNA from nearly every race on Earth—all combined into one!

This type of person is heavily used in Sexual Magick Rituals that involve imprinting all races of humans simultaneously. This ceremony involves many males ejaculating in or on this person to boost the energy of the specific thought-form being projected. Then, this person is ejaculated so that the combined energies of all other participants is subsequently thrust out into the physical world to connect to all races on Earth for manifestation of the thought-form.

This person is closely watched and guarded by the Windsors, who control the United States. It makes sense that he is an extremely valuable asset to them in their quest for global domination which can be more easily accomplished with acquiescence from all nationalities. He is indeed a "master key" to them.

During his process of deprogramming, many issues related to top Illuminati families has arisen. He has also been placed in a position to travel to many global locations which facilitates the energetic dispersals in the physical world necessary to imprint actual areas of the Earth.

This male Monarch also has animal alters that are used in various rituals. One of these is a fawn, which helps to perpetuate fear and targeting of the global population. Conversely, this animal alter is a derivative of the person's actual original mind-pattern to which the programming is hooked. This individual needs to release the fear and victimization thoughts to unhook the attached programming.

Fortunately, this male Monarch is aware of what he has experienced and is consciously on the lookout for triggers and individuals sent to him for a function and ritual preparation. However, when it comes to sexual triggers, most people easily fall into the patterns for which they were programmed as sexuality is a primary and base function for creation. In other words, most people give into the primal urges without thinking of the consequences. The Illuminati programmers count on that so that their agenda is always served.

It is best for this individual to stay away from all situations that could lead to triggering and rituals. Physically removing oneself from such sensitive situations is often the first requirement for beginning the deprogramming process. Elimination of symptoms allows the programmed person the opportunity to have the presence of mind, without sensory input, to work on these profound issues.

This male Monarch's "demonization" process allows for astral entities to appear in his environment as either a warning, trigger or prelude to ritual. Using violet as protection and verbally banishing these entities is an aid to clearing out the energies.

In addition, this male shows indications that he has Dragonfly and Scorpion Programming as described in my book, *True Reality of Sexuality*. Many rituals are based on these types of programmed males.

A Dragonfly slave can be either male or female. In fact, many are females. However, to contain this type of function, bisexuality is an absolute must. This is because the Dragonfly individual is used sexually with androgynous Reptilians that can shapeshift or use holographs to appear male or female, depending on the need.

It is likely that in ritual functions, this slave type sexually performs with both sexes simultaneously. This is considered by the Illuminati to be the epitome of sexual function and ability. For one to be so sexually versatile is considered to be extremely high-level and valuable.

Sexual ritual has nothing to do with eroticism or desire; it is merely an energetic formula created to achieve a specific result to manifest on the Earth plane. Human bodies are used as step-up transformers via their sexual energies.

The Dragonfly program is also a play on words for "flying dragon." In Reptilian culture, the dragon is the leader and God who must be obeyed. It is the highest energy of their society. The White Winged Dragon with icy blue eyes is their "Christ." A male often portrays this role in ritual and can be represented by a tall, muscular blonde man with blue eyes. There are versions where red-headed males with green or blue eyes are used, but such rituals are reserved for astral possessions.

It is an absolute treasure for the Illuminati elite to find a human with the amazing genetic mix as this man has. In ceremony and ritual, his energetic emanations can be broadcast globally with great affect on the population, especially when amplified by scalar satellite boosters.

Dragonfly males are almost always ready for sexual activities. They are able to ejaculate more frequently than a "normal" male and have no qualms about the type of sexual activity in which they participate. Basically, they can and will do anything, anywhere.

Their body type is usually very masculine, meaning muscular and with body hair. They tend to be slim and take good care of themselves. They are extremely particular about the way they look and appear in public, similar to the Presidential Model. The commonalities are related to the high-level of persons with whom they are in ritual. They prefer only the best of everything and can even appear to be snobby at times.

They tend to date or have relationships with the elite, or those with lots of money and power. They like the unusual, conventionally and unconventionally. They also attract very harsh experiences and people. Conflict is their rule of life. You can always count on them to speak up loudly and confrontationally.

Dragonfly programming can only be entered into a matrix if Monarch Programming is there as a base. Scorpion Programming can only be entered if the prior two—Dragonfly and Monarch—are already present and functioning. Monarch input is through the pineal gland. However, Dragonfly Programming is entered only at the reptilian brainstem and is centered there. This is why so many Dragonfly slaves have neck and back issues.

Scorpion Programming uses both the pineal and the brainstem. It also uses the gonads and is quite painful when entered. Scorpion Programming is the deepest, darkest, and most intense of all sexual programming. Anyone having this must, by necessity, be quite physically and mentally strong.

The Scorpion slave flirts with death a lot. It is always fighting, which is why it is mostly a male program. There are some rare females who have it, but there is a tendency for them to be Lesbians or bisexual.

Scorpion slaves like rough and dangerous sex. They often use drugs and/or alcohol to achieve a sexual state of being. They are terrifically defensive and protective of their sexual organs and tend to have huge genitalia. For the male Scorpion slave, his erect penis is his stinger. He is programmed to use it for pain and pleasure. Any of his sexual partners, male or female—as the Scorpion is always bisexual—will find his penis almost too large for them to handle for any length of time.

The Scorpion sex-slave desires numerous sexual partners and experiences, with many scenarios placed in his matrix by his programmer. All Scorpion slaves must have a balancing program or animal frequency in them in order for them to have any kind of normalcy in their lives. This is often either Dolphin or Lion frequencies.

Interestingly, the Scorpion male slave often has a temper, yet he avoids confrontation. He knows that when his anger is up, death can follow—of the one who angered him! So, since all Scorpion functions have confrontational Dragonfly as a base, this can create many problems emotionally.

Therefore, as a layer of programming, the Scorpion is kept as a loner or frequently isolated so that there is little room for problems. Part of deprogramming for this individual is to work heavily on his foundational anger issues that enabled such programs to be inserted in the first place. No program can be entered unless there is a natural basis in the mind that allows it to take hold on fertile grounds.

Deprogramming such an individual is a long and tedious process, more so than any other type of programming. There is deep self-sabotage and self-punishment that is capped with a virulent suicide function that must be monitored round the clock.

The individual in this case study is quite unique in many facets and has come a long way in understanding and working with his programming. He needs to be more consistent and communicative about his process, but this is a common issue for people like this.

Also of interest is that despite the numerous sexual partners, rituals, and chance-taking of such individuals, rarely do they contract any diseases or illnesses from their experiences. It is as if some sort of immunity connected to the Dragonfly and Scorpion frequencies helps them maintain strong health and protection.

Case #6
Disney Programming

As an adult I read the Montauk Project book series. Until then I was unaware of the time-travel experiments held there. The idea of time-travel intrigued me. I read each book in a matter of a few days, waiting impatiently for the next one to come out so I could continue to learn the story. On some level I felt a strong connection to it and needed to know more.

A few years later I met two of the key players in the project, as well as the author of the books. I eventually recalled memories of a hidden life of which I had previously no conscious awareness. It was with this new knowledge that I began to discover who I was and why I was here. Little did I know at the time that I was part of that incredible story and connected to those in it.

Learning the Language of Hyperspace, taught me how powerful the mind is and how to be in control of my own mind so others were not. I began to look at my life from a whole new perspective and discover my true nature. I also discovered how important I was from a programming perspective.

Reviewing my early years, I was a painfully shy child with many fears growing up. The most prevalent fears were of heights, enclosed spaces, and the fear of being away from home.

The second-born, I was constantly sick and eventually hospitalized and had major surgery at two years old to repair a malformation that caused all the illnesses. I would later learn the number two plays an important role in my life. I was a very quiet, withdrawn child who never spoke to anyone but my immediate family.

While growing up in those early years, I remember having these very scary dreams that always occurred prior to getting sick. It was always the same dream of me hiding from a big green hand while my father slept next to me. I felt unprotected and very scared.

The walls of my bedroom had Disney characters hung on them from the popular movies. My all-time favorite movie growing up was The Wizard of Oz. I was even "Dorothy" for Halloween one year.

I never enjoyed being in school; most of the time I kept to myself because I was too shy to make new friends. If I had no one with whom I was familiar to be with, I spent recreation time alone. Every day I couldn't wait to get home. I feared not being able to get home because I might miss the school bus.

I consider my teenage years average. I was a little more outgoing by this time, but still had many fears, preferring to hang out with a small close-knit group of friends. My parents separated during this time, so I found refuge with my friends. We hung out mostly in the neighborhood, and did some experimenting with cigarettes, alcohol, and marijuana. I was an average student in school and could have done better if I applied myself. I daydreamed frequently, doodling a lot along the sides of the class notes. Spirals, daisy flowers, scrolls, and ivy were among the most common. I discovered my artistic side, eventually pursuing it as a career.

I was always open to things not of this world, mostly life after death, and UFOs, although I had great fear of seeing both. My friends and I used to do the Ouija Board, always scaring ourselves silly. After the death of my father, I had many experiences to support my belief in the astral, and pursued it with a passion from then on.

Graduation from high school and beginning college brought a newfound freedom. I met many new friends in college, one in particular a young woman who years later I was to discover is my programming twin. We lost touch after college but did meet up briefly after we each had our first child, and then again later after our third. The similarities in our lives at that point were so startling that we needed to find out more.

We continued to share with each other our lives and how they unfolded through the years we were apart. Our reunion soon lead to a partnership in our work as well as our self-healing through self-awareness.

It was through our self-awareness work and a dream that we first learned about programming. It was a shock at first, than it was like a puzzle falling into place. The more I learned through my visualization work, the more began to surface. I questioned every-thing, but as I began to recall events I was shaken to my core. The emotions that surfaced were so powerful! There was no denying there was something to this. Still I had a hard time believing it.

My exploration took me back into my past. I looked at various events and understood them to be part of the program-ming process. What happened in my physical reality was a mirror to what happened in my nonphysical reality. The death of our pet white rabbit had new meaning. Near-death experiences during surgery and a near-drowning by being held under water enhanced the programming process. I went back further into my family tree and found more connections. Some extraordinary family history suddenly made sense as well as resonance with particular people and places.

Even with guidance, the self-deprogramming process is dif-ficult at best. Many times after my deprogramming visualizations memories surface in my dreams. I get little snippets of informa-tion. Later, I have to go back to try to explore more. Many times I do not want to go back into the dream because the memories are too horrific. You just can't make these things up.

It is a constant struggle to take back my power. As I merge together the pieces I find, my programmers delete, add, or rearrange. They know all the codes while I still have to learn them all. When I deviate from the plan they punish with ELF. I am plagued with severe headaches, bouts of depression, and suicidal thoughts. Many times I want to just forget it all. What you must face in this process is what they count on being enough to stop you. I refuse to let them win.

I see signs of different alters in pictures of myself and in my handwriting from different time frames. Sometimes, I even catch myself changing alters during the day. I am like a detective looking at everything to figure out this puzzle and put it back together.

It is the unknown areas that concern me most. All the memories compartmentalized in different alters that I have not accessed yet. What will I find? Every day brings a new experience and something to learn. I have only scratched the surface of the job ahead, but if I don't do it no one else will. Some times I need to take a break and not do my deprogramming work for a while, but eventually I get back to it. Still I move forward.

Case #6 Analysis
Disney Programming

> This woman lives in an area not too far from the Montauk Project location. Mostly males were used in that experiment since females absorb energies, while males project out energies. The programmers at Montauk were seeking ways to broadcast/project out various mind-control functions that were developed at the site. Sexuality was one of these methods.

This woman was used in Sexual Magick Ritual numerous times with many of the primary males who worked as psychics for the project. Close physical and emotional bonds were necessary to develop a smooth and growing energy flow. This makes it easier to download energies from the rituals and experiments.

She remembers the activities and faces of the males during that intense time period which made most people in the area feel "weird" all of the time without knowing why. Her comments along these lines are common for those young people who lived there in the 70s and early 80s.

In order to facilitate her use in the Project, a combination of Disney/Monarch/Alice In Wonderland Programming was used. In those days, many variations and combinations of programs were used to see how the different alter types fit together and what effect they had on the daily functioning abilities of the participants.

It was because of this that the Disney World Theme Park was opened on the East Coast to enhance the programming for all of the new programmees at the time. This woman was kept activated via the use of Disney marketing items and a white rabbit, which is a standard triggering icon.

With these programs in place, the alters developed from them, such an individual can be used to create fantasy-like events in rituals as well as be used for alternate reality connections. The person becomes like an anchor and vortex portal for connecting to many other alternate time lines or dimensions.

Deprogramming involves the use of a delta-T antenna at the crown which is brought into the pineal. Instead of her programmer controlling the functions, she now takes charge of it, destroying the construct in the matrix that enables this use of her.

She must also do heavy work with the Monarch Butterfly as a focal point at the pineal gland to remove the sexual ritual uses and preclude any further use. She also has Tinkerbelle Programming which keeps her young-looking and viable for an extended period of time—which could be many decades.

As in all such cases, personal relationships are at best difficult. She has experienced this during the course of her life and has also passed on genetic programming to her children.

Her husband is/was also programmed. Such matches are doomed for failure unless both parties make a serious effort to deprogram and overcome their issues. It is also wise to work with the children of such a marriage to circumvent further fracturing of their personalities, thus discontinuing the generational cycles.

Fear of what is inside of your mind is the main reason people do not continue the process. This woman has made valiant efforts to move forward in her deprogramming and has made tremendous strides. As always, sabotage and self-punishment arise. This is standard procedure. She is learning to stop, reset, ground and balance, merge, and move on.

Women with this combination of programming tend to be a bit scattered in thinking, with a lot of emotion that they suppress until it builds up into a great depression. They tend to find diversion in their work or career, as this woman has done.

People with Disney/White Rabbit Programming tend to be extremely artistic and love to decorate. They usually go into jobs that involve artistic creating and manipulating colors and words. This is an outgrowth of the symbols and alters in their matrices.

Disney Programming is used for quickly altering a person's perspective, hurling them into a virtual reality cartoon world where nothing has any real meaning. This serves a purpose of diversion of an individual or masses of people—as seen at any Disney Theme Park—so that while the diversion is in force, the ones in power can be actively and physically creating an event without being seen or stopped. This has happened at times of war and in catastrophes all over the world.

It is interesting to analyze what television and movies are playing whenever a global tragic event takes place. Transmission of cartoon characters via ELF from satellites at night produce cartoon-like dreams and mental images that send a person into their virtual matrix world for a time or at least switch them into an alter that is childlike and easily diverted in attention and reaction.

For a child, to think that he/she is in a cartoon world is so fascinating, that the child does not realize that some inappropriate sexual behavior is taking place with this character that is actually imprinting and programming them.

Then, as the child gets older, any time they see or hear of this character or groups of cartoon/Disney figures, the programming is triggered. This causes the person to act out any function that he/she did when he/she was as a child with this image.

White Rabbit Programming is related to Disney because it uses cartoon figures for the most part, but not exclusively. White Rabbit is used to access alternate realities and dimensions, usually astral, for the purpose of creating a doorway between realities. Sexual ritual is a heavy aspect of this as anal intercourse, or even rape, is a common pathway to allow the energies for demonic-astral entities from using a human body to experience the physical world.

Children are more participatory in such activities when a cartoon/Disney character is present or even the one perpetrating the rape or abuse. In this way, the child learns a perverse sexual gratification from Disney figures and this stays with the child for life.

The towers on all Disney Castles in all theme parks are phallic. The hats worn by many cartoon/Disney figures are also phallic. Many symbols in all the cartoon movies have phallic symbols from the dancing broom to Mickey's magician hat.

When deprogramming, a person like the one in this case study, must first start with the basic Monarch deprogramming techniques using the butterfly images. As the individual progresses, then she can start with White Rabbit images as a second layer, finally easing into the various cartoon or Disney characters that each person may see during the deprogramming process.

The symbols, colors, and figures that the person reports are a clue as to how to proceed and with what deprogramming methods. Jumping too quickly into another level can bypass many important alters that need to be merged. Moving too quickly in the process might also cause the person to overlook constructs within a virtual world of the matrix that need to be dismantled. Extreme patience using slow, methodical techniques are the only ways to handle a multi-layered programmed individual.

When dealing with cartoon characters and Disney figures, the programmer has a multitude of possibilities from which to choose. Each person has his/her own unique nuances from their particular programmer. Never assume that all Disney or cartoon programming is the same in each person. There are always numerous differences. People undergoing a programming process should not compare themselves, their results, or procedures with others. This only creates sabotage and blocking issues. Just as humans are all unique, so is each person's programming.

I caution all people with programming like the one mentioned in this case to avoid watching Disney films and cartoons in general until they get a grip on their own situation. Visiting any Disney theme park is a major setback in the process, as this only enhances the programming that the person is stopping.

Case #7
Green Star Programming

After forty-two years of living a life of extraordinary events I have come to realize that my life was meant to be what it is. I was born in a crazy and underprivileged area. My tormented life began when I was around three years old. I was constantly visited by small grey aliens in my crib at night., This went on for many years, continuing to this day.

I remember these greys put things up my nose all the time which caused me a great deal of pain. I suffered constant nose hemorrhages until I was about twelve years old. I have now found out through my own research that these procedures are pineal gland implants for special people.

These greys took me to a strange place which was just a big round room all the time when I was about three to four years old. I was in this room with many other children just sitting around on the floor like in a dream state. There were usually about thirty to forty kids just all staring at one another. Some were crying. There was always two or three greys around the outer walls. To this day I still don't know what this gathering of children was about.

As I got older I told my mother about these things. She said that the greys had a strange interest in me. When I was around five years old my father left my mother to get on with his own life. This was hard for me to accept as a child but what choice did I have? I often cried myself to sleep as a boy.

My mother was the best mother anyone could ask for; she was a mother and father in one. Back in those days times were very tough. We lived on a pension of thirty-five dollars per week. With four small children you can only imagine how hard times were.

My mother was a psychic who practiced a lot of strange things: astrology, numerology, tarot, witchcraft, voodoo, séances, and so on. I believe that many of these practices brought in strange entities that started my terrible experiences as a child.

I saw my mother will a man to fall off his horse one day, before my eyes. She just kept on repeating fall off, fall off, fall off, quietly. The next minute he was on his backside. I just looked up at her and she smiled. I said, "What was that all about mum?" She replied, "I will not tolerate anyone being cruel to animals." I saw her do this sort of thing on many occasions. I also have a sister that can will things to happen. She practices this all the time. I, too, can will bad on people but choose not to practice this harmful manifestation.

Growing up with a mother and a sister with psychic ability was strange. My mother held seances every Saturday night. Through these seances I saw some of the most amazing things happen before my eyes: ghosts, spirit entities, things levitating in mid-air, strange figures standing in my room, lights going off and on, taps turning themselves on ,and the sounds of footsteps running over the roof – it was never-ending.

I used to tell my mother about all these things. She said that I saw these things because I am psychic. My mother told me since I was a child that I was psychic like her and my sister; that we all had the same astrology signs. My mother and I have almost identical planetary placements. All my mother cared about in her life was her children. We were, we were blessed to have a mother as good as her. She was a brilliant cook and a very clean and tidy person.

When I was around six to seven years old I started noticing changes in her. She would go all strange. The house would get all messy and the food was not the same as the usual. When I tried to talk to her she just mumbled and did not make much sense. Then one day I was just looking at her and I said to myself in my mind, "Something is not right with Mum lately."

She spun around and looked at me with full black eyes as all the whites of her eyes went black. She just stared at me very evil. I also saw this happen when we went shopping one day. My younger brother was in the pram. I was walking next to it holding on as we were going to the supermarket. My mother stopped robotically for about five minutes staring at a strange person across the other side of the road. I asked her what that man was looking at. She spun her head around that fast like a robot and stared at me with full black eyes , I have never been so scared in all my life. The memory of that day will stay with me forever.

I now realize that my mother was being replaced by a clone throughout my childhood. I also believe that she was being used for breeding purposes throughout her life on several occasions. As a young boy I used to ride my pushbike around the neighborhood. Cars would stop in the middle of the road. Strange people stared at me with strange eyes. This happened often till I was about twelve years old.

When I was about eight years old, the dental van came to my school. This is a government-funded dental program and, of course, is a FREE service. It is a very large van that goes to all public schools and does very unnecessary dental work on children. I remember sitting in the seat of the dental van and being told to open my mouth. This tall, rather unusual-looking, man was surprised to see that I had previous dental work done. He called out to his colleagues to come look at me but the amusing thing was that this man spoke without moving his lips. The other dentists approached and they were all standing around me having a conversation. None of them were moving their lips!

They knew that I could hear them on a telepathic level. These are the hybrids that are putting tiny microchips in the teeth of our children on a mass scale (chipping the populace for the New World Order). For the remainder of the week that the dental van was at the school, these two men and two women stood outside the van at recess and lunch time, staring at me with the most evil eyes you could ever imagine. They knew that I knew that they were not human.

As I got older I tried to disassociate myself from all of this. I tried to put my past behind me and forget everything I had experienced, but this would just not be. I have a very strong sense of perception and my past just keeps coming back to haunt me I continually question myself as I know things that were been taught to me. I tried to find interest that were so far away from the paranormal as possible.

As a child, I pretended that these things did not really happen to me. I found friends that knew nothing of any of this strange behavior. But, as I got into my twenties, I could no longer ignore what was going on around me. I can tell when things are not normal around me through this energy field. I pick up on so much around me that is unexplainable. I see spirits, ghosts, spinning orbs, Reptilians, and some of the most amazing things that I cannot even put a name to.

There is a golden eye that watches me constantly. Everywhere I go, this eye is a manifestation of a technology being used to monitor me. If I go to someone's home and there is any spiritual activity when I walk in, things become activated. I am absorbed by this energy and strange things start happening around me. There are many people around me that have witnessed this energy activation and are lost for words, when things start moving around the room. I have spirits tapping into me all the time because they know that I can communicate with them. This is why they hassle me. It's like I am being used as a medium between two worlds but choose not to participate.

My wife and I were in a department store one day looking at pots and pans. As we walked down the aisle we passed these sets of cutlery on display. The knives started vibrating on the shelf. We stopped to see what was going on. One knife bounced off the display stand, spinning in the air, just missing my face and landed on the floor next to where I stood. My wife looked at me, shaking her head. I believe that these are signs to let me know that my energy is not suited to certain areas.

I can be in my living room at night sitting there reading a book or watching television when suddenly the atmosphere in the room changes. I start seeing these dark entities around the room monitoring me. There are times when I am in the bedroom at night doing what mature people do. I see up to five tall dark figures from the roof to the floor around my bed. Through my own research I know that these Reptilian entities do this to steal the sexual energy.

A friend visited me one evening at dusk. He knocked on the door, walking in with a look of fear on his face. I said before you say a word, let me tell you what you saw. I proceeded to tell him that he was followed here by a tall dark figure. He was shocked that I knew, but I told him I could still see it when I looked out the window. I told him that the next time he saw it to emit love to it and it would go away—they thrive on your fear and that is why it kept following him.

One afternoon while driving home from work, I pulled into a service station. As I was walking in to pay for the fuel, I noticed a lady and a young girl walking toward me as I was about to enter. When I looked at this young girl I saw that her face was half torn off and was a horrifying sight. I closed my eyes for a second shook my head to look again only to see this young girl's face was normal. I know what I saw was a premonition of something that was going to happen in the not too distant future. How could I tell this poor child and her mother? They would think I was crazy. I see this type of thing in people, especially when there time is almost over. I sense their nonphysical departing from the physical. This is very emotional for me as I have seen this many times.

Sometimes while lying in bed at night drifting off to sleep, I see in my third eye area a metallic disc 20 feet in diameter by 6 feet in height pull up just outside my house, hovering about 50 feet in the air. I can see the two greys standing there, looking out the windows. I spring up out of bed, awake for the rest of the night. I have had this all my life. I have taken many trips in these crafts with the two greys, traveling at awesome speeds. I remember being on the floor of the craft screaming, looking up at them, and the skin on my face pulled back tight from the speed, so unbelievably fast that always knocked me unconscious.

When we got to our destination, I was brought to my conscious state. A high-pressured door would open quickly and loudly. I was met by two Reptilians in black cloaks with cat-like eyes, who I followed. I was always put into a trance state. I know I am not meant to remember these gatherings, but these events would always come back to haunt me. I was placed on a table where a fine needle was inserted into the base of my penis to give me an instant erection. Then a dark-haired woman was on top of me just riding me slowly. These places were always dim and cold.

I have been abducted throughout my whole life and experienced some of the most shocking things done to me that I wish were not true. I have woken some mornings with bruises on my body with the sorest rectum one could only imagine, and take up to three days to recover for supposedly no explanation. I believe that I was used in these rituals throughout my life because of my genetics. My mother said when she was alive that Lord Louie Mountbatten was her grandfather, so this explains why I am used in these rituals that mainly take people with the blue blood genetics. I am not proud of having these genetics as I know through my own research that this Mountbatten was a pedophile, a 33rd degree Mason, and a shapeshifter.

For the last twenty years, I have lived in a small country town. My wife and I had a road house for five years in the town. Through the business I was introduced to a lot of people in the community. At the time, I did not know that most of these respected men were Freemasons. There was one particular man with whom I became close. I found this man to be interesting and very knowledgeable in all areas of life. He seemed to be on the same level as myself and was very understanding and kind to my wife and I.

I knew a little about the Freemasons when this man asked me to join. He said the other men who I had knew nominated me to become a member of this fraternity. I found out that this is not something that you can just sign up for, because you must be chosen or have people who support you to join. This one particular man who was a 33rd degree Freemason, and a member of the Grand Lodge of Melbourne.

I have spent large amounts of time with this person as he knew things abut the world that no other did. I talked to him about my experiences. He knew that I was not crazy. Most other people that I talked to about these issues did not take me seriously. He always appeared to be surprised and even upset at the things that I knew, telling me that I should not know these things.

As I knew there was more to these men than they were telling me, I decided not to join. In March 2003, I had an extremely disturbing experience. I was put into an altered state and abducted from my home by two hybrids and this 33rd degree Freemason. I was met at my front door at approximately 3AM. The Freemason held a sword and marched like a German officer. I followed him with the two hybrids, one on either side of me. One held a black box that holds my semen which contains my vibrational frequency which was used to manipulate and alter my state of consciousness, lowering it to delta state, which enables them to have full control of me. This is also known as psychotronics.

I was walked to the bus which was parked in front of my home. I was taken ten minutes from where I reside to an underground facility at the military base. Here I was placed on a table with five masked people around me, dressed like surgeons. They operated on me. They removed my left eye from my eye socket, threading things through the optic nerve of my eye. Other things were pushed down the back of my throat. A fine needle pushed up through the table where I lay and inserted into the back of my neck. There were monitors all around the room. As they proceed through this operation they viewed it on the monitors. I have some of the most sophisticated, state of the art technology integrated into my body.

Afterwards, I went to this Freemason's home and told him of this whole event. He was just dumfounded that I knew about what happened to me. I do not need hypnotic regression. I have a recollective memory. This is why I remember almost everything that has been done to me throughout my life If this is what the high degree Freemasons are up to, I am thankful for not joining. In my opinion, they are the main driving force behind the New World Order.

I believe these procedures performed on me were an advanced way of monitoring us. In this way, they are able to see what I see, hear what I hear and speak. This makes me a prisoner inside my own existence. I do not believe that I am the only one with this technology integrated within. I believe this is being done rampantly throughout society to certain individuals who may be a threat to their agenda.

When these rituals are going to happen, I have noticed previously that I have a visitor in the form of a owl. I have taken a great deal of notice that at times of these events this owl hangs around my home day and night. It is on the power lines, on my aerial and one time sitting on the step of my house staring in the window at me. This is a sign that I am about to be abducted in the not-too-distant future. It is never ending in the games they play with me.

When I was about nineteen a friend and I went out spotlight shooting at a place called Pyalong . It was in the middle of winter. We often did this to get the best fox pelts in their prime. As we drove over this mountain, I noticed this strange pulsating orange light in front of us. I had never seen anything like it before and I have been shooting around this area since I was a kid. We kept on driving and spotlighting for over an hour. This strange light kept on moving with us.

Everywhere we went it followed above the car. Finally, I pointed the high-powered rifle at the thing and it disappeared. Then, all of a sudden there was two of them following us. When I put the spotlight on, three of them appeared. This started to spook me a bit but Phil said to keep spotlighting. Suddenly, a fox appeared. When I shot it at 100 yards, the orange lights disappeared. As I grabbed the fox out in the newly ploughed field, three orange lights came up over the mountain at me.

I dropped the fox, running back to the vehicle faster than I ever ran before in my life, feeling like my feet were not even touching the ground. I felt like I was hovering over the 100 yards at an abnormal speed. At the same time, something was pulling so strenuously on my testicles that I thought they were going to become separated from me! I hit the fence so hard that when I stopped, I tore all my abdominals and the barbed wire on the top strand snapped.

We got in the car, driving away at speeds in excess of 100mph. No matter how fast or slow we drove, the lights just stayed with us. This incident happened near the Puckapunyal Military Base between Seymour and a small town called Tooborac. I now know through my own research that I have an implant in my left testicle, causing the magnetic pulling effect on my scrotum via the ELF emitted from the lights.

Another night while driving home about 1:30AM through the bush, I was cruising along when suddenly I felt a strange energy in the car. I glanced in the rear view mirror to see a thin black figure sitting in the back seat of my car staring straight at me in the reflection of the mirror! I will not forget that night, especially the eyes on this thing. It had bright yellow eyes like a cat.

I have had many experiences on that road. About a year later a friend and I pulled up in the middle of the road. I turned off the lights on the car and we sat there looking up at a plane in the dark sky. I told him to take note of the time we stopped. After we talked awhile, I asked him how much time he thought had passed. He guessed about nine minutes. I asked if he thought it was strange that the plane was still in the same place. When he realized this, he wanted to get the hell out of there!

There was a time when I really believed that I was going crazy, but others saw the same as I, so I knew there was more to it. I am constantly followed. At last I came to the conclusion that these people are hybrids. Even I found this hard to believe – how could they look so much like us? But it is more than the way they look. When they are about to come near me I feel them. In most incidences I get a knot in my stomach, feel totally sick like I am going to vomit, feel lethargic, and I begin to hyperventilate. I feel my etheric body separating from my physical body. I feel a tiny needle going into the crown of my head. Through this needle I feel an electrical current entering into me. In most cases, I feel the needle first. It is very thin, like a strand of hair.

Even on the highway, I can always feel when these hybrids follow me. I have pulled over to see a whole car disappear in front of my eyes. Another time I was in a supermarket and saw one walking up the aisle. My wife and I stopped. The hybrid also stopped where we were standing and turned her head, just staring at us both. There are many incidents where they have taken my memory for a short amount of time. I stare at them and when they are gone I do not remember where they went. I always talk to them telepathically, at least 80% of the time. My friends have been with me and seen these hybrids. Once in the parking lot of KMart with two friends, we watched a hybrid drive past us. All three of us saw him shape-shift to a female right in front of us.

Another time I was driving late at night. I felt the bombardment of the negative energy of these creatures all around me. The car in front of me slowed, then stopped. When I tried to go around him, one car pulled up on each side of my car, with another behind me. I was trapped on all sides. This road was quiet and it was late. Not one of these so-called men would look at me. They all looked straight ahead, robotically moving in sequence. I was a little spooked as I thought this it. I felt this crushing sensation in my chest as the amount of energy they put toward me that night made me feel completely helpless.

They also monitor me with a high-pitched ringing in my ears, similar to an extremely loud screeching. I believe for years now they have tested my ability to feel their presence. They know that they can not evade me because I am too sensitive. I can feel one in a crowd of 200 people. Over the years, I have learned that there are many types of hybrids. There must be some type of levels within the species, as there are types that go unnoticed in society. Even when I felt their presence, sometimes they avoid me at all costs. Here are others that I see with an electrical energy around there heads and a strong white energy coming out of their pineal gland chakra spinning in an anti-clockwise direction.

Then there are the ones who are just blatant. They stop to stare at me with their unemotional eyes. I speak to them telepathically, telling them that they are no good and that I know what they are. But they just continue to stare, then walk away, stop, and turn around to stare again. They are in all nationalities and races. Recently they spoke to my wife, telling her that no one would believe her, and that humans are becoming outnumbered. They told me telepathically to mind my own business and to get one with my miserable life.

There are also the black-eyed ones, who I consider to usually be the best-looking and most human-like. Their presence is more difficult to determine. If I could not pick up their energy, they could very easily fit into a crowd. When Stewart Swerdlow was here presenting a seminar, we stopped at a restaurant where I frequently go. We were enjoying our meal when a couple came in quite late and the restaurant was almost empty. I did not take much notice of these two as I was trying to enjoy my time with my friend, but it started. I suddenly felt so nauseous that I had to stop eating. I pointed them out to Stewart, who could also feel their energy. When I stared at the woman, she glanced over to us, allowing the whites of her eyes to turn black. Stewart also saw this happen. Then the couple left, but as the woman walked out the door she glanced back at us with a smirk. I have such strong senses to these hybrids as I feel they have no soul, and nature does not produce clones.

Then there are the ones that look like a hybrid. I believe these are the lowest form as they do not have a great deal of energy. These are the creatures that I believe are put into every day society in our rural areas. We have a great deal of people who are just not right. They look strange with offset eyes, large ears, and strange hair growth. People in society call them lower class and uneducated, but the amount of people like this is abnormal. These hybrids are here to program the young of our country, the teenagers who are easily led and may have difficulty at home. These hybrids work in places where the rebellious are.

These lower forms are in the low wage sector, in hospitals, fast food outlets, youth centers, social security offices, legal aid, etc. I remember one day answering a knock on the door only to find it was two hybrids saying they were Jehovah Witnesses. I will never forget their faces when I spoke to them telepathically.

Australia is the original land of the Reptilians. It is this country that is hot and dry, with less and less rainfall each year that passes. This is their agenda. We have lakes that are dry. These lakes held millions of liters of water and are now barren waste land. We have strict laws. Australia is the land of being honorable. Our government gives rewards for informing on your neighbors. We have created a population of civilian police. For me it is nonstop annihilation. These hybrids can not intimidate me with their brain-scanning so they use their puppets. Over the years they have sent law enforcement officers to my home and my place of business, concocting stories, putting me through court cases, then later dropping charges as they couldn't come up with any evidence.

I was raided once because I covered what I believe is a two-way television. When the police came, the senior sergeant in charge of the operation who was a 33rd degree Freemason, walked over to the television and asked me if I was a smartass – so that answered the question right there. I am continually prosecuted for the crime of knowledge. On this charge I pled GUILTY. I refuse to stop showing people that these hybrids are everywhere. They are like a plague, moving in slowly and unnoticed until it will be too late when everyone opens their eyes or should I say, their senses.

Where I live is very rural and there are no street lights or high-rise buildings. The sky is always clear at night and the stars are bright. You can go out about any night and the UFOs will give you a show. When Stewart was staying here they put on a nice display for him. They know they can do what they like here and no one will take much notice.

I have a friend who is closely monitored at times. He first noticed it when a small black helicopter followed him wherever he went. These are the size of a toy helicopter but no toy could follow you on a 100km trip. I have been followed by the same thing on many occasions. But they come in all shapes. There was a time where I was sitting at home and I heard a strange noise. I went outside to see a full-size helicopter on silent mode hovering about 5 metres above my roof. This is the reason why the government ordered the eradication of asbestos in homes here in Australia, so they can use thermal imagery and monitor everyone in their home. Asbestos blocks metal detection and thermal imagery.

I was out in my shed talking with a friend one night. I felt there was something around and the dog was barking like crazy. Then I saw hovering inside the shed a black figure in the shape of a snake. It was about a metre in height but was not on the ground. It danced in mid-air, roaming around the whole area. I heard my mother's voice say very tactfully, "What are you doing here?" My friend also saw this and was completely spooked.

Then my friend and I took my daughter into town and came straight back home. I saw a car with a man sitting in it parked not too far from my home. I pulled over to talk to him but he would not communicate back with me. His face was horrendous. It looked as though he had facial tissue removed and glued back on. My friend could not believe this man's face. She was horrified as she had never seen anything like this in her life. He was a shapeshifter who had not been able to return to his human form properly. I felt that he was the entity that split into a nonphysical form, watching me in my shed, trying to project negative energy toward my friend and I.

I do believe that my purpose in this life is to bring the truth to as many people in society that I can. In my 42 years of living, I have experienced a great many things. The one thing that I have learned is the hybrid breeding technology is in such fast progression. I saw this hybrid not long ago. She was beautiful and so powerful in her projection of power that she stunned me. This is proof to me that they are getting better at human-looking and alien-powered technology. I have come to live with the constant 24/7 monitoring from these hybrids and the abductions.

I have been with many different people who witnessed these interactions so if I am crazy all those people are also. Only 1% or less of our population knows the truth. My purpose, no matter what, is to increase that number, I cannot emphasize the fact of this whole outcome and how strong it is in its programming of the population. This planet is being taken away from us right under our noses. I do believe that if these hybrids did not want me to know this knowledge that I am instilled with, then I would not be here to talk about it.

Nothing happens by chance. They are everywhere. The most common symptom that I see is people going into so-called "daydream mode." It is at this moment when you drift off that the hybrids insert energy into the mind-pattern of the person/persons. Everyone is becoming more militant, negative energy is everywhere, we are all selfish, people have no morals anymore, we are loosing love, and creating hate. This is the agenda of the DRACO. They turn us all on each other. The more negativity out there the stronger their energy becomes.

Once the reality of their presence is believed we can only stop helping their agenda by helping one another. We are the ultimate consumers, greedy and ruthless. We are becoming the hybrids of the future. I personally have no faith in the future as our army is small. I live always in the present, never thinking of tomorrow. The future is too hard for me to process and build upon, as the past has been such a struggle. The only thing that gives me faith is the knowledge that there is a beyond.

As I lay by my mother's side, her body only functioning by machines, and when her soul finally was released by a switch, she told me in spirit that everything would be okay. Everyday that passes I ache to have her near me and her simple gestures. The only comfort that I get from her passing is her frequent visits to me, her guidance spiritually has helped me over my bumps in the road and her knowledge that the greatest challenge gives the best rewards. So as much as my life is turbulent, the satisfaction of inner awareness is the only reward I seek.

These beings need our energy to survive, so it is our choice to give it to them or not. Each day they bombard me with the energy, but a year ago when I met Stewart Swerdlow he changed my life. We have come to learn that we have shared many experiences together. With this I call him my true brother, a person with whom I feel unequal to any other. Before my interaction with him, I was ready to jump of the world. What little hope I have, he is the person that has given it to me, as ignorance is the offspring of mystery.

Case #7 Analysis
Green Star Programming

⟩⟨   This Australian man tells a story that is the most unique in all of the experiences that I have had in deprogramming. Australia is a land that is the largest piece of Lemuria left above the ocean.

For this reason, there still remains intact vast parts of the underground structures and equipment that were part of the Lemurian civilization that was destroyed by the Atlanteans tens of thousands of years ago.

The US maintains a deep underground base in central Australia known as Pine Gap. All Australians are aware of this place which is basically off limits to citizens of that country and manned mostly by American soldiers and scientists.

I can verify all of his story as I personally witnessed these hybrid beings who can shift their eyes to deep black when they perform with their mental/physical supernatural powers.

Australia is a giant laboratory for the Illuminati since it is so isolated and with a relatively small population. Most of the country in desert and uninhabitable, therefore, the largest percentage of the 20 million people live along the eastern and western coastlines.

The laws in Australia are extremely strict with regards to herbs, vitamins, and unconventional treatments. Very little is allowed. It is as if they are trying to keep their experiments uncontaminated. What works in Australia is then imposed on other continents.

This man is part of the experiments in his country. He is a product of a long line of Illuminati families and has the typical blonde hair, blue eyes of programming necessity.

His frequency is reminiscent of the Montauk Project "boys." He may well have been used in the Australian version of this. I recognize a lot of myself in him. Beyond the fact of feeling like brothers, I feel that he is also a programming twin of mine.

He displays the characteristics of a Monarch Male as well as having a lot of various alien programming related to End-Times. He is working on all of these. In addition, his wife is an exact replica/clone of my "first wife," Mia, who I wrote about in my book, **Montauk: Alien Connection.**

Australia is the home of very strange hybrids who have robotic-like behavior and display the characteristics of humans, Reptilians, greys, and Sirians all combined. They seem to have a mental connection to some specifically programmed people in Australia who also appear to be a target of these hybrids.

This person's deprogramming is challenging as he has many issues with which to deal. His mother is also a product of this hybridization program and he may be the next phase in the humanization of alien genetics as a forerunner of a new human race in the future.

He is doing very well in his deprogramming techniques and has made great strides in understanding who and what he is. A further investigation needs to be done in Australia concerning the intentions and purposes of the hybrids and their interactions with the general population.

This person is still a very unstable individual. He still waivers back and forth in being completely of sound mind and then goes into bizarre states where he experiences the incidences mentioned in his story.

People who have been subjected to such types of physical and mental manipulation often find it very difficult to determine the difference between what is actually happening and what is a virtual mind experience. To them, it is all the same. Of course, this brings up issues of what is real, anyway. To the mind, there is no difference between the dream state and the waking state.

I have seen both males and females from several continents who describe events happening to them similar to the ones described here. All of them seem to have similar characteristics. Each of these individuals have extreme sexual urges and would be considered to be promiscuous, especially the males. This is because that as part of the downloads to expand genetic capacities, such programs as Monarch, Dragonfly, Scorpion, and White Rabbit have been input.

To the general population, if they met any one of these people, they might see them as deranged, hallucinatory, violent, unstable, and perhaps even vulgar at times. All of them have a multitude of what is usually considered vices, such as drinking, smoking, drugs, gambling, and heavy sexuality. Living life on the edge appears to be a common trait.

From a deprogramming perspective, it is my observation that all of the people in this category have several demonic/astral attachments to their programming matrices and can easily be triggered into hosting or bringing forward such entities.

Interestingly, most of the ones I have met over the years appear to be much younger than their chronological ages. This indicates Tinkerbelle Programming which makes sense for them. It took a lot of time and effort to achieve this virulent mix of genetics and programming. These people are walking laboratories and contain a plethora of functions. They are valuable. Therefore, they are intended to be used for an extended period of time, hence the need for Tinkerbelle Programming.

Another interesting commonality for this type is that their genitals all have some sort of marking or abnormality of different kinds. For example, some of the females report that the opening to the vagina has been cut, extended, or changed in some way—often in a painful manner.

The males report lumps or bumps on the scrotum or shaft of the penis which may indicate implants or some other type of surgical alteration. Both the males and females can have multiple orgasms. Very few, if any, that I have worked with are gay or bisexual. They all appear to be completely heterosexual, which in itself, is an aberration for ritualistic purposes.

This indicates to me that they are used for reproductive purposes and are not used ritualistically in the same way as most other sexually programmed people. However, all of them have extreme relationship issues and find it difficult to stay with just one person.

Another commonality is that almost none of them can hold a job or even make their own businesses. They constantly fail financially, often depending upon the government and/or others to help them get by.

As with the person mentioned in this case study, ultimately, almost all fall away from the deprogramming process, choosing instead to remain as they are, floundering through their lives. They rarely take responsibility for anything, tend to overreact to all information, and exaggerate facts and experiences.

I suppose that all of this is part of their programming designed to make people stay away from them and be wary of whatever they say. In this way, such programming types remain isolated and unexamined by conventional society.

A concern of mine is that once the Illuminati has gotten all the information that they need from these people regarding alien experimentation, then they will most likely eliminate them since they could be a liability. Suicide programming is very strong in these people and must be monitored closely.

Case #8
Elite Descendent Programming

When asked to contribute to Stewart's book concerning my genetic lineage as a Wilson, I thought a great deal about what would be the most helpful and to whom. From my personal perspective, it would be rather boring, lengthy endeavor to detail my life. I have similar lessons to learn and weaknesses to overcome as everyone else does.

Yes, it may well be true that my genetic make-up has placed me in a particular stream of experience and learning. I can say that in my journey through this life, my life has not been usual; even by the standards of unusual life's experiences of others in this particular time line.

Having said that, where could I begin to share my life's experience in a way or ways that make a contribution to others? What are the signposts along the way, the turning points, the choices and the exposure of true knowings which have brought me to where I am at this time?

For me, the first crucial point of change of focus or "awakening to" the deeper truth of life here on Earth came when I was ten years old. It was summertime. I happened to walk out onto the hill behind our home. I looked out over the valley; the sky had a heaven look to it – one of those extraordinary plays of light and streams of golden light that to me meant God. At that time I knew

I was looking at God and angels. I simply knew. In that moment every cell of my being declared (and I said this out loud), "I am going to find out all the secrets of this place." God definitely heard me that day. Such a proclamation was to have its results from that moment on.

Later in my life I began a "formal" course of study. This was one of those package deals, as I call it, of a particular meditation coupled with a specific style of journal-keeping. With these two methods and their related techniques I was able to better facilitate and harness my already very active "psychic" abilities. These methods enabled me to redirect my consciousness to the Christed aspect of myself.

My proclamation at ten years old definitely had its results. Looking from now to then I understand my Soul knew and agreed to not only my genetics but also to the exposing of truth and secrets. The addition of truth became an important quality – a quality added consciously when I began my journal-keeping with its related meditation.

Some of these results felt akin to Pandora's Box or worse – worse in the sense that most of my difficulties occurred out-of-body. My physical body was unwell and my emotions were totally tormented.

As a child, living in a rural setting, I caught myself being put back on the road outside my home. More quickly than expected, I regained conscious awareness of headlights in the air just above me. There were no cars around, no streetlights. There were no "ordinary" explanations for this.

Jumping forward to three or so years ago, my exploration into this aspect revealed a constant and consistent taking of my consciousness into other realms for somebody else's purposes. Again here is where the teacher and methods showed up to help me through this period of my life. Approximately three years ago is when I met Stewart & Janet Swerdlow. Their work and support have been extremely valuable to me. I thank them from the bottom of my heart.

Because I was practicing through the years techniques and methods to realign my consciousness to my Christic and Divine Self I was also confronting genetic programs as well as interfering sources of control. These confrontations brought to the surface very strong counter programs to keep me in my place, so to speak. I became physically ill, emotionally drained, psychologically challenged, and always feeling alone. For some reason, I have a strength which has kept me going in the direction of wholeness. At every step of the way there always comes the resource needed to allow me to see choices and the potentials of their outcomes. I guess it is my mind-pattern.

Returning to age ten, I set in motion a mind-pattern, a pattern which held within it many mind-patterns. The strength of my emotions, feelings, and determination (will) was so strong that singular event created for me a pathway to re-create, heal, align, and resolve my version of separation from the Divine Source of myself. To show these by example would be an autobiography far beyond the intentions of this book.

Simply put, but not necessarily easily done, choices were presented to me, the skills and teachers of those skills arrived in my life; my desire to truly correct myself to living as best as I can attain the highest qualities of my creation is what I do. This may well be the Wilson genetics and the Illuminati. May this be the return of both to the finest qualities of the Christed Frequency and God-Mind balanced.

Concerning my current life as a genetic Wilson, it is rather like being at the forefront of discovery, a constant reframing and re-defining of the constituents of daily living. My personal definition and experiences of life are definitely changed from years past. Following along the applications of the basic principles of facilitating change and growth, I experience a very full and meaningful life.

Is my life productive? Do I affect others? Am I worthwhile? Such questions could be expanded to create a very long list. The answers to these questions depend upon whom you or I ask. Another question could be if any of those questions are truly important. If they are, then to who or what are the answers meaningful?

By consistently focusing my consciousness in the balance of my True Self created by the Mind of God, then I am gently led each day into and through relationships which allow me to know myself, accepting myself and thus others as we truly are.

By keeping this focus I continually find that indeed all needs are met upon all levels. My mind-patterns attract to me qualities and situations allowing me to experience life beyond survival. Often I laugh with myself concerning a challenge I have given to myself. Purely as entertainment – an ego-based desire.

Where does such an occurrence of my creation lead me? Simply for what it is. The importance is to realize it was ego created. I did it. The next step is giving such an experience over to a higher principle; transforming me into a more attuned human being to God-Mind. This allows my life experience Source to be from a base of corrected thinking.

Living life from such a perspective, the "burden" of ego-based decisions and perceptions of events is changed. I, as a Soul-Personality, follow in freedom the initial God-Mind based original thought, which is dissolving of all "other" based thinking.

Allowing the True Source of me to use this physical body; using physicality to communicate itself with others focused in this dimension, freedom is given from any worry concerning well-being or long term planning. As corrections in thinking occur, the mind-patterns and any supportive structures are dissipated. I allow for the corrected mind-patterns and their supportive structures to be expressed according to my Oversoul for me.

Case #8 Analysis
Elite Descendent Programming

⟩⟨ This woman is a Wilson. Many readers may remember
that important name from the Montauk Project series of books
that mentions the Wilson family as being instrumental over the
last few centuries in mind-control and programming projects both
in the UK and in the US.

The Wilson family is associated with the Windsor family in
Britain. This means that she inherited quite a huge stash of programming and has had major programming installed subsequent
to her birth.

Although she was born in the US, she spent many years in
England raising her only son. He also is programmed in a major
way and is working on his deprogramming issues conscientiously.

This woman once showed me a plate that her family brought
from Europe when they came to the US. On it was depicted a huge
dragon with wings. This plate was a family heirloom. It did not
depict the Reptilianized lion as most European elite symbols show,
but a pure dragon. This indicates an extremely pure lineage.

In the process of her standard deprogramming, she has discovered an amazing connection to the Lion Frequency. She has
become quite proficient in it and accesses incredible information
for herself and others. The winged lions that exist in this frequency

help her to speed the deprogramming process and integrate her personality fragments rapidly.

It is quite likely that her affinity to the Lion Frequency comes from her close Illuminati descendency. In my book, ***Blue Blood, True Blood: Conflict & Creation***, I mention that the Reptilianized lion of European coats of armor and city banners is a mix of the pure lion energy of the Magdalene lineage and the dragon of the Khazar lineage. Therefore, the reason she so easily connects to Lion Frequency may be genetically directed from her Lyraen side. This also implies that she can easily connect to the Reptilian/dragon frequency as well. This makes her a perfect ambassador between the human race and the Reptilian race as she contains the best of both. Her programming has been brought to new phases by the Illuminati since the late 80s onward. There should be next generation versions of her walking the Earth these days.

I have met a few clients like this woman who are very direct descendents of either the Illuminati or the Committee of 300 families. All of them are highly educated, even if from economically deprived branches of the "family". They all seem to have emotional neutrality, meaning that they do not seem to go too overboard one way or the other with feelings. This makes it easy for them to leave people, places, and things behind. Despite originating from the elite, there seems to be a minimal attachment to nostalgia and "things."

All of their programming is related to receiving information from nonphysical realms without the need for ceremony or ritual. It just comes naturally to them. However, these people work well with hyperspace techniques as you can see from this case study.

As with other programming categories, this type also has relationship issues, but always manages to have one or two children that they raise by themselves. Their children tend to be extremely creative and independent. They also inherit programming and the ability to connect to nonphysical sources.

This elite group live in areas known for ritual and where "blue blood" genetics are predominant. These locations are usually in hilly or mountainous regions outside of major cities.

All of these program-types have extremely pale skin, are very physically strong, and mentally powerful. Nothing bothers them too much and they do not allow others to get them upset. They do have somewhat of an air of superiority, but without blatant arrogance or prejudice.

Deprogramming such individuals is easier than you would imagine since they take to the work so well, progress quickly, and do not feel threatened or antagonized by the Illuminati or other elite groups. In fact, they know many of them personally and often socialize with them.

The deprogrammer who works with such people may feel odd, like walking into the nest of the reptile, but at the same time, receiving a sense of understanding and respect for the culture and lifestyle that led to the programming in the first place.

Case #9
Failed Termination

I sit here in wonder and amazement after a Personal Consultation with Stewart which revealed, according to my program, that I was supposed to have died February 1, 2000. I reflect over my life and the times leading up to the event and obstacles that I overcame on many levels, conscious and unconscious. This explains feelings that I have of my life looping around and not seeming to make any sense. Now, following this event, the programmers do not know what to do with me. With his expertise in handling matters such as this, I now have a plan of deprogramming and cutting the loop so I can continue on my way to really savor this lifetime and move forward.

As a youth, I was different from many children in my hometown, much to my parent's dismay. I was defiant and extremely headstrong. This behavior continued through my childhood and into college. As was expected for the women in my family, I pledged a sorority and found myself miserable because of the rigid rules and rituals. Even at that age, I was resistant to the program and didn't conform to the world of Greek sisterhood.

I grew up in a small Texas farming and ranching community and discovered that people were labeled according to the church they attended. Even though my parents were not active members, they were raised in the church and insisted that I be exposed to Christian teachings, which was also encouraged by my grandmothers. So I joined the Methodist Church and even became very "religious" in junior high school. As I moved into my high school years I wasn't as devout, but was still active in church activities.

I married a rancher, who in accordance with his German heritage, was traditional and conservative in his ways of thinking and behavior. Certainly we were never to discuss spirituality. In his opinion, it was the church and the minister's job to fill that need. I sat in the pews, disillusioned with the sermons, feeling an urge to seek my own truth. I began to explore by ordering spiritual books which I literally read behind brown paper wrappers, pouring over every shred of information and ideas I could find.

Different concepts were interesting and new. My appetite for expanding my world was endless. Then a huge fight ensued with my husband. He was very uncomfortable with the ideas and the murmurings I was expressing along the way. He forbade me to discuss newly discovered concepts. I was not allowed to read my treasured books, so to avoid any further confrontations, the books were stored away in the attic. But, I still could not resist the urgings, so in the early 60s I enrolled in Silva Mind Control. This was my first introduction to meditation. Through the techniques, I was able to heal the migraine headaches that plagued me for many years. The marriage ended in divorce. Symbolic of my freedom, I dumped the books that were stored away onto my bed in my apartment and slept with them the first night.

My spiritual journey has taken me to many exotic places in the world, from the Himalayas to sacred sites in India; to the temples in Thailand; to the caves and villages in Java. I sat on woven mats in an artist village in Bali carving a ceremonial mask. I took a camel trek across the outback of Australia, discovering aboriginal cave drawings of space ships and unusual space creatures covering the walls of obscure caves from centuries past. I have participated in rituals and sacred dance in far flung parts of the world listening to the ancient sounds of their ancestors. All the time my soul was stirring with an insatiable appetite for more. I questioned what made these people so attuned to their gods and why couldn't I evoke the gods of my lost tribe?

My quest took me to Egypt twice. I layed under the chin of the mysterious Sphinx at midnight and chanted in the Kings Chamber of the Great Pyramid. I explored the grounds of sacred sites, and inside temples along the Nile with a curiosity and eager anticipation for answers. I listened to sages, teachers, and lamas whom I hoped would unravel the mysteries, thinking that perhaps they would soothe my restless soul.

Each time I would imagine my understanding had deepened, but there was never any resolve. I swam with wild dolphins in the open sea. I listened, mediated, laughed, and played with them. There was a definite connection on some level, which I carry with me to this day. There were many more journeys throughout the world and experiences too numerous to mention that enriched my life. I have developed a profound understanding and respect for many people I have encountered in my travels, sometimes connecting in very deep and powerful ways.

During the Christmas holidays of 1999, my nephew extended an invitation to me and his mother who is my sister, to join him in Morocco in January 2000. She was in agreement that it would be fun and exciting, and that this trip would fulfill my desire to visit northern Africa again. Morocco held a definite fascination for me. I had taken hand with a Sufi Sheikh a couple of years before, so I embraced all that Sufism had to offer. My sister, also a student of Sufism, and I were invited to meet with a Sheikh in Fez and participate in zikrs, dance, and ceremonies.

After much preparation, we embarked on a life-changing adventure. My nephew's wife also joined us, which completed our family foursome. Everything about the trip was in harmony; it all worked seemingly without a glitch. An overland trip at midnight via a taxi from Casablanca to Marrakech set the pace for an exciting adventure. We explored and bargained in the markets of Marrakech. We visited the tourist sites, laughed and ate our way through the city, exploring the Kasbahs, as well as weaving through alleys and back streets fascinated by sights and sounds of this intriguing city.

Since my nephew had been in Morocco for a few weeks and had driven over many of the roads, we decided to rent a car and begin our journey to Fez. We took side trips off the beaten path, visiting and lodging in many Kasbahs. We loved the people, the food, the dress, and of course, all the interesting vistas along the way. Most of the things we experienced were not the typical tourist activities and, for the most part, were spontaneous.

We drove through the Atlas Mountains for days, coursing around the oftentimes treacherous hairpin curves, savoring the beautiful landscape surrounding us. The weather was cold, clear, and sunny, which made it very pleasant. We were cozy in the small rental car, our bags stored in the hatchback. The soft daypacks cushioned our heads in the backseat where my sister and I sat. I made a mental note that there were no seatbelts in the back, but I never buckled up in the back seat in the states so I wasn't concerned.

We spent the night in a village at the base of the mountains, quaint and charming along with a bonus of unexpected entertainment. The evening temperature was dropping into the 20s. The warmest spot in the inn was in the main dining room around a roaring fire. Many of the guests gathered around to listen to the local Moroccans drum. My sister was in her element, having led drum circles in California; she also taught drumming and drum-making classes so she especially appreciated the rhythm and their unique style.

Not to be undone, a travelling French orchestra brought in their instruments and there was a showdown contest. Without question, the Moroccans won, hands down. So much fun and so many nationalities shared the stimulating evening. On our way back to our rooms, my sister and I sat down on one of the comfy sofas, continuing our ongoing sisterly conversation. She confided to me that she had decided the ideal way to die was with family, doing something she loved and laughing. Little did we know her wish was about to be fulfilled.

The next morning, February 1, 2000 at 9AM, we waved good-bye to our friends, piled in the little car and sped on our way. It was another beautiful, clear, sunny day. As we left the village, I remarked to my sister that we missed shopping in this village, noting some yellow scarves hanging in a store window. My nephew's frequent comment when we missed a shopping opportunity was that "we will see it in Fez!" That was the last I remembered. The following account of events was later related to me.

As we traveled along the way, at approximately 11AM, two military trucks in tandem, approached us from the rear. As the first one got close to our bumper, my nephew pulled over so they could pass. When the second truck came barreling around us, my nephew pulled over onto the shoulder of the road. With that, he lost control, the car making the first flip that threw my sister out one side and me out the other. After the car flipped the second time it came to rest upside down on the rocky, sandy field. Terribly shaken but uninjured, my nephew crawled out the broken windshield. His wife sustained serious injuries with a lacerated forehead and a deep gash on the top of her head, but was still conscious. He began to look for his mother, eventually finding her on the side of the road, dead.

She appeared as if she had just laid down, taking nap. The only external injury was a bruise on the side of her face. Then the search began for me. Finally, after following moaning sounds, I was discovered under the car, my clothes shredded and large amounts of blood covered my body. The soldiers helped to remove me from the wreckage, gather our personal belongings, and placed us in the back of the truck. We were taken to a village several miles away where my nephew attempted to seek medical help. There was none available, so we were transferred to another vehicle. We were then driven to another village where there was the possibility of scheduling an air ambulance at the cost of $6,000.

The immediate response was that he could manage with credit cards, but it wasn't that easy because this service was available for cash only. Discouraged, he rented another vehicle and we proceeded to Marrakech. After arriving there, he was able to obtain a helicopter to fly us to Casablanca. I later learned that had I flown in the airplane with a punctured lung, the pressurized cabin would have killed me. Upon our arrival at Casablanca, the embassy was contacted. He was given the name of a small orthopedic hospital which turned out to be the best place we could have wished for under the circumstances. My injuries were serious, life-threatening, and complicated.

On admission to the hospital, it was discovered that I suffered a broken neck. All the time of transporting me from place to place it was not detected and my neck was never constrained. I am grateful every day that I am not paralyzed. Besides the neck injury, I suffered a crushed left arm and nerve damage to the right arm which left it frozen to my side. My ribs were broken and the sternum cracked. I also suffered a broken pelvis and ankle as well as lacerations on the back of my head and a deep gash over my right eye. My oldest son and his wife came immediately to the hospital from Texas and that is when I woke up after days of unconsciousness. They told me later they didn't recognize me when they approached my hospital bed because of the heavy bruising on my face and body.

I have very positive comments regarding the medical facility. The physicians were trained all over the world in their specialties and all but one of the surgeries were performed in that hospital. My broken body was expertly pieced back together with screws, pins, and plates. The hospital staff and embassy were especially sympathetic to our situation and literally took us under their wings. I mentioned many times there were places in the world I didn't even want a hangnail. But I believe by Divine Intervention I was guided to the appropriate place, to the right people, at the right time and it was consistently true throughout this ordeal.

After several frustrating days with my son and the ambassador's aide attempting to make arrangements to fly a gurney patient home, at last we were on our way via Air Morocco. One of the physicians even flew with us as far as New York. We then chartered an air ambulance to my son's city of residence in Texas where I was hospitalized for several days then on to a rehab hospital where I stayed for four months.

While in the hospital some amazing revelations occurred and my deep soul searching took another turn. Since I was unable to walk or move even slightly without assistance, I was at the mercy of many just attending to my basic needs. I experienced bouts of anger, frustration, grief, fear, and feelings of despair, not to mention, extreme pain. I was experiencing the dark night with a knowing this journey was to be long and arduous. Without the wonderful care and encouragement of family and friends, I shudder to think where I would be today.

As part of the rehab routine, I was required to be present in the central therapy room twice daily, even though I was unable to participate in the activities. With my right leg and foot uninjured, I devised some innovative and unusual methods of therapy which passed the time. When I was in my room the depression would overwhelm me. I could not read, watch TV or even listen to books on tape because I simply didn't have the strength to press the play button and I couldn't see without my glasses. So, while lying there it dawned on me to finally put all the information I had read, learned in seminars, and been taught by all the teachers I studied with along the way, into action. So, I began to be quiet and meditate for very long periods of time. The amazing fact of this is I discovered all the information I had sought outside myself was inside and with that revelation, the real journey began. I decided in order to get my attention, the universe had to get pretty creative, dramatic, and drastic, and it appeared to be working!

When I returned home from trips outside the country my habit was to do a parasite cleanse. While in the hospital, I knew the normal routine of this would not work so my son and I researched essential oils. We came upon bergamont, discovering it was native to Morocco and used for parasite cleansing. Meanwhile my daughter-in-law discovered a brand new unopened bottle of bergamont in their bathroom cabinet. She didn't know what it was, much less the use, and of course had not purchased it. To this day we do not know how that bottle mysteriously appeared! Three of my grandsons visited often and decided they would like to do something to make me more comfortable. One placed his hand under my hand and arm that was in a cast and pat me with his other hand. The oldest massaged my feet with the bergamont. The youngest attended therapy sessions with me, acting as my stand-in for the exercises. They all had an active participation in my healing process.

This is a long, ongoing journey of healing as well as a time of self-discovery. With sheer determination and a strong will I have defied odds and reached a place of almost total independence. There are still parts of me that don't work exactly as I wish, but I see the progress I've made in four years as the healing continues.

At times I find myself in denial and overwhelmed with the idea of deprogramming and I admit I find the work daunting. But after meeting Stewart and Janet, attending his workshop and the ***First Annual Expansions Conference*** along with phone conversations, I know there is support. Their books and website are fascinating as well as helpful. I am attempting, with Stewart's urging, to begin the process using the guidance and information they provide.

My goal is to travel again because I love the rich experiences and interacting with different cultures. Now I know there won't be the frustrating endless search for peace and resolve when all my answers are inside and my God-Mind and Oversoul are available 24/7.

Case #9 Analysis
Failed Termination

Having spent time with this woman in her home in Texas, as well as meeting with her for consultations, it becomes obvious that she has several types of programming within her. She has had relationships and marriages that are common to Monarch women. In fact, she is one of the earlier versions of Monarch programming that was characteristic of the late 40s and into the 50s.

In addition to this, she shows signs of New World Religion programming that led her to Sufism and that form of guru worship for awhile. Her constant quests of going to native-like cultures and joining in on their practices is a sign of a person who must learn about these religions to help incorporate them into the local area after the New World Religion (NWR) takes effect. In other words, since the NWR is comprised of many of these religious practices, people are needed in every little town and village with first-hand knowledge of these cultural nuances that can explain and promote the belief system.

Somewhere along the way, she became a liability. Perhaps her old version of programming was no longer viable. Things change. Both she and her sister, who was also programmed, were scheduled for elimination. The military vehicles are a common method of slave destruction. Morocco is also an old base for programming Air Force personnel in both the US and UK militaries.

Perhaps her connection to her Oversoul saved her. It was not her time, but as far as the Illuminati were concerned, she was dead. Her sister died instantly, and she was supposed to die as well.

It was the catalyst of the "accident" that propelled her to realize that something was not right in her life and that there were other hands in her affairs—and in her mind. Her deprogramming work has led her to many self-realizations. In addition, she is also working on healing her body in unconventional ways.

I recommended to her to work on the religious aspects of her personality while going through the deprogramming process. She also needs to work on the Monarch Programming which is foundational to the rest of what has been programmed into her.

I also suggested that she concentrate on doing the Green Spiral Staircase Visualization from my book, *Hyperspace Helper: A User Friendly Guide*, to help focus on the accident scene since most of her memories were wiped clean of this event. In a simple amnesia case, at least glimpses of what occurred would have returned by now. But her memory is completely wiped. That is a sign of the programmed alter who experienced the "death" is no longer being "alive" in her programming matrix, so the memory died with the alter.

When she is able to recapture this via reintegration of personality, then the larger programming picture will become apparent and a greater self-realization will occur. This is a case of a deeply programmed slave no longer useful, but becoming a liability, so there was a need to discontinue the life process. You saw this before with famous slaves like Marilyn Monroe and Jayne Mansfield. In recent years, there have been several young, high-level Monarchs who were successfully eliminated, such as the singer, Aliyah, as well as Linda Lovelace, both of whom died in crashes.

The Monarch in this case study is also one who was from the time of programming experimentation. Case Study #4 is similar to this one, in which a female was used as a walking laboratory to test and retest.

This lovely woman went through agonizing physical pain and emotional torture. In many ways, she experienced a living death. She was not able to concentrate on anything in life except getting better. She had never even heard of programming or deprogramming before finding my work.

Of course, there exists always the question, at what point does such a Monarch become a liability and need to be eliminated? What is the chain or course of events both personally and globally that create the decision for removal? We are in End-Times Programming activations. It could very well be that the early, experimental Monarchs did not have these types of functions or alters that could be utilized during End-Times.

If this is the case, then these women become a liability when compared to the activated, modernized Monarchs. The older Monarchs function at a different level that can more easily trigger the newer Monarchs into "non-End-Times" behaviors. This is a liability from an Illuminati perspective.

It makes sense that female Monarchs who are devoid of End-Times Programming need to either be reprogrammed or removed. This female appears to have a form of New World Religion Programming. However, it is connected to an Islamic version which is in the process of being eliminated. It is also possible that her intended death, as well as the death of her sister, were part of a symbolic ritual of removing the Islamic population from the Earth.

It is symbolic that her near-fatal accident occurred inside an Islamic nation in the middle of a desert. That is a message that her belief system, programmed or not, is going to be removed from the general populace. It is also symbolic that at least one of her children and his family are Fundamentalist Christians. Now, that is in alignment with what is to come spiritually. It is also interesting that during her long recovery period, she spent time in the home of the fundamentalists. Could this have been an attempt to reprogram a termination failure?

I have seen a few times that after a termination failure, which is extremely rare, there is a repeat attempt to kill the Monarch, often as an illness. The reverse happened in the case of Linda Lovelace, the pornography queen Monarch who was also experimental. She had liver and breast cancer which she survived. Then she was suddenly killed in a head-on car crash in Colorado. If at first you don't succeed…

The other factor in this particular case is that this woman lives Texas, an area that does not match her frequency. This implies that no matter what her health, life becomes a struggle anyway. When a person lives in an area that does not energetically match their frequency, there is always conflict and struggle. In this way, keeping a failure termination in a place that is restrictive in many ways, creates a diversion anyway from interfering in the activations of her peers.

This woman is doing extremely well. Via deprogramming techniques and engaging in alternative healthcare, her injuries are almost healed and she is in extremely good condition on all levels, body, mind, and soul.

She continues to do her work and move forward. Attitude is paramount when deprogramming. Hers is exceptionally positive despite the pressures she receives from relatives and friends who do not share her outlook or belief system.

In order to not just survive in this circumstance, but to surpass and improve, you must be motivated to continue your process no matter what is thrown at you. This is especially true if your programming was original, experimental, and/or incomplete, meaning that it has no validity in modern times.

Back in the 1940s and 1950s when these original Monarchs were being created and tested, the programmers and Illuminati believed, based on life at that time, that these women would be dead long before End-Times came into play. They never realized back then that they would have to consider a cadre of older females who would become liabilities. Even the powers that be make huge errors.

Case #10
Androgyny Programming

)(I was born in the 60s. My mom became very ill the day I was born and was hospitalized for the first eighteen months of my life. My godparents took care of me while my dad cared for my siblings. They did not name me. They called me "baby." There is no first or middle name on my birth certificate – only a last name.

My brother sexually assaulted me from the time I was five until I was seven. My mother was on heavy medication. She slept twenty hours a day, thus unaware of what was going on. My sisters knew, but told me that I was doing something wrong. They threatened to tell our parents if I didn't do their chores.

My dad traveled for two weeks at a time, came home on the weekends, and regularly beat my mom. He threw her out windows, kicked her vagina, and hit her with metal baseball bats. When the police came, my dad and sisters would leave for the evening to stay in hotels, swim, and buy new clothes while I stayed with my battered mom.

At age nine I lost about three hours of time and to this day I don't know what happened. The abuse with my parents went on until I was eleven when my parents divorced. My dad, sisters, and I moved to California. No one was ever around to take care of me. When I was twelve, I became deliriously sick. My dad refused to take me to a doctor. Instead, he set the house on fire but I made it out. The next day an insurance man phoned and assumed I was my mom. When he said, "Sorry for the loss of your daughter, " I realized that my dad had tried to claim me as deceased.

During this time my dad often took me with him to Mexico, which was just over the border. There he picked up some white powder in a bag he then make me stuff down my pants until we crossed back.

My mom came to live with us again when I was fifteen. My dad still beat the hell out of her frequently. I started getting stoned a lot and leaving the house to do "daredevil" skateboarding. I left home when I was sixteen because I couldn't take dad's abuse of my mom anymore. I got married to a man when I was nineteen (although I am gay) and long story short, he works for the government. One of the houses we lived in was owned by a former member of "the flying tigers." This man asked me if I wanted to do some yard work around the complex for a reduction of rent. He told me that I would find the tools that I could use on the grounds of the property.

When I started exploring, I found files: government files. There were files of the Patty Hearst kidnapping and files of deeds of properties. For some reason, I took the files to show my husband. This was a mistake because my husband and I all of a sudden started being followed. We were almost killed a couple of times. Once, we hopped on a flight to New Mexico. After arriving, we were told the airport was closing. I called a friend of mine who lives there to beg for help.

While I was on the phone, my husband told me that there were two men on either side of the phone booth dressed in blue Air Force coats pointing guns at me. We made it to my friend's house and stayed there three months. During the first month, we frequently saw men dressed in the long blue Air Force jackets observing the house. I never went outside alone. My husband and I divorced when I was twenty-six. We no longer talk. There is only one person in my life who I talk with who has known me for longer than ten years. There is a lot more I could write.

Case # 10 Analysis
Androgyny Programming

This brief but intense story is actually typical of a programmed slave in training with a father-handler. This woman has told me more stories about her earlier life. Many times she would be placed in the presence of a wild animal and left to fend it off. She was also beaten and sexually abused. Although she was married, she now feels that she is a lesbian and lives with another woman, who is also programmed.

This is a typical story of a person who was used experimentally. She told me that her father worked for a drug company. He brought home many types of foods and chemicals for her to try to see her reactions. She knows that much of what is placed in the ingredients of food and drink are designed to enhance programming as well as alter the genetic structures of those who ingest the products.

She was, for all intents and purposes, a human laboratory designed to see what would happen to the public if certain items/chemicals/drugs were given out en masse. Her sexuality was purposefully designed to be androgynous so that a wider perspective could be studied in just one target human. There are males used in this way as well.

Another purpose for this woman was as a prototype for the bisexual/androgynous human that the New World Order promotes. Such a person can be used in a variety of ways. Sexual ritual is available for all categories of ceremony. The person becomes as an android/robot that is multi-purpose in function and programming.

She has gone on to have a successful relationship with another woman. She assumes the "male" role by working and supporting her partner, dressing like a man. She keeps her hair short and her emotions in check.

I have encountered a few more women like her since I first met her. They appear to cross racial barriers and cultural borders. The commonalities are a dominating father and a weak mother figure. Often, there is a military connection for the father.

These women also appear to have been placed "on ice" since there is very little further programming developed with them, i.e., no changes, upgrades, or reprogramming performed.

All of them have financial difficulties and low self-worth issues. They live in smaller apartments or houses and take jobs that are way below their capabilities. They usually have difficulties in maintaining a relationship, going for females that are more feminine than they are.

The programmed females are extremely slender, almost to the point of emaciation. Their bone density is extremely low. They compensate for this by wearing bulky, masculine clothing that makes them look bigger.

I have seen their gay male counterparts. These males seem to attract "daddy" figures as mates who take care of them financially, but who are not good sexual partners. I noticed that the males are constantly cheating on their partners while the female versions remain loyal. This indicates that although they are programmed to support androgyny, sexually they defer to their birth gender's propensity for sexual activity. Males tend to wander while females tend to remain faithful.

Deprogramming in this category takes patience and great understanding. The standard methods are used, but ultimately, the androgyny must be changed. It does not matter if they choose to remain same-sex orientated, but they must be conscious of their birth sexual preference before making that decision.

From my observations of the females, I firmly believe that they are not naturally lesbians. As we read in this particular case, this woman was initially married. In almost all the cases of this type that I have observed, the females start out attracted to males. It is only after the father/programmer experiences that there is a switch to same-sex partners.

Most of these women can revert back to heterosexuality after deprogramming is underway. However, almost all of them stop the process after a few months. Their Internal Programmer kicks in to stop the process and sabotages them.

With the males, they do go a lot further, but they often remain same-sex oriented. My feeling is that they were imprinted with males during the early programming process since all programmers are male. Because females get their initial imprinting from males, their initial sexual experiences are heterosexual. Therefore, it is the females in this androgyny category who can have conventional lives whereas the males remain in alternative lifestyles, continuing to relive their male-to-male initial sexual imprinting.

Both situations are fine as long as this is what the person desires. The main point is to reintegrate the personality so that the individual is in charge of his/her own mind. When this is underway, life choices can be made without outside interference and from a conscious perspective of true self-identity.

Case #11
Monarch Breeding Programming

)(I was listening to the radio yesterday to an interesting interview with Isabel Allende. She was speaking about the terrible years in Chile after her father was overthrown and Pinochet came into power. She was fortunate to have left Chile two or three years into the holocaust, escaping to Venezuela. When she returned fifteen years later, after the overthrow of Pinochet, she found that no one wanted to talk about what had happened. Many people were badly traumatized. Others had relatives and friends who had just disappeared. Their experiences were horrendous. None of them were willing to talk about it – to anyone! They just wanted to forget.

In sitting down to write my story, I understand how they feel. I also don't want to talk about it. I don't want to go back there; I don't want to touch it. It is very painful. However, in seeing how important it was for the Chileans to "witness" their story for the world, I begin to realize how relating my story can have the same kind of effect.

Of course, no story begins in a vacuum. There were roots that grew long before these actual events unfolded. My feelings of low self-esteem, weakness, doubts, lack of self-assuredness, and confusion were already present. When I pinpoint the beginning, it was at a good time. It was 1959. I was living in Baltimore and my husband was finishing up his Ph.D. at Hopkins. I had just delivered my first child, a son. I was feeling uneasy and unsure of myself as a new mother.

I knew whom I wanted to use as my baby's pediatrician. I had heard of him and his excellent reputation. I was drawn to him – straight as an arrow. I knew he was the one to take care of my baby and me. When I met him for the first time, I felt a strange affinity. I can't say I was crazy about him, but felt a certain attachment. He was a great help during those months with a new baby: Motherhood 101.

I became pregnant again about two and a half years later. Into about the eighth month, I began to experience uterine contractions and the baby was born prematurely. He seemed fine at first, weighing nearly five pounds, but shortly after birth he developed hyaline membrane disease, a breathing disorder of preemies, and died two days later. My doctor (I'll call him H) assured me that he would take care of everything and that it would be better if I didn't see my baby. Being Jewish, I thought perhaps we needed to have a funeral but H. assured me that it wasn't necessary or best. My father consulted a rabbi who agreed with this plan. I never saw my baby again.

I feel so ashamed to say this but after the death of this baby, I found myself madly in love with this doctor. I became obsessed with him. He filled my every thought. I continually fantasized about him. I couldn't get him out of my mind. I didn't tell him, or anyone, about my feelings as I was ashamed. I believed he could never feel the same way about me. I lived for months in this split: my fantasy life with him and the deteriorating relationship with my husband. I am convinced that I became pregnant for the third time while having sex with my husband and fantasizing madly about H. I have always felt guilty about this and worried about the effect it has had on my child.

My third pregnancy was difficult. Around the seventh month, I began having contractions again. I received delilutin shots, which is progesterone, I believe. This was given to prevent early delivery. I was confined to bed for the last two months of my pregnancy. Even though I delivered three weeks early, the baby was healthy and still considered full term. This became a very happy time for me having this baby and seeing H. often. My fantasy persisted.

It was then that my husband found a new job in a new city and we moved away. For me this was the straw that broke the camel's back. I did not want to leave my family, friends, and H. Saying good-bye to him was torturous. When I said good-bye I had one of the most unusual moments of my life. I have never experienced anything like it before or since. I began to kiss him and entered into an altered state where reality shifted for me. Suddenly I could see and hear the roar of the walls crumbling around me. They crumbled down about halfway. Then it all stopped. Complete silence. I could not see over the tops of the crumbled walls. A feeling of pure ecstasy came over me. I wanted to stay there forever. When I left the room, the scene started to fade back to reality. By the time I walked out into the sunlight, it was gone completely. However, the memory was not. I spent months and years yearning to return to that place.

It never happened. I slipped into a deep depression instead. Looking back now, I believe this to have been a post-partum depression that kept deepening. Alone in a new town with two babies and cut off from family and friends, I moved into a fantasy life that became an escape from a dull existence with my husband. I never received the emotional and psychiatric support I so desperately needed. I began having nightmares of mirrors and glass fragmenting. These nightmares frightened me greatly. I was spiraling down and began to fear for my sanity. I needed to speak to someone. I needed some reassurance that I was okay.

My mother had a longtime friend who entertained patients at a private mental hospital in Baltimore called Taylor Manor. I am giving the name of this place because I believe it to be a hall of horrors and a mind-control center. It is still in existence. BEWARE! At that time at least, all they did was electroshock therapy – for everyone. I did not know this fact. My mother's friend (sure!) recommended a psychiatrist, so I went to see him.

He prescribed a sleeping pill that I took. I awoke, walked to the bathroom, felt totally drugged, and passed out. "They" decided

I needed to be hospitalized. My husband signed for shock treatments on the advice of the doctors. My diagnosis was "Psychoneurosis, Anxiety State." I was given three months of shock treatments, three times a week. I recall coming out of the treatments with the others in a sort of basement. This felt like being in a roomful of zombies. I clung to whatever sanity I could muster. How I survived, I will never know.

But I did survive even though my memory and mind were totally wrecked. Two moments stand out as I think back on leaving the hospital. One was the parting words of my psychiatrist: "Do your own housecleaning." The other was a small voice in my head as I pulled into the driveway of my home. It said that everything would be okay now. I couldn't understand how everything could possibly be okay after all I'd been through, but it was. Of course, I was never the same again but I prevailed. I have spent the rest of my life learning to heal.

Case #11 Analysis
Monarch Breeding Program

◟◞ This is another case of a woman who was among the first in the United States to be programmed for the earliest of the Monarch programming agenda. It was common in those days to traumatize via death and injury of those around you. It was only later on that electromagnetic trauma and torture was available.

This Dr. H was most likely this woman's handler. It was and is still a common reaction for programmed Monarchs to fall in love with their handlers since the handler's energy is imprinted in them. When the experiment on this woman was complete, she was moved to another location with new handlers. The fact that this woman fantasized for such a prolonged time over this man indicates a possibility that they participated in sexual ritual together. It is even possible that Dr. H was the father of the baby that supposedly passed on.

The death of her second baby could have been a cover for her. There is a strong possibility that the infant was the product of a genetic test and needed to be studied. The baby's body was taken away without being seen. I am sure that any grave supposedly containing this baby would be found empty. I have heard similar stories all over the world, but particularly in the United States.

It is also a possibility that the infant was used in ritual or even that it lived and was given to another programmed family to be raised. The documents shown to me of the death are vague and incomplete. I know several women in my years of deprogramming who are searching for taken babies. They were all told that their babies died although never allowed to see the baby. There have been many stories of women, who years later, feel the need to see the truth about their dead babies. I once saw a documentary on television where one such female had her baby exhumed after several years only to find that the tiny coffin was totally empty. No baby, no bones, nothing!

Where did this child go? Could the woman in this case study also have a child out there that was taken from her under the guise of death? I have heard these types of stores countless times during my years of research and deprogramming.

In many cases, the death certificates, autopsies and burial information are either mysteriously missing or completely altered. My feeling is that some of these infants were given to more "appropriate" families for raising, some were used in sacrifice rituals, others were used for testing various genetic and mind-control procedures, while others were sent off-world in a colonization program.

This woman needs to do the original Monarch deprogramming which requires the use of the blue butterfly—the original symbol. After so many years, the programming, which in this case was left unfinished due to the time period involved, becomes corrupted in the mind and fragmentation can be permanent. As age becomes a factor, it becomes more difficult for the mind to reintegrate completely and emotions can become an issue. Heavy release work is a prerequisite in such cases. This becomes a process of patience and letting go.

The woman had two other male children, both of whom have severe emotional issues in life. The oldest son remained in her home city and became a medical professional. He never married but hooked on to a rather large older woman who may very well be his handler. He never had children and refuses to consider any alternative explanations for what has occurred in his family. He is not very close to his mother, instead, clinging in an unusual dependency to this older woman who basically controls his life.

The younger son lives in a large East Coast city with a gay life-style. Again, he has a warm to cool relationship with his mother and has gone into the arts world and the world of entertainment. She is concerned for his health and laments over the fact that with these two sons, she will never have grandchildren.

Her relationship with her long-term husband is one of room-mates at best. The husband rarely leaves the house. Most of the time he seals himself in his room doing odd things on the computer, hardly ever seeing the light of day.

The woman of this story is bored, depressed, and constantly looking for diversions in her life. She spent a great deal of time deprogramming and was very successful to a point. Then, she suddenly switched to new "gurus" who talked her out of deprogramming. Now she is off on another tangent totally obsessed with other "teachers."

Of course, on the surface this appears to be her choice after becoming bored or disenfranchised with deprogramming. However, she is a slave who has been "put out to pasture," as the programming term goes. She is valuable enough not to be termi-nated, but not important enough in the scheme of things to be reprogrammed or activated.

From observation of such types, it is my deprogramming opinion that she is a "test case" for the programmers to see what happens when an older former breeder is allowed to "wander through life" trying to find herself. My feeling is that they are observing "bleed-through" possibilities where programming information may come to the surface and cause a liability. This may be why she now clings to "New Age" types of teachers who discourage her deprogram-ming, instead steering her on a course of nothingness.

With her current path, she gained another false sense of iden-tity. As of this writing, she still has not uncovered any more infor-mation regarding her original personality or programming. She was determined to uncover the truth about her second child who "died." Her family urged her not to pursue it, so she has given up her search. This is all understandable, but shows situations where the deprogramming process is diverted by "well-meaning" family and friends who themselves are programmed to divert energy away from self-discovery.

It is possible that at some time in the future, should this woman live long enough, that she will return to her deprogramming process and reintegrate more. This will help the soul-personality in the next phase of existence as well in whatever lifetime it chooses in the linear future.

Eventually, these older Monarchs will pass away. The information and stories within them will be lost forever unless they are encouraged to deprogram and research their own lives. This is comparable to the stories of the Holocaust victims who survived the Nazi camps. When the last one dies, the original stories will be gone with them. How interesting it is that both situations have the roots and creations in the same people.

Case #12
Cult Programming

As the effects of the peyote drug wore off our son started getting delusional from time to time. One weekend while I was working, my husband told me that our son had been talking to himself and acting strangely. He recovered but a week or so later he told us about the "voices" in his head. He often broke down, crying for hours.

At this time I was involved with "channeling." I have always been a soul searcher. The entity channeled was the Egyptian sun god "RA." He did not have any good news about insanity! He said that it can be cured by Western medical procedures or by naturopathic means. The only other advice I got was not to study the subject or "it would scare the living daylights out of me."

Intuitively I knew that I was not going to get any help from this channeler or entity so I stopped asking and dropped out of the "New Age." At the same time I did not feel comfortable about getting our son into "the system." My Aunt had died from electric shock treatment, but perhaps this may have been a great relief for her.

I managed to look after our son at home hoping that a quiet, peaceful environment would help him return to "normal." My husband agreed for a while but was not happy about this approach. Our son got worse. He stayed up all night being noisy and became increasingly more delusional. My husband watched him take the sharp large kitchen knives out of their container and was afraid. We agreed to get our son some kind of medical insurance. That involved getting him to an interview with a lady who could determine his mental state and treatment needed.

She recommended that we should take him to the psychiatric department of the hospital right away. I could not see any other way. I knew that my husband would not agree to the naturopathic approach any more because we had tried that. The doctor who I found at the time was not trained in orthomolecular medicine and not that experienced with mental cases. My husband was concerned about being "knifed" in the middle of the night. I was desperate and agreed to the hospitalization. My only hope was the thought that maybe once our son became more stable we could gradually introduce naturopathic methods.

Meanwhile I resolved to find out as much as I could about mental illness so that whenever my son was ready, I could help by showing him various healing options. Then it would be his choice. Even the choice whether to heal or not would be his. I prayed that I would meet someone who could help me with him. I even read in one book that the Tibetans have healed their mentally ill people by giving them "Yeti" meat to eat. I do believe in looking "outside the box." Of course, I'm not inclined to hunt for "Yeti!" My son is still in the system.

So far this has been a sad tale which seemed to start about ten years ago. I knew there were lessons to be learned from my involvement and role as his mother, I prayed for someone who could help him heal himself. About five years ago I went to a lecture with a friend. I had no idea that I would have such a profound change in my life or find the person that would really help me feel some hope and be the answer to my prayers, He's the author of this book!

After reading **Montauk: the Alien Connection** by Stewart, I realized that my son is programmed. With Stewart's help I started using the techniques to help him. This was not easy because my son attracted a handler who was busy triggering him as fast as I could clean him up. There were all sorts of heavy reflections to learn from. My husband wanted my son to live outside our home. My son rebelled by refusing to obey the rules in the group home.

He moved in with his "handler," then promptly got kicked out of her apartment as he was too triggered to live with. My son lived on the streets, on drugs, and went to Raves where the drug ecstasy is used. Then he disappeared. Finally, he goes to jail for assault. Apparently he frightened the person involved, but did not hurt her badly.

The next big change was my son's acceptance into a big hospital for the mentally ill. Not the way I really wanted "things" to work out, but the best under the circumstances. My husband was not open to other solutions and the other alternative was for him to be in jail for a year.

He started to do better in the hospital. I think the routines and discipline helped him. Although street drugs have even found their way into mental hospitals, my son managed to avoid them. Finally, I could go to sleep at night knowing that he would not be out on the streets or controlled by his handler.

After the hospitalization, my son was accepted into a group home not far from his father and brother. I get along well with my son's case manager and visited him recently. Last year I left my husband. My son was about to get into the group home and was much more stable. I hoped that my son would relocate with me, but he did not want to. It was hard to leave my boys but I felt I needed to move. I endeavor to follow the guidance of my Oversoul, even if it does not seem to fit in with conventional thinking. There's a lot more that could be written about my move. For now, I know it is in their best interests and that they are in good hands. The story about those "good hands" is another "miracle" which would not have been possible without Stewart's help.

There are so many people to thank who have helped me on this journey. Janet Swerdlow is one of my most inspirational teachers. Her articles, books, and seminars have helped me through a lot of dark times with my son, especially the article entitled *All Experiences are Neutral*. I am totally grateful.

Case #12 Analysis
Cult Programming

✕

This person was involved for years in a popular international cult that was started by a writer in the United States many years ago. She left her native country to come to the US to live with this cult, where she met her future husband. She and her husband were completely programmed in this cult to the point where they were unable to make decisions about their lives unless the cult was involved. This particular cult is called a "religion" in some countries and is actually banned in others.

The use of drugs and programming in cults is standard procedure. People are often matched up together to produce a child of a certain genetic mix, which is what happened here. Sometimes, the inherited programming from both parents is an overload for the developing brain, so the child is born with mental and emotional issues which is what happened to this child.

This woman was previously married in her home country where she had a child there with her first husband. As a young woman, she displayed characteristics of a typical Monarch as it relates to the original version mentioned earlier in this book. Her foundational programming input was created at Tavistok Institute in London, UK.

A child such as hers is pre-fractured mentally, so additional programming goes in easily. It is the overload issue that is a particular problem for programmers. If the child is valuable in other ways or has special talents that are usable, medications and other mental techniques are used to either block or divert the inherited programming so new ones can be overlayed. These children grow up to be troubled adults, many of whom are diagnosed with a fabricated ADD or ADHD. Then, more medications and treatments are devised for them that tweaks their new programming or blends it with the inherited programs and alters.

Of course, the parents act as the handlers, until the counselors or group home leaders take over when the child becomes a young adult. This makes deprogramming difficult because there is little physical access or communication with the person.

I recommended to the mother to do Oversoul deprogramming at a distance and to talk to her son as often as she can about it during his more lucid moments. With her permission, and his, I was often able to do mind-to-mind links to direct his actions and thoughts in a more beneficial nature. This worked well for a time until when the doctors saw he was improving, triggered him into a semi-violent mode, drugged him heavily, and institutionalized him for a period of time.

It was only with great effort on my part and the mother's that the son finally came out of the institution and went into a less restrictive group home with cooperative counselors. The father was extremely hostile toward me, the deprogrammer, during this entire process. The father was still heavily leaning in the cult-mind direction and refused to alter his actions toward the son or to admit he was programmed.

Many men feel like they are failures or inferior if they admit that they created children with these issues. In such circumstances, it is important that BOTH parents are involved not only in the deprogramming of their child, but of themselves. In this instance, only the mother was willing to do this and did wonders for herself, eventually escaping this marriage, thus uplifting her mind and surroundings.

We are still working on the son. He has come a long way. There is still a long way to go, but progress is still progress and should be applauded. The mother often expresses her programmed self via her artwork which is magnificent. Outward manifestations of alters and programming is a great step in removing it from the inside.

Interestingly, in this woman's artwork, there is a preponderance of red dragons and mask-like faces with odd expressions. This may indicate the type of ritualistic programming that was input into her, as well as describes possible functions as a vessel or "Priestess" status in the ritual hierarchy.

Most people who get involved in cults generally have New World Religion Programming. It becomes evident that such people are monitored as a control group for the entire global population. In this way, reactions and cracks in the programming system can be observed so the programs can be fine-tuned for use with the general public.

When a cult, or members of a cult, fulfill their purposes and become a liability, they are eliminated. For example, during the passing of the Hale-Bopp Comet in the late 1990s, cult members committed group suicide in several countries as their activations came to an end.

Massive suicide and murder are also common as per Jim Jones in Guyana. It is not far-fetched to see hundreds and possibly thousands of cult members perish in one manner or another as their section of the experiment is completed.

From programmed cult members we can learn the types of characteristics expected of the global population when the New World Religion is imposed. From years of working with such individuals I can categorize the following traits and behaviors:

» Total obedience to the cult/religious leader.
» No ability to think or interpret doctrines on your own.
» Memorization of cult/religious slogans and belief statements.

» Labeling of behaviors and thoughts with a cult/religious "lingo."
» No independent will.
» Monitoring others for non-cult/religious behaviors and reporting on that.
» Removal of self from prior family and friends, and keeping a distance.
» Sexual interest in others who may be committed to a permanent partner.
» Soft-spoken most of the time, but hostile when challenged.
» Semblance of being meek, including passive/aggressive behaviors.
» Willing to be subservient to the "leader."
» Appear to be completely unemotional at all times.
» Speak in a monotone manner and always smiling.
» Eyes can appear to be glazed over when speaking.
» Having an artistic talent or ability that is often not used for financial gain.
» Mostly look much younger than their chronological age.

These are just a few of the main traits and the ones most often employed for deprogramming. Many report that when they are in the midst of deprogramming sessions, there is a great realization that they had given up their identities and lives to become robots for the cult or religion.

This woman has made tremendous strides and is gaining a huge semblance of who and what she really is in life. She has even gained insight into her simultaneous existences and her artwork now reflects this.

She has been strong enough to disconnect from her cult past and associated individuals, despite many threats and warnings from those people. She has stood her ground and is exemplary in her attitude and mental work.

Interestingly, cult people are a bit easier to deprogram because they are so used to being disciplined and using mental visualizations. Their progress is actually faster that other types of programmed people. They also remain more loyal to the process and are determined to regain their original self back.

As is standard, relationships are always an issue for these people. Work is also hard for them to secure. It is best that they remain independent in living and working for themselves at least while they are deprogramming. Connecting too much to others seems to trigger their cult behaviors and can throw them back a few paces.

Case #13
Vigilante Sleeper Programming

I was born on a hot July day in Fort Worth, Texas in 1972. My birthday would have been sometime in August if the doctor, who wanted to go on vacation, hadn't induced labor two weeks early. When my mother tried to breast feed me, it made her sore, so after a few days she moved me to formula. I was an angry baby and cried a lot.

When I was two years old, my brother was born. I was jealous of him because I thought my parents started paying more attention to him than me. One time when he was crawling around on the floor, I walked up and kicked him in the head. That was the first of many physical offenses I committed on my brother. Around that time my family moved to a small town in east Texas because my father, who is a minister, went to work at a small country church in the town. We lived in a small house behind the church, which was the church parish. During the summer my parents ran a box fan in the house which scared yet fascinated me. I even had nightmares that it was chasing me and trying to kill me.

There was also a man I feared who came to visit my parents, but the memory is very dreamlike. My parents say they don't remember him, but I think his name was either "Norman" or "Gordon."

When I was five, my family took a summer trip to the Gulf of Mexico where we went on a tour of a docked WWII Navy ship. I still have vivid memories of this ship, as I was quite in awe of it. It seemed familiar to me, and I didn't want to leave. During that same trip, I remember walking down a street and into an open garage where another child was playing with a metal child-sized hammer. I took the hammer away, and hit the other child in the head with it. I still don't know to this day why I did such a thing, but it seriously injured the other child.

After that, I started kindergarten, but I don't remember much about it. All I can remember is that when the children first arrived in the mornings, we all met in the cafeteria, leaving our lunch-boxes on the counter. We lined up, single-file, and marched out the door and down a hallway. I don't remember actually learning anything or what the classroom looked like, just vague memories of lunchtimes and naptimes. Halfway through the school year, my family moved to Eugene, Oregon. I have clear memories of the classroom there, and actually learning things.

When we moved to Eugene it was 1977 or '78. This was a vastly different environment for me. My father had grown up there, and his parents and a few other relatives lived there. However, during the sixties and seventies, Eugene was known as a kind of Mecca for hippies and "fringe" people in general – sort of a Berkeley for the Northwest. There was a much more permissive and diverse atmosphere there than in the rural South. I think it made my parents uncomfortable, as they were both strictly religious in the traditional sense.

Needless to say, I started learning things about the "grown-up" world pretty fast. Across the street from our house lived a house-ful of lesbians who chopped wood outside while topless. Down the street lived an older boy who invited me and my brother to his house to play with his toys as well as to look at pornography and participate in homosexual relations. He told us it was called "friendship." I was always curious about sex, asking my parents difficult, detailed questions about it. They usually answered the questions in a very dry, matter-of-fact way, but always reminded me that it was forbidden by God outside of marriage, and to even think about it was a sin.

My father did not work as a minister during our stay in western Oregon. The church my family attended was very large and labyrinthine, holding a certain mystery and wonder for me. Over the sanctuary was a large dome split into twelve segments, There were many ornate stained-glass windows around. The floor of the kitchen and dining area in the church basement was covered with black and white checkered tile, identical to Freemasonic halls. I believe something may have happened there.

Grade school was filled with many challenges and hardships. Since I was already an angry child and a loner, sometimes I didn't get along very well with my classmates. I excelled in the coursework, reading and articulating better and faster than most of the others. I always seemed to attract the school bullies, who picked on me relentlessly. I, in turn, went out during recess to harass, insult, and physically assault those weaker than me, namely the "special ed" children. Then I would go home to argue and fight with my brother, and the vicious cycle would continue.

I was very mean to insects, pulling the legs off spiders and the wings off butterflies, especially Monarch butterflies, as they were abundant in Western Oregon. After I tortured and eventually killed the insect, I always felt sad, and eventually I stopped. I remember reading a fictional book in third or fourth grade about some kids who learn how to telepathically mind-control other people after traveling to another dimension. This influenced my thinking and daydreaming greatly. I also took up stage magic as a hobby, lasting well into my teenage years.

After finishing the fourth grade and shortly before my tenth birthday, my whole world was uprooted and radically changed once again, as my parents decided to move the family to a small rural town in Eastern Oregon so my father could take over a congregation there. I did not want to move to this unknown place, leaving my friends and many relatives behind, I screamed and cried about it to my parents, all to no avail, or course. This new place was closer to the town where my mother was raised in a Freemasonic household, and where most of her family still lived.

Soon I was starting fifth grade in a town 1/10th the size and diversity of my former home. This only further intensified my anger and depression, and drew even more bullies eager to pick on the new kid. That year, our school class was taken on a field trip to various natural and man-made landmarks throughout the eastern part of the state, as well as a bird refuge. One of the landmarks was called Malheur Cave, which contains the largest underground lake in the world. It is the main meeting/ritual location for, and owned by, the state's Freemasons. We were taken about a quarter of a mile into the cave where the meetings were held on bleachers at the edge of the underground lake. I think this was for the purpose of triggering certain children. There was also a summer family trip to Disneyland, complete with the midnight Disney parade.

For the sixth grade I was switched to yet another school as my family moved from the church parish in town to a farmhouse in the country several miles from city limits. More feelings of depression and isolation ensued along with more conflicts with rednecks and bullies. My bedroom, as well as my brother's, was in the basement of the old house, and sometimes I had night terrors there. One of them was of a floating demon-head coming through my doorway, which scared me intensely. During this time, I became fascinated with the Nazi swastika and pictures of Hitler, as well as military weapons, fighter jets, Navy ships, astronomy, and technology in general. I also developed obsessive-compulsive behavior, doing things like checking the doorknob at least three times after locking it, avoiding cracks on the sidewalk, repeating certain movements multiple times, etc.

The junior high years were harrowing, to say the least. The onset of puberty, combined with the constant onslaught of insults, violent confrontations, and sexual embarrassment from my peers was just the "icing on the cake." After reading George Orwell's "1984" at the age of twelve – in the year 1984, the book was being criticized by the news media – I became even more depressed. Whenever I saw the smiling face of Ronnie Reagan on TV, I got the distinct impression that the world was run by forces operating in darkness. This "revelation" sank me into deep despair, driving me to serious thoughts of suicide and homicide, although not in that order.

I hated my parents for bringing me into a world filled with corruption, lies, and bleak hopelessness, often plotting to kill them and my siblings, followed by suicide. I also worked out elaborate scenarios in my head to kill certain students at school by sniper fire, the ones who picked on me, of course! And of course, (hasn't everybody considered this one?) the "faking-your-own-death" plot was a popular one for me.

At the age of twelve, I had my first wet dream, which was Oedipal in nature. After that, I began masturbating excessively, often four or five times a day, becoming obsessed with achieving orgasm whenever and wherever possible. I stole pornographic magazines from my grandfather's closet whenever we went to visit. I exposed myself multiple times to both male and female classmates, not caring about the consequences, even when I was caught. This obsession with masturbation and exhibitionism lasted well into my twenties, blocking most healthy relationships I might have had with females.

It was also during the mid 80s that I became exposed to information about the Philadelphia Experiment, again at my grandparents' house, while watching cable TV. There were reenactments of the ship disappearing and the soldiers coming back insane, very ill, or dead from having molecularly "merged" with the ship. These images caused me to feel feverish, and became burned in my memory.

Like many children, I grew up watching a lot of television. My favorites included the original "Superman" series (I thought the actor was actually Superman), "Batman", "Spiderman," "Star Trek," "Twilight Zone," "Land of the Lost," "Bugs Bunny," Disney cartoons, the list goes on and on. My whole family got excited every year when "The Wizard of Oz" came on, and watching it became a family event. By the end of the movie, I always had a headache or nausea, or just feel completely exhausted.

I could never sit through a whole viewing of "Alice in Wonderland." When I started taking karate classes, I became obsessed with ninja TV shows and movies, and fantasized about being a ninja assassin. Pretty much any show that had a vigilante hero made it onto my "must-see TV" list. This list included superheroes, cowboys, Captain Kirk, etc.

I had many dreams about being in some kind of training facility with other kids my age. We all did various relay like standing long jump, and playing games like tag, much like physical education class in school. The only difference was that whenever we would run or jump, we had to bend our knees, tucking our legs up under our bottoms, and literally float or fly towards our target at great speed. I did not think much about it at the time as it seemed like a fun fantasy, but about twenty years later I was talking to a friend who claimed to have memories of being involved in some kind of Superman training as a child, and his memories matched my dreams, down to the very last detail.

In 1985, ten days after my 13th birthday, my last sibling was born, a baby sister. One night my parents were away and I was babysitting. As I sat outside on the front step holding her in my arms, I began having visual flashes of being in a ritualistic Satanic ceremony with my sister, and being forced to have sexual intercourse with the infant. At the time, I considered the flashes to be the work of the Devil, trying to weaken me as a soldier in God's army. But I never forgot that night, or those horrible visions.

During junior high and high school, I excelled at math, science, and computer programming, as well as most of my other classes, but tended to be a loner. I was overweight and not interested in sports. As a result, I was labeled a "nerd" and shunned by most of the school. I did have a small, loosely knit group of friends who were also misfits, class clowns, computer "geeks," etc. My relationships with them were usually mercurial, vacillating between harmony and discord. Needless to say, I was one of a small handful of kids who did not attend the high school prom.

In my senior year I decided to pursue mechanical engineering as my major in college. I briefly considered joining the Navy, as they were keenly interested in me for their nuclear engineering program, but my belief in nonviolence kept me from going in that direction. After toying with the idea of attending Boston University, I settled on a state school that was cheaper and closer to home. High school graduation was a relief. I was ready to get out of "Dodge" and experience new things.

College was a challenge as well as a turning point in my life. In addition to my major coursework, I elected to take classes in various other subjects based on the idea of having a "well-rounded" education. Some of them required research that branched out into other fields of study. Soon I was studying things like philosophy, ethics, film theory, cyber-punk, psychology, radical feminism, sociology, the Frankfurt School of social critics/engineers, and other "left-wing" political issues and counter-cultural agendas.

I started to think of myself as a disillusioned idealist and free-thinker. I quickly became more interested and excited by these subjects than by my dull and tedious engineering courses. After the first year, I gave up Christianity and switched my major to "undeclared – liberal arts." Of course, it is nearly impossible to get financial aid for an undeclared major, so I was only able to attend two-thirds of my second year before dropping out from lack of funds. This, coupled with having to move back to my parents' house in that small town, sent me into a new downward spiral of depression.

There was considerable tension when I came back home. I fought with my brother because he had moved into my old bedroom. My parents sided with him. My parents were also upset because I had abandoned their religion and resented their politics. I felt totally alone and unsupported. In my boredom and despair, I decided to take some courses at the local two-year college. I started working with their drama department, building stages and doing other behind-the-scenes work, even acting in one of the plays. I started smoking, drinking, doing drugs, going to rock concerts, hanging out with my brother's friends who were still in high school, and drifting in and out of employment.

The next several years are a blur of moving in and out of my parents' house, in and out of jobs, new friends replacing old, loud music, parties, more parties, excessive drinking and drug consumption, over and over like a vicious cycle. I felt trapped and sad and cynical, all the while clinging tenaciously to my long lost days of cheerful, energetic idealism. I became a staunch atheist and "debunker" of all things spiritual or paranormal, feeling that humankind was an absurd accident and that nothing lie beyond the physical realm.

However, I was still devoted to the idea that humanity is responsible for making the world a better place, but that a small and inhumane group of powerful people is intent on impeding this forward movement. This conviction led me into further research on the history and modus operandi of imperialism and powerful governments, as well as comparative religion and the use of religion by the state to control the masses. Naturally, this course of inquiry eventually led me, thanks to the wonders of the Internet, to numerous sources relating information about the New World Order and mind-control projects and the Illuminati families who control it.

Soon after I started to investigate this information, certain events began taking place that confirmed its veracity to me. I was followed by helicopters, first the black ones, then several white ones, even one that was camouflage. I saw a "UFO" in broad daylight, which I believe was a "Blue Beam" holographic projection. A couple of years prior, I started to get painful lumps under my skin in certain spots on my body, and now they appeared much more frequently. They usually appeared under the jaw line, on the neck, shoulder blades, armpits, chest, around the nipples, lower abdomen, and pubic area. After one had been around for a few weeks, it would usually dissipate. I still get them occasionally.

As soon as I found the Montauk material and the work by the Swerdlows, I knew I had hit on something major. The information from ***Expansions Publishing*** was unlike anything else available on the subjects of energetic healing, mind-control, programming, and deprogramming, and metaphysics, among many other subjects. Their explanation of God-Mind was one that I could actually understand and accept. I was quite fascinated by all the detailed information they had about Illuminati programming, but never suspected at the time that I might actually be programmed.

My first personal consultation with Stewart Swerdlow changed all that. During his scan of my body's energetic field, he noticed a very pronounced energetic "marker" above my left shoulder that is found in specifically programmed Illuminati slaves. This revelation stunned me at first, and made me angry, not at Stewart for telling me, but at the fact itself. But it also helped me to make sense of many events in my life and motivated me to learn as much as I could about my condition, and how to counteract it.

Since that time, I have been working on deprogramming myself and balancing my mind-patterns, with the kind and generous help and support of the Swerdlows and everyone else involved with Expansions. I now live in the Midwestern US. Although the deprogramming process can be tough and frustrating at times, it is also very rewarding and educational, especially with a support system of like-minded and caring people from all around the world. I am far from being completely deprogrammed, but I feel I've at least been given a fighting chance. Thank you to the Swerdlows and everybody else who has helped me to better understand myself.

Case #13 Analysis
Vigilante Sleeper Programming

This is a most fascinating and honest depiction of a person who has been switched into alters of all types over the years. The religious and Masonic family background makes his story even more classic and intriguing. There is a definite progression from violent small child to depressed young adult. What he perpetrated on insects and other children was because he was acting out the scenarios that were done to him, or programmed into him to perform at ritual or when activated into vigilante mode.

The fascination with the Nazis and Hitler is a standard imprinting for those with End-Time and New World Order programming. It is generally embedded in the soul-personalities of those who participated in World War II in some capacity. It might be more clarifying to also read my story in my book, *Montauk: Alien Connection* to get more detail on the types of soul-personality transference and embedding. Though sounding like science fiction, this technology is available. Admiration and understanding or compassion for the Nazi regime and Hitler is a common theme among certain mind-controlled males.

This individual has made enormous strides in his deprogramming. The mere fact that he is able to so openly discuss his most hidden and disturbing thoughts is a clue that he can fully deprogram. Once you are able to talk about your deepest secrets and experiences, you are able to face the deep darkness of your programming and undo it!

Sexual encounters with other children of both sexes and of various ages is part of the training and desensitization process so that the slave is willing and able to perform sexually with all types of bodies, even with animals. This is a clue that there is Dragonfly or even Scorpion programming entered. Often in such individuals, there is a fascination in all sorts of pornographic materials and a desire to try different types of sexual activities. The individual mainly does not prefer one method or another, but remains versatile in many sexual formats, though at times, this can be a source of confusion.

Exposing oneself without fear of consequences is also part of an entrainment to allow yourself to be "on stage" in front of ritual audiences to perform a sexual ritual. This, then, inhibits "normal" relationships so that the slave is a loner and thus available whenever needed. The need to expose oneself can also originate in sexual ritual where the naked body is on display at all times and the audience at the ritual is supposed to view and participate in the action.

Therefore, such a programmed person feels the need to be on "display" for the crowd around him or herself at all times. There is no sexual gratification in it, but a desire to fulfill a subconscious role or command that is always active on some level.

This is also one of the cases where as part of the final deprogramming boosts, such an individual may need to participate in sexual encounters of similar nature only under mutual consent and direction. In this manner, a positive experience and memory overrides the original imprinting and use. Only then can the slave become free sexually in every way. He can make the free choice of which type of sexual relationship he/she prefers. The individual can now experience his original versions of the sexual techniques as an overlay of the programmed version. Then a free choice can be made for preference and lifestyle.

Always keep in mind that most programming is entered in a sexual procedure and it must come out in the same way. This is how the mind can undo what was done in the first place.

"The Wizard of Oz" reactions are also common, as well as "Alice in Wonderland" reactions. This indicates a use as an interdimensional conduit and a facilitator of stepping-up programs for others. This case is another example of how many large programs can be placed inside of the matrix of the mind for many uses.

It is clear that this person must be both mentally and physically powerful for such a diverse array of programming to be placed in and activated in so few years of life. His genetics must be of a more pure strain with just the right mix of other types of DNA that strengthen the original. You can compare it to making a metallic alloy that is stronger than just the pure metal by itself.

This person has a long road in front of him but he is certainly making his way down it with conviction and focus. Such an individual, at some point, would make an excellent deprogrammer himself since he has experienced the wide-ranging gamut of what is out there. He would have the understanding and compassion necessary to help others go through the deprogramming process.

The hostility toward the sibling is also common as it helps to create family detachments that aid in ritualistic techniques. If you can harm your own brother/sister, then you can easily harm a stranger. Release work is necessary as part of the mental/emotional corrections. Connecting to family again via Oversoul methods would enhance this and make relationships stronger in the future.

These traits are very necessary within a Vigilante program so that the alter is able to function as required without concern for morals or emotions, especially of others. The alter always feels as if it is doing the correct actions. Vigilantes have been in the media a lot in recent years. Sniper shootings, school attacks, mall shootings, even kidnappings and domestic violence are all associated with Vigilante activations since the mid-1990s.

Most of the perpetrators of these crimes have been described as quiet, law-abiding citizens with no prior record or convictions. Most of their families and neighbors are totally shocked by the actions and say that this person would never do such a thing. Usually, the Vigilante is killed or commits suicide before any real questioning or investigation can begin. This is designed on purpose since the programmers will never allow the information to be revealed. Sometimes, the Vigilante tells the authorities that he hears voices in his head or does not remember any actions.

In the case of Timothy McVeigh and the Oklahoma City bombing, the suspect said he had been mind-controlled in Kuwait while serving in the army for the first Gulf War in Iraq. It was shortly after he made that statement that the government executed him, permanently silencing his story.

Vigilante types are usually slender and powerful. They have low-paying jobs with very few marketable skills. This keeps them in a subservient mode and in a struggle all the time. That mind-set allows for programming to take hold more firmly and builds anger, hurt, and frustration like magma under a quiet volcano that one day comes spewing forth in fury and death.

The Vigilante can snap at any time. Deprogramming must be maintained at a low level to start and build slowly until the individual gets a solid grip on his emotions. Over 90% of Vigilantes are males for obvious reasons. In fact, some of their functions are to rape both males and females as "punishment" before murdering them. We saw this with the BTK killer in Kansas.

The events on the media involving this category of programmed slave have for the most part been a test of the system. Those considered expendable or liabilities are activated to see how the signals are working. This indicates a full activation in the near future. The Illuminati will use these people to clear out all those who oppose them. It eliminates the need for prison camps or re-education centers. Though these will still exist, they will not be crowded with political dissidents.

The suicide or death function of the Vigilante also eliminates the need for the authorities to capture and try a suspect. The entire category of programming is tied up in a neat package with no loose ends. The dead suspect is labeled an insane person and the case is closed. Often, the media refers to an abusive childhood. This summarily wraps up the explanations as to why a quiet and meek individual suddenly turns into a bloodthirsty monster on a killing rampage.

This group is overlapped with an Assassin programming where the slave is sent to various parts of the world to assassinate a targeted individual in power who is in the way of the Illuminati. One such group is comprised of Black women who pose as tourists. They are expert marksmen know as the "Black Angels." They are a rare group, but one with deadly aims.

Still others are expert at poisoning, a la the Russian agent in Britain killed by radiation in 2006. There are those who create "accidents" for various people and can make a heinous murder look like a suicide.

Unusual Programming & Experiments

Section 2

Chapter 1
Destroyers

There is a class of programmed people that are a subdivision of the Vigilante and Stalker Programs. These individuals, both male and female, have the mission to destroy or redirect the lives of their targets. First, they endear themselves deeply into the life of the target. Once they gain the target's confidence, the destroyer undermines and sabotages whatever the target does. The destroyer also disrupts and/or destroys everyone's life with whom he/she comes in contact. Then, the destroyer abruptly vanishes.

Many of you have read my story in **Blue Blood, True Blood** about my experiences with the New World Order agent I called, "Rosie 2." She was a female example of a destroyer combined with both Monarch and Stalker Programming. She subsequently targeted another hierarchy slave, ruined that person's business, and stole money, which is a standard procedure for these types of operations.

Destroyers have levels of awareness of what they are doing. Many are only subliminally aware that they are hurting another person or group of people. The alters within them that come forward at triggered times are programmed to go after specific individuals. Often, there is a transmitted ELF trigger to the destroyer that refreshes or adds to existing programming.

Destroyers usually work by setting up a disaster for their target. When the target needs help, the destroyer is amazingly present at the correct time and place to "save" the target. This proves them in the target's mind to be a friend and savior. Great promises are made to the target with no intention of ever fulfilling them. When the destroyer thinks that the target is now loyal to them, the destroyer pretends to pull away because it is "best" for the targeted person. This causes panic in the target who "coaxes" the destroyer to stay, intensifying the bond between the target and destroyer.

In all cases, the destroyer uses sex as a means of downloading the programming into the target. That is why the destroyers are usually the opposite sex of their targets. However, with gays or bisexuals, which are common in programming, it can also be same sex. The destroyers are always bisexual in order to be more useable.

It does not matter if the target is married or in a committed relationship. The destroyer sabotages with intent to destroy, suggesting that the mate is not being faithful, the relationship is obviously bad, and only the target cannot see the reality of the situation. Basically, the destroyer makes the target think he/she is stupid and not in touch with reality.

The next step is to isolate the target by putting wedge between the target and his/her loved ones. The destroyer sets himself/herself up as the only one who understands the target, fabricating lies and stories about family and friends. At this point, the destroyer attempts to physically remove the target from familiar surroundings and loved ones. The destroyer becomes the buffer between the target and everyone else. The target is now actually living in a falsely created "protected" environment from the outside world. Thus begins the redirection of the target to coincide with the agenda of the controllers and programmers.

Alcohol and narcotics are given to the target to dull awareness of what is going on. Programming-type environments are created to enhance the installation. For example, a room may be too hot or too cold, then suddenly switched to the opposite temperature. This is a trigger for the programming. Food and sleep deprivation are employed as well as cigarettes and olfactory stimuli. The destroyer knows the code words and numbers of the target to bring up willing alters. These processes activate the alters of the target so they may be reprogrammed.

Female destroyers are always experts in sexual activity to keep the male target hooked. They may be inappropriately sexual, catering to every whim of the target. They buy the target expensive gifts and expound upon the real or perceived strengths of the target to everyone, especially strangers.

Male destroyers are handy around the house and know about technical things that the female target may not be able to do. They become a chauffeur, cook, handyman, and bodyguard all rolled up into one; "a woman's dream."

Both male and female destroyers move in with the target, often saying that they maintain another residence to go to should things not work out. They often fight or argue with the target to keep life anxious and unsettled. They always threaten to leave, telling the target that he/she will be on their own since no one will else will ever want them.

If the target becomes difficult or if the mission fails for some reason, the destroyer will vanish abruptly. If the mission is accomplished, then the destroyer leaves with an excuse that sounds reasonable to the target. No matter how it ends, either the destroyer is never heard from again, or surfaces somewhere else trashing the target, saying how the destroyer was hurt or jilted by the target. The entire episode is always construed by the destroyer as being the target's fault. If you ever meet such a person, go the other way and never look back!

Chapter 2
Name Changers

Name Changers are actually more common than rare. As you know, there are 2,197 compartments that can be programmed within the human mind. Many have different names than the original personality.

I often come across people who constantly change their names. Usually, the names are both culturally and family inappropriate. This means that a white person may take a Chinese name or Indian name. Some people take names that are colors or numbers. These are related to their programming codes.

Sometimes Name Changers assume the names that come forward with their alters as their primary name. Some change them relatively frequently depending upon whatever triggers evoked the name change.

Other people use first names or only one name, such as Stream, Star, Red, Sunshine, and Rainbow. All of these names are associated with either constructs within a programming matrix and/or a code to access an alter or an alter group/family.

Some people take Egyptian or Hindu names, saying that their "guide" has given it to them. Their "guide" is none other than their own Internal Programmer or the satellite transmission that activated it. Your birth name is your true frequency. It is not an accident. Even if you do not like your name, you chose it and it is still it is who you are.

Name Changers switch to different alters in order to perform a particular function in their program. Often, Name Changers group together in communities in major programming areas. Some places you most likely are familiar with where Name Changers congregate include Sedona, Santa Fe, Taos, Mt. Shasta, Yelm, Maui, Los Angeles, Ashville, San Francisco, Long Island, and New York City. In the 90s and 21st Century, this also occurs in Australia, the UK, Germany, India, Norway, Brazil, and Ontario. All of these locations have huge programming sites and pull in these types of programmees for monitoring.

It is extremely challenging to have intelligent, coherent conversations with Name Changers, as their topics often lean toward New Age philosophies, the "coming Golden Age," or some other channeled prediction.

Most Name Changers are running away from their original identity and soul-purpose, making them extremely receptive mind-control targets.

Chapter 3
Channelers

Channeling is probably the most common form of programming that exists. While channeling has been around for a long time, efforts were intensified in the mid-1960s by the US government when it decided to create the "New Age" as a form of disseminating disinformation to the public. This was a brilliant idea, although one with an evil intent.

Masses of people were programmed with alters that came forward after the original personality went into a trance or left the body. The casual, untrained viewer might even say that it looked like a form of possession, which it would be if it were true.

In these cases, at least one alter personality is designed to come forward after some type of trigger prompting by the original personality or another person. This alter always has another name, which is usually angelic, alien, Atlantean, Sumerian, Lemurian—you name it. This alter or group of alters has the appearance of some kind of "light being" who decides to help humankind by disseminating information. The person whose body is used is always described as the "only" one who is allowed to channel this high-level information to the public.

After each session, the original personality "returns," usually unaware of the conversation that took place. Most of the information is of the "love, light, and peace" category coupled with the fact that humanity is always about to go into a great epic of peace and prosperity.

When Alien Programming is used, the channeled information usually states that they are high-level beings from some other galaxy. One popular alien program involved the Plaeidians who want to lift humankind to new heights. The story is that the Plaeidians do this out of the goodness of their hearts because humankind is almost "ready" to join with the other brilliant "space-brothers."

Often there is talk about a Mother Ship high over the Earth that no one can see except the "enlightened" ones who believe the channeled information. These entities are always in the process of saving humanity from some calamity or giving out strange historical or future information.

There are also channelers who only speak with Jesus or Archangel Michael or even Mary. Nowadays, there is a big business with those who channel Princess Diana and The Ashtar Command.

Categorically, all of these are computer-generated programs funneled through satellite transmissions to the targeted channeler. These ELF signals activate the alter who channels the information to those who follow. Technologically, it is a simple process, but one that enables the New World Order to reach large numbers of people with similar programming. The words are carefully orchestrated to download new programs. The people are even instructed to gather into groups for group meditations, rallies, specially-worded prayers, and affirmations as well as physical actions that are related to Neural Linguistic Programming (NLP).

There are many famous channelers. Many of you know who they are and what they say. Most of the information is the same. The majority claim a unique status with the channeling entity. There are limited occasions when a person is possessed by an actual entity, but the energy or personality must always come from the same Oversoul as the possessed person.

The main thrust of channeling as a programming methodology is to disseminate instructions to the public for the onset of New World Religion, Staged Alien Invasion, and End-Times Programs.

Chapter 4
Walk-ins

"Walk-ins" is an extremely misunderstood term that has been bandied about by the New Age crowd for the past thirty to forty years. This is a favorite tool for programmers to use. Programmers brilliantly trick people into believing that this is all about soul-personalities who leave their bodies into which they are born. Then another, more advanced personality takes its place for higher purposes.

This idea is also used by savvy con artists who consciously decide that they are no longer the person who was born into their body, and are now some highly advanced soul-personality who has come to save humankind. They change their names and walk away from their old life, including debts, families, responsibilities, and criminal charges. These people should be called, "walk-outs," not walk-ins!

In reality, this is a programming methodology and mind-control function. Keeping in mind that the programmed person has a matrix comprised of 2,197 pieces or compartments, these can be grouped into quadrants and families of alters that come forward upon trigger prompting.

A "walk-in" is actually a "back" alter who is prompted to come forward to become a "front" alter, now in command of the body.

The original front alter was no longer useful and is relegated to back status or decommission, possibly permanently.

The new front alter is programmed to tell the public that it is a walk-in who took over this body, complete with wonderful teachings to share and uplift humanity. Sometimes it may say that it is an alien, an Atlantean, etc. The point is, there is some function that this alter performs for the purposes of fulfilling an agenda related to the New World Order.

It is important for you to know that a soul-personality can only maintain a physical body if it has created the DNA for that body. Obviously, a walk-in of the New Age variety is not capable of doing that.

The "cure" for this type of programming is to use the basic brown merger archetype at the pineal gland in order to reintegrate the overall personality. In addition, use medium green and the Green Spiral Staircase Visualization from my book, *Hyperspace Helper: A User friendly Guide* to bring up the memories of the original personality that animated the body which will hopefully prompt it to return to full control of the body again.

When a person is legitimately in a walk-in alter, this front personality will not consciously know family and friends. He/she will act quite differently than the original personality. You may even see a different hairstyle, body weight, clothing preferences, sexual preferences, changes in dietary choices, and even in residence locations.

Of course, it is difficult for an untrained person or one who is unfamiliar with the subject matter to determine if these changes are the result of programming, mental illness, conscious choice, or actual possession.

Chapter 5
Religious Fundamentalists

If you have ever known anyone who suddenly became a religious fundamentalist, then there is a strong likelihood that this person has a religious alter which is part of the New World Religion scenario. These people go into alters who are determined to convert others or scare them into going to hell if they do not believe in their religious ideas. The programs generally involve functions related to the staged Second Coming of a Christ figure who will save the world and declare the New World Order His New Holy Empire.

The Illuminati already have a cloned individual waiting to assume this role which will be accompanied by aerial displays of the Blue Beam Project which can transmit holographic images to anywhere in the atmosphere or on the ground. The people with religious programming will become triggered by news reports of sightings of Mother Mary, Jesus, any of the Apostles, or any of the apocalyptic images mentioned in the New Testament.

The newspapers and news reports will play up the mysterious events as they are reported all over the world in specific sequences. Religious leaders will be quoted using certain terms and words that will trigger a function in a particular group associated with the New World Religion.

One of the major icons of the New World Religion, other than the Christ figure, will be Princess Diana who is the female counterpart of the male/female duality. This comprises the balance of the androgynous aspects of the Reptilian-based religious belief systems.

The people who are programmed in this way may respond to the triggers in various forms. Some may leave their families to follow a particular religious or philosophical cult or organization. Others may actually assume the identity of the "Holy" figure, claiming to either be either that person or a disciple of him/her.

The New World Religion programmees will band together to help usher in this wonderful new life that the "Savior" now presents to the world. They will do everything in their power to promote these new ideas and religious understandings to their loved ones, friends, and strangers, even if this means violence.

There is a sort of Stalker/Vigilante Programming associated with this that means the individual will purposely seek out and identify those who are nonbelievers. The "infidels" will be targeted for brainwashing or destruction.

Before all of this occurs publicly, it will be simple to identify the programmees by their behavior and belief system. Many will become immersed in different kinds of religious psychoses. They will become strong fundamentalists in Christianity, Judaism, Hinduism and Islam. Many will join in the New Age belief system, starting to channel religious figures or angels. Some may even claim that God speaks to them directly, giving them orders. In programming vernacular, the Internal Programmer is often referred to as "god," so this really is not completely inaccurate!

Family and friends of the programmees may actually be content with the sudden changes or "improvements" within the person involved. Often, programmees have major emotional issues or may even have a criminal tendency. Suddenly, the person appears to become pious, kind, and religious. Who would you prefer living with you? See how the front alter can be more acceptable than the original personality?

There will be name changes involved with this type of programming activation. The new front alter most likely will assume a Biblical or angelic-sounding name. Often, only one name will be used instead of a first, middle, and last.

Implementing a deprogramming process with this category of programmee is extremely challenging because the programmees believe that only Jesus or an angel can help them. Religious deprogramming methods, i.e., immersion in Bible statements, or even exorcism, can be a circle leading back to the programming itself. Deprogramming these type of people is like trying to put out a fire with bacon grease.

The best thing to do in such cases is to work strictly on the Oversoul level. Confronting the person or trying to convince him/her of programming issues or the invalid nature of their beliefs will only serve to push the person further away, perhaps even disappearing entirely from family and friends. These people are best helped with trained deprogrammers.

Common Programming

Section 3

Chapter 1
Seeding Programming

The Seeding Program is a little-known program that was devised toward the end of World War II when the Germans realized that they were going to lose the war. They did not want their eugenics program to fail so they carefully created a plan to secure it into the future.

The Nazis wanted to create a super-race of humans who would be the next phase of humanity. In their opinion, the ideal person would be tall, very white-skinned, blonde-haired, and blue-eyed with Teutonic genetics. Basically, the Nazis were attempting to create the Lyraen civilization with the corresponding genetics.

In Germany during the war, couples were paired together to produce the desired type of offspring. Toward the end of the war, Dr. Josef Mengele, who was in charge of this operation, decided that it would be best for safe-keeping if the children of this eugenics program were farmed out to "safe" places so that the project could continue unhindered. Many of these children were then placed with "appropriate" families to be raised in a prescribed manner conducive to the Third Reich.

Recently born children, or the very young, were sent to live with Germanic families in Scandinavia, Poland, South Africa, Germany, Austria, Switzerland, Britain, and Ireland. The women who were still pregnant with the fetuses were sent to America, Canada and Australia as refugees needing help.

Dr. Mengele oversaw the entire network. He lived until the 1980s in Brazil where he died. He established camps or ranches in remote places in Brazil, Paraguay, and Argentina where he continued genetic research on native people in the area.

The women brought into the USA were told to give up their babies to adoption agencies, then either killed or sent into prostitution of mind-control experiments in the 1940s. Mengele gathered appropriately-gened people in the US for the continuation of the experiments.

He arranged within his American network for certain males to mate with certain females for the production of a specific type of human. These babies were placed into the adoption network organized by Mengele and his cronies, to be placed with families of Teutonic lineage all over North America.

The adoption agencies used were generally located in Tennessee, Texas, Illinois, Missouri, and Arkansas. In Canada, the agencies were located in Ontario and Quebec. The placements of the babies were usually made in Minnesota, Wisconsin, California, Manitoba, Saskatchewan, Michigan, New York, New Jersey, and Montana.

There were other locations for both agencies and placements, but these were the most commonly used. Most of the placements occurred in the late 1940s, 1950s, and into the mid 1970s when the project ceased due to circumstances and logistics.

These adopted, genetically-programmed children were raised under strict rules by programmed families who abided by Nazi rules and regulations for the upbringing of such important people. All of these children inherited programming from their ancestry with more added during the course of their lifetime. They are programmed to activate in the early 21st Century to facilitate the onset of the New World Order.

There is a twist to this scenario. When the initial programming was entered, the world situation was quite different. The factions of the Illuminati were on the same side. Now, infighting has rendered some of the programming invalid, posing a problem.

The Fourth Reich, located under Antarctica, has a network that spans North and South America, Europe, and the Middle East. The Fourth Reich is working to usurp the plans of the established New World Order by reprogramming many of the Third Reich's progeny to thwart the plans of the Rothschilds and Windsors. The Fourth Reich is a separate column within each of the countries that took in these children, now adults.

Some of these adults will attempt to come to power politically and economically. They will most likely refuse any deprogramming techniques, leaning toward fanaticism in their belief system. They will all be blonde-haired and blue-eyed with very good body types. They will speak ill of the US and UK governments to endear themselves to many.

The new agenda programmed into these progeny by the Fourth Reich is extremely racist accentuated by extremely harsh personalities. These people tend to appear friendly and helpful at first. Once they pull you into their sphere of influence, they proceed to undermine and criticize you.

I have met several of these individuals in North America and Europe. Only a few are consciously aware of their ancestry and purposes. Some do not even know that they are adopted or that they have a "glorious" life planned out for them.

Another interesting twist in this scenario is that there are certain Black people who are part of the Seeding Program. These individuals have direct ancestry that can be traced by the Illuminati to the genetics of King Solomon and the Queen of Sheba. Many of their ancestors were brought to North America as slaves centuries ago. The Illuminati hold a high respect for them because it is they who will play a major role in the installation of the New World Religion. Only the descendents of Solomon and Sheba can be used to rebuild the Third Temple in Jerusalem and usher in the new Messiah. I have met a handful of these Black people who have Ethiopian backgrounds who cannot trace their direct ancestry. It is the Falasha Jews of Ethiopia who were transported back to Israel in the 1980s in order to fulfill the prophecies of the temple rebuilding.

These people will become triggered and activated when the Dome of the Rock, a Holy Islamic site in Jerusalem built on the Temple Mount, is destroyed, making way for the rebuilding. Already, the walls of the Mosque have weakened and partially collapsed. The Israelis are helping this along by digging underneath the Dome of the Rock to get to Solomon's Stables where one of the Holy Arks was stored.

Interestingly, the Black adults who were part of the Seeding Program are extremely open to this idea of who and what they really as compared to the seeded White adults who are more resistant to any ideas outside of their programming.

Chapter 2
Suicide Programming

Suicide Programming is a sub-routine of all other types of programming. All programmed people have this within the overall composition of their matrix. This means that even those with ordinary subliminal programming could also have these instructions transmitted to them.

The programmer installs this in each programmed individual as a self-destruct mechanism. If the functions become invalid, the person no longer is useful, deprogramming gets to close to the true core personality, or if there is a programming failure, the person can be activated to self-destruct.

Almost 100% of the people I have worked with in deprogramming have suicidal thoughts or even attempted suicide at some point. Fortunately, in all the years I have done this work, only one male has actually succeeded in his attempt. I never want to experience that again.

One of the challenges of Suicide Programming is that this function causes the person to reject the deprogrammer at times. The person's programming instructs him/her to hide his/her true feelings, so it is difficult to know what the person is planning until it is almost too late. Often, it is not known what the person is thinking until they are close to doing something. For this reason, it is extremely important that the deprogrammer insist that the client communicate at all times about his/her feelings.

People who are deprogramming must be aware of this function, so that when any suicidal thoughts, visions, or attempts surfaces, he/she makes every effort to speak to the deprogrammer, or even a close friend. It is highly likely that such individuals have suicidal alters which surface to sabotage all attempts to deprogram, especially if there is an active function or a function is about to activate.

The suicidal person must remain in violet at all times surrounded by brown. This flushes and filters the program, as well as ground him/her. The brown merger symbol must be placed at the pineal gland until the suicidal urges are completely dispelled. After a day or two when the person is off-guard, the suicide programming usually surfaces again, perhaps even stronger than before. For these reasons, the violet and brown merger symbol must be used exclusively in such cases for at least a week to ten days to diminish and override the programming.

Suicidal Programming can be attached to all layers of the matrix cube so do not think it is over when you are through only one episode. Be vigilant, understanding that it is common for it to repeatedly surface as you go deeper into the deprogramming process.

Despite the feeling of not wanting to continue the process, it is important that you consistently use the violet flushing with the brown merger symbol to maintain balance and grounding as you work your way through to the other side of this particular function.

Suicide Programming seems to be more strongly attached to the right brain/emotional side, thus more volatile with females. In general, females seem to be more vocal about suicide plans, making it easier for the deprogrammer to help her. On the other hand, males seem to internalize the function, silently making suicide attempts. Identifying suicide plans beforehand is much more difficult in males. To keep males in balance, they need to access the female side of the brain. Deprogrammers need to be aware that males are more likely to successfully accomplish their plans for self-destruction than females.

The deprogrammer can assign specific mental tasks to both male and female programmes to distract them from the suicidal thoughts. The deprogrammer must be absolutely certain that no physical harm is played out by the programmee. This takes dedication and perseverance on the part of the deprogrammer.

Chapter 3
Green Star Programming

Green Star Programming is an umbrella program that covers a lot of territory. Within this genre of programming are those who have alien abduction scenarios, alien contactees, Star Wars Programming, Star Trek Programming, Alien Ambassador Programming, and most importantly, Staged Alien Invasion Programming.

Each of these subheadings contain even further delineations and breakdowns that pervade every walk of life and every possible function that can be conceived in relation to the idea of alien beings and the interaction between them and humans on Earth.

The New World Order hides behind masked memories imposed on people who think that they were abducted by alien beings. In fact , they were really taken by government programmers to have their minds altered and subliminal routines entered into the virtual world of their programming matrix.

UFO researchers estimate that over 5 million Americans have been abducted by alien beings that take genetic samples and perform various mental and physical tests on them. "Abductions" appear to be generational, meaning that if your parent or grandparents had an "abduction" experience, then it is likely that you and your children will also have these experiences. Understanding that these "abductions" really involve mind-control and programming logically explains why "abductions" are generational. Eventually, programming becomes part of the DNA. This makes it easier for the programmers to work with a pre-programmed person who inherits lots of programming that can be added to and altered.

Many abductees become angry when confronted with the idea that their experiences were not what they believed them to be. They prefer to accept the scenario that aliens took them on board a spacecraft. In a way, this makes them "special" or "chosen," and often the envy of friends who also want alien experiences. For this reason, many reject the truthful scenario that they were taken to a programming center where a masked memory was imposed into their minds. It is also highly likely that most people who have had these experiences have implants placed in the body. What truly is alien is the programming technology and procedures. There are some cases where an actual alien abduction does occur. This is extremely rare since the late 1970s when this planet was blockaded by the Illuminati so that only a select few alien cultures are allowed to physically visit here.

The world government, in an effort to use the idea of a common threat with a need for a global central administration, conceived the idea of staging an alien invasion in the 21st century, after the threat of terrorism dissipates. With this "threat to Earth," the civilian population would easily acquiesce to the demands of a unified world government that would save them from this unknown alien invader. There are plans for a second alien group to suddenly appear to save Earth. This pre-planned "savior" group will be the Reptilians who will then explain how they colonized our world and how the Illuminati are their descendents, are the rightful leaders of Earth.

To build up to all of this, decades of UFO sightings, abductions, and alien contacts were staged on this planet to imprint the concept of alien life into the human psyche. This is further enhanced by television and movies depicting aliens in a science-fiction genre. In addition, the media is rife with carefully planted reports of crashed saucers and secret government contacts.

Many Green Star programmees will believe that they have children with aliens and that these children are amazing hybrids that can change the world. There is a preoccupation with pregnancies and genetic variations within the human species.

There is also a preponderance of drug use and narcotic abuse amongst the Green Star programmees. Many of them start with something seemingly innocent, like sleeping medication. This often leads to prescription antidepressants. During the course of the person's lifetime, this can escalate to an increasingly amount of prescription drugs. These types of drugs only enhance the programming that was initially administered via drugs and narcotics.

On my website, I invited a person with Green Star Programming to keep a running dialogue of his process. He easily fell into the use of medically prescribed drugs to help his "mental illness." He decided that these drugs provided an easier route than continuing his deprogramming work. His excellent progress with deprogramming was destroyed by his sabotage alter that activated to steer him in a direction of despair and perpetual mental care.

One major subroutine of the Green Star Project that gained in popularity during the 70s and 80s was the Ashtar Command cadres under the leadership of "Jesus Christ." In this program, Christ was named "Sananda." He piloted a fleet of invisible Mother Ships that orbited the Earth, supposedly monitoring the human situation.

Ashtar Commanders, who were human, told their Earthling protegees that they had come to save Earth to teach some of them how to pilot their ships. The people who are in Ashtar alters vehemently defend their leaders in space, refusing to even entertain the idea that this is all programming and that the conversations occur within the virtual world of their matrices.

The name "Ashtar" is a derivative of the Babylonian/Phoenician goddess named "Ishtar," who had to do with fertility. A play on the words "ash" and "tar" give you a clue as to the thought behind the name given by the programmers. Therefore, according to the Illuminati programmers' ideas, Ashtar Command really represented a fertile ground for destruction and paving over a mind-pattern. They do not choose their names and words lightly.

There are several other alien groups that the Illuminati use for mind-controlling their slaves. In the 70s and 80s again, depicting Plaiedian aliens as saviors of humanity was a big aspect within the Green Star umbrella.

There were and still are countless communicators of Plaeidian entities who claim that they are the ones who seeded humankind. They say the Plaeidians have returned to help the people of Earth uplift to higher dimensional realms. There is even technology given out to Earth "scientists" that supposedly recalibrate the human energy field and brain.

Chapter 4
Monarch Programming

Monarch Programming is probably the most well-known and comprehensive programming system ever devised. Monarchs were developed by the Nazis in WWII as a method of using sex-slaves as human tape recorders and carriers of information. In this way, a beautiful female is used to access secret information from enemies and friends for her handlers.

This type of programming was brought to North America after the war by Dr. Ewen Cameron of Scotland. He arrived in Canada where he began experiments on mental patients in hospitals via torture and narcotics as well as using sound and vibration.

The tests were so successful that the Americans brought him to the US to develop the Monarch Program. In those days it was called Project Bluebird. This morphed into other projects before finally being called the Monarch Program in the 1960s.

Over the years, Monarchs developed into many subcategories depending on functions. They have been given designations according to Greek letters from Alpha all the way to Omega. Within each category are subcategories by color codes. Within the color codes there is a further numerical breakdown so that for example, a Monarch slave could be designated as a Beta-pink-7. This implies a sexual slave whose purpose is to retrieve files to complete a mission.

Each slave also has a numerical identification within the vast cadres of Monarchs in the world. The identity code for any programmed person has built into it the birth date, programming center code, the Illuminati family to which they belong, and the number of generations the slave's family has been a part of the program.

During deprogramming, it is a great help to ascertain these codes and designations so that the deprogrammer can decide which techniques is best, but this is not an easy task. Not every technique works well in all Monarch Programming categories. It can be a slow and tedious process to litmus-test various techniques over time. If codes are determined, it shortens the process significantly.

Monarchs are the most difficult programmees to work with because they are so volatile. They can snap in a split second because they have so many triggers programmed into them that they can easily be activated at any time.

Monarchs, especially the females, have deep suicide alters that surface when programming is "tampered" with or any type of deprogramming takes place. The Monarchs have many different suicidal methodologies programmed into them. The most common types for females is car accident, drug overdose, and self-stabbing.

About 85% of Monarchs are females. The rest are males who may lean toward bisexuality. In fact, most Monarchs are comfortable sexually with either sex or even in group sex.

Monarchs are used heavily in ritual, especially in Sexual Magick Rituals. They tend to have a capacity when drugged, for multiple orgasms. They can participate in lengthy sexual activities. They tend to be extremely sexually motivated, even to the point of jeopardizing their "standard" relationships.

Some of you may have read the ***Diary of a Monarch*** that was on my website several years ago. This started as an attempt to prevent a suicide by a programmed sex-slave. Our emails quickly evolved into a long conversation and deprogramming session, so we posted the process on the website for a while. For a short time copies of the diary were sold as an aid to understanding the issues and emotions that are common to those with Monarch Programming, as well as deprogramming techniques specifically designed for this type of Monarch. The diary has since discontinued, as the person went into a subroutine of her programming that did not allow for further progress.

Monarchs who attempt suicide accomplish in a different way than the females. Male Monarch suicide is usually done with a gun or rifle, poison, or some kind of exotic herbal overdose. I suppose this is because of the way the male mind works that allows the suicide programming to be entered via these methodologies.

Monarch sex-slaves tend to congregate with each other, even if they do not realize their own status in programming. They pick up a resonance with one another that causes them to flock together. Real Monarch butterflies also flock together. These beautiful creatures all migrate to Mexico in the winter. As many as 35 million to 50 million butterflies congregate together in the valleys of Central Mexico to spend the winter and breed.

These butterflies do not intermingle with any other butterfly species and move back to the United States all at the same time. The Monarch sex-slaves also tend to stay together and travel in the same circles. The programmers are very specific as to why they name a category of programming the way they do.

Of course, keeping in mind the Illuminati's love of playing with words and symbolism, "Monarch" also refers to kings and queens, or the leaders of the people. Monarchs are often the true leaders of the people of Earth who have been picked up and manipulated from birth and sometimes while in the womb. The Illuminati enter programs that divert the soul-personalities from actualizing their potential and accomplishing their goals and missions. With persistent and constant deprogramming, the Monarchs can reclaim their own internal power, going on to accomplish the purpose of the soul-personality in this linear lifetime.

Deprogramming

Chapter 1
Deprogramming Techniques

The very basic deprogramming techniques have been given in the body of the case studies in Section 1. These include the brown merger symbol, the white rabbit, the Monarch butterfly, the green spiral staircase, the matrix cube and the variations thereof.

Here I will outline some more complex techniques that should only be used after the basics that have been outlined. I will refer all readers to the DVDs and Study Guides on mind-control, programming, and deprogramming before using advanced techniques. It would also be wise to read the *Hyperspace Helper* and related deprogramming articles on the website.

Black Rabbit

This technique is performed exactly like its sister technique using the white rabbit, only a black rabbit is placed at the pineal gland and then followed to a compartment for observing, flushing with violet, and then brown-merged.

People who have the black rabbit as a deprogramming icon are those who have very deep and secret programming that is related to Sexual Magick and hidden rituals. Often, during the black rabbit technique, other animal alters arise or images of animals arise that may have been used in ritual with the person. If a particular animal or creature appears frequently during these sessions, then that animal should be used as a focal point at the pineal as a deprogramming technique separately.

Apparently, this icon brings up a lot of sexual sensations and images. It most likely is used during fertility rituals where heavy sexual activities are performed. It might be wise to alternate the black and white rabbit techniques to get a more balanced picture of the programming.

Merging the Cube

In this exercise, visualize the matrix cube at the pineal gland. It may appear in red, olive green, navy blue or many other colors. No matter how it appears, flood the entire matrix with deep violet color.

Next, see a brown merger symbol inside each of the compartments. Obviously, you probably will not count all of the 2,197 compartments, but imagine it as best as you can. Then, when all of the compartments are violet and have a brown merger symbol in them, see all the mergers merging together in the middle, forming one giant merger symbol with no compartments noticeable. You just see a large violet cube with a brown merger in the middle.

Then, place a brown merger at your pineal gland, connecting to the merger in the cube. See them both come together and move up through the crown chakra to the silver infinity symbol, representing the Oversoul.

Now, balance your T-Bar archetype and put your entire body in brown.

 ### Lion Frequency

This is the highest frequency possible on the Earth plane that can be sustained in physical reality. It is extremely powerful and totally activates the God-Mind energies within. As such, it can easily help to override programming issues when using this frequency in conjunction with other techniques.

Visualize a violet diamond shape lying flat on the crown chakra with a point facing forwards. Next, visualize a golden aleph standing straight up on the violet diamond platform facing forward. Then, create a small royal blue circle at the center of the golden aleph.

Start moving your consciousness through the royal blue circle and just observe what happens. Or, you can just focus on the entire archetype symbol without moving your consciousness and just observe.

Reactions will be different for different people. Often, the lion energy helps to break through blockages seen in deprogramming. It also helps to deconstruct sections of the matrix and clear out programming from alters. Since this frequency is so connected to God-Mind, it is much more powerful than any program that can be entered into the mind-pattern.

After a while, there may be physical changes that accompany prolonged use of the frequency. These can include hairiness on the body, a slimmer waistline, fuller hair on the head and face, sharper vision, deeper voice, increased chest size, large genitalia and a need for more heavy proteins as part of the diet.

Mental changes include a slightly higher aggression toward those who irritate you, a need to be in a group instead of alone, being more creatively expressive and finding solutions at a faster rate to problems that arise.

When you end any Lion Frequency work, it is important that you stay in a deep brown for a while as this energy tends to make you want to stay out of body. The sensation of flying and being powerful from a nonphysical perspective can be overwhelming and many programmed people prefer this feeling to the one of being controlled and manipulated all of the time. So, balance this frequency with grounding and by doing something physical afterwards like gardening, exercising, or writing.

Bear Frequency

This energy was used by the ancients and especially by the Cherokee tribe of North American Indians. The original purpose for using this was when the shamans of the people would go into a sometimes drug-induced state and a vision or speak with non-physical elders or guardians.

Basically, this frequency is for going within the "cave of the mind" in order to retrieve information to bring out to the public. From a deprogramming perspective, it is to attempt to connect with the true core in order to overpower the programming and the false cores.

Again, the preliminaries are the same. Then you hold the archetype symbol at the pineal gland and simply observe. In many cases, there will be memories coming up about bear ritual during Illuminati ceremonies. Allow these to surface, and flush with violet and brown merge them.

The ritual memories for males and females will be different. Females will remember being on a platform or altar while one or more males, wearing various types of bear headdress are having sexual relations with them. These rituals are ancient and designed to bring up information for the participants to use in their manipulations.

Males may remember wearing the bear costumes or skins in rituals. This frequency is mainly used with males as it requires a large, hairy man who is burly (bearly) and has great physical strength. The body changes accompanying this frequency are much more becoming on a male rather than a female.

There is usually an aggressive mode that is part of this frequency along with deep hunger and need for sleep. It seems to be more conducive to those with genetics that are Eastern or Central European, American Indian, Eskimo, or Middle Eastern.

The bear technique enables the person to go deep within the programming matrix and observe what the various layers contain. It also allows the deprogramming person to retain the information in the waking state and helps to block further activations or reprogramming.

During ritual, many Bear Frequency males are paired with female Monarchs who are of French/ Merovingian lineage. This may have something to do with the symbol of the bee for the Merovingian lineage, and the connection of both bees and bears to honey, which is used during Sexual Magick Rites with these participants. Seeing, tasting, and feeling honey are common triggers for Bear Frequency people. Honey also represents semen.

Many deprogramming individuals use the bear energies to dismantle constructs with in the matrix or even to keep guardian alters at bay. At some point, the bear frequency can be used to eliminate the Internal Programmer and access that stored information.

The Bear Frequency archetype symbol, although suggested here in golden brown, can also be used in black, white, red and darker brown. These are all variations or subgroups within the overall frequency. Use each one separately and keep separate notes on each type. Although they are all under the same umbrella, the deprogramming may be different, like the differences that can come up between the black or white rabbit.

The Dragonfly

This technique is extremely powerful and should only be used after the other exercises have been thoroughly played out. This technique is specifically useful to high-level Monarchs who are Betas and Presidential Models.

After the standard preliminaries, center your consciousness at the reptilian brainstem in medium red. Place a dragonfly sitting on the brainstem with its wings out. Simply concentrate on the body and wings of the dragonfly, especially on the tail section. Let the mind go. There is no telling what you will see or experience. Just do not participate in anything in front of you. Observe only. You may feel like you are falling or going inside of the brainstem. Anything can happen.

When you are finished with the session, evaporate the dragonfly from the brainstem. See the pale red "Y" symbol for balancing the Reptilian brain at this location. Then, see the T-Bar at the pineal gland in whatever color it appears. Then, bring the two symbols together at the mid-brain region for complete balancing. Then, place a brown merger at the mid-brain, go to brown, and come out of it.

I do not suggest staying too long in this technique at the beginning. You need to build up to it slowly. Generally, Dragonfly is a separate but related programming to Monarch. It is for upper eschelon sex-slaves who participate in sexual ritual with pure Reptilians or with shapeshifters who perform ritual as Reptilians.

Since in the Reptilian form the being is androgynous, the sexual activity tends to stay more in the astral levels and is extremely energetic. There tends to be a blending of mental and instinctual energies and very often, the human participant feels violated at the deepest levels, way beyond just sexually.

It feels almost as if sexual intercourse of a violent nature took place in the brain. Dragonfly women are often referred to in ritual as "Dragon Ladies." Males, though rare in this category, are referred to as " Dragon Slayers."

Slaves with this programming have a tendency towards bisexuality, migraine headaches, shoulder and neck pain, are resilient towards most diseases, and are multi-orgasmic. They are also extremely intelligent and considered by others to be cold emotionally.

This deprogramming technique should be used at an advanced stage of deprogramming when the actual core is truly within reach. Side-effects will be nightmares, instinctual fears and aggressions, flashes of ancient memory, and back pain. There may even be frequent skin irritations and feeling physically cold a lot.

Remember, the true core of a personality is located at the reptilian brainstem. Everything in your programming as well as your original personality are located here. It is also a key to your genetic memories.

Wilhelm Reich Procedures

This methodology, sometimes also termed "Fellowship" is illegal in the US and most countries, especially the ones that employ programming as a way of life.

The information about these procedures are available in my manuals and DVDs on ***Mind-Control, Programming & Deprogramming***. You should also refer to our book, ***The True Reality of Sexuality***. Please refer to these for more details.

Chapter 2
Technology Techniques

These methods require working with a professional deprogrammer who is capable of using the equipment. Of course, any electrical device emits some form of ELF, and therefore, can be a problem when used with deprogramming methods as this could trigger or activate the deprogramming individual.

There is, first of all, the use of Radionic Machines which use specific frequencies to transmit healing or other energies to a person, place, or thing. This is related to "Psychotronic Devices" which the government uses to send mind-control waves to the public or a specific target.

For deprogramming purposes, a witness of the programmed person must be used on the Radionics Machine. This could be a recent photograph, hair sample, nail clippings, or any other item that has the individual's resonance.

Then, a template of a brown merger symbol or any other deprogramming symbol or technique can be placed on the transmission plate. The energy of the deprogramming item will then be transmitted to the programmed person. This does not replace the actual mental and physical deprogramming processes already mentioned.

It may be a good idea to keep the witness and the transmission on the machine for several days or even weeks at a time to ensure that the technological deprogramming is in place all of the time. It is recommended that this method only be used as a temporary "filler" for someone who may need a break from the other mental techniques, or for someone who is having difficulty in mental concentration work.

There are other technologies that can be employed in deprogramming. From Europe comes the Quantum Machine which can read frequencies and pick up programming issues. This would be more of a diagnostic tool rather than an actual deprogramming method.

There is also the use of a standard personal computer software that works on balancing the two hemispheres of the brain and may open up various programming alters and functions to be worked on.

If this method is used, it is extremely important that both a computer software expert as well as an experienced deprogrammer be physically present with the programmed person so that any triggers can be dealt with immediately. There is always a possibility that a person can be stuck in a sequence and not have the ability to know how to get out. Better safe than sorry, so have a team that works with you available.

Color and light frequency can be used in deprogramming. Here, the actual frequency of each color is produced, rather than just having a mask of color over white light. This would especially work for Monarchs and related programmees whose triggers and functions are specifically color-coded.

Again, it is advisable that you use this methodology with a trained and experienced deprogrammer physically with you so that decisions can be made on timing and sequences of colors via observation of the individual as well as the knowledge of past deprogramming history of the person involved.

Careful notes and detailed documentation must be part of all of the above methods. This is not only for future use in deprogramming in order to get a base line scientifically, but also to aid the specific individual and help that person decipher their programming codes and triggers.

It may also help in the deprogramming process for counselors as well as their clients to watch the Mind-Control/ Programming/ Deprogramming DVDs in order to learn about possibilities and types of programming that could be revealed.

Chapter 3
Elixirs

This is a very ancient technique that gained popularity in Ancient Greece, but actually has its origins in Atlantis and off-world. The idea is very simple. It is nothing more than embedding the frequency of an emotion, thought, or physical object into distilled water, which the replicates this in the person without the side-effects of the item itself.

For example, if arsenic will kill a virus in the body, and it is dangerous for a human to ingest arsenic, an elixir of the frequency of the poison can be made for the person to consume or rub on the skin. The individual will receive the benefit of the arsenic without the detrimental effects.

Expansions has had created an entire line of deprogramming elixirs which works on the emotions and conditions that commonly arise in the deprogramming person. For example, we have an elixir called "Guilt." This works on the issues of the frequency of guilt and helps the person to deal with this emotion as it arises.

The elixirs can be ingested and then will replicate internally to cover the cellular memory and DNA information storage. They can also be placed in sea salt baths where they will enter via the auric field. They can simply be rubbed on the body and enter through the pores and can be enhanced by the person's chakra system.

Every emotion, thought, and word has an energy that can be resolved down to a frequency vibration of a specific numerical value. If the frequency calibration of these are known, the reciprocal frequency can be determined, thus cancels out the condition.

Elixirs can be tailored to the individual based on the specific deprogramming needs of that person. Work with your deprogrammer to determine which elixirs would be of benefit to you.

Chapter 4
Deprogramming Training

The only way to have a person be prepared to become a deprogrammer, is for that person to have undergone the process himself. I use the masculine term here, not out of chauvinism, but out of safety and reality.

In my sexuality book, I wrote that males project energies while females absorb. This becomes an issue in deprogramming because by the nature of it, a female would download the programmed energies of her clients. Therefore, a female can be a deprogramming coach, but should not be an actual deprogrammer. A female coach should not be physically present during an actual deprogramming session, since she can easily pick up the energies like a sponge and severely trigger or activate herself.

The process can be long and complicated. There is little chance that the deprogrammer-in-training will be fully deprogrammed. But the person must be well along the way, and able to recognize his own triggers and activations, and stop them quickly, or even prevent most of them from happening.

At that point, deprogramming training can begin slowly. It is wise for the training person to continue with his own process while working on others. This is because it is very likely that during his training process as well as when deprogramming others, the client will trigger him and cause issues to arise.

The key to the entire deprogramming training process is lots of experience in the work both on self and others, plus a willingness to do whatever it takes to get to the next step for yourself and those you are helping. Everyone lives within their own comfort zone. But in this type of work, it is necessary to go outside that box and be prepared to do and think as you never have before. You must be open to all possibilities and release all feelings of guilt or shame.

I also do not recommend keeping notes on clients since deprogramming is technically illegal in most countries. This is because programming does not "officially" exist, so therefore, deprogramming should not exist either, according to most governments. You should suggest that each client keep his/ her own journal for personal use and also suggest that this journal be kept in a secure location away from prying eyes.

Never put anyone through an exercise or procedure that you have not done yourself several times. You must know and experience as many possibilities as you can so that you can be aware of what the client is feeling and seeing mentally. It is best not to predispose the client by telling him/ her of what may be experienced. Allow them to tell you afterwards and remind them to document this in their private notes later.

When choosing a prospective deprogrammer-in-training, emphasize that all work is done in a professional manner only and in total privacy. It is helpful if the trainee has had experience in dealing with the public before, has a lot of patience, and a good sense of humor.

It is most helpful at some point in the process to do play-acting in common situations. Create scenarios where you are the client being deprogrammed and spontaneous issues arise during a session. Make it difficult and intricate, because this will happen in real circumstances. A good deprogrammer must be prepared for anything—including physical violence and health emergencies.

The trainee should not have any sexual hang-ups or judgments about any type of lifestyle or sexual behavior. The deprogramming trainer should also not be shy in explaining methodologies or in demonstrating any technique or procedure. Both parties must be totally honest and blatant.

Self-defense techniques that do not harm the client should also be learned. These are interventions that would be applied when a person being deprogrammed goes into a violent or suicidal alter. It may also be wise to have a cell phone handy to call someone to help you should the session become too much for one person to handle. This is of special concern when the client is rather large or powerful.

The trainee should learn to always remain calm and not get excited about what may be seen or heard in a session with a client. The deprogrammer must never have any medication, drugs, or alcohol in his system when operating a deprogramming session. Phones should be off and no noise or external intrusions should be allowed. The client should be in an environment of security, comfort, peacefulness, and neutral energy.

Deprogramming rooms should have non-threatening art-work, mild colors, and be a warm, but not hot, temperature. It is best to have no windows that could distract the client or deprogrammer. There should be no items that could become dangerous to either party. Lighting should be soft and with no equipment on. Smells should be neutral so that minimal or no triggering can occur. Do not allow pets to enter this room when a session is in progress.

Supportive Articles
by Janet Swerdlow

Section 5

Chapter 1
Layers of Mind-Control & Programming

Most people do not realize that they are programmed from birth, beginning with parents who dictate all kinds of rules and regulations. Your conscious mind is clear and ready for imprinting. The first time you experience anything, you are imprinted and therefore greatly impacted the rest of your life.

In order for the initial imprinting to occur, there has to be something within your soul-personality that pulls these experiences to you. As you go through the rest of your life, these first imprints are the "pea in your mattress" a la "The Princess & The Pea" story—no matter how many mattresses are stacked together, the Princess can always feel the pea. Those imprints, or peas, are felt through all experiences.

This means that if you are taught that humans live approximately 75 years, this is your imprint, and you will fulfill that. If you are taught that God is a man sitting on a throne in the sky to judge you, you skew your life in that direction. At the early age that you are taught these things, you do not consciously have the tools to question—you are led with blinders on down the path of your life. You really do not have a choice to do anything but follow. Consciously, you know nothing else.

You do as you are told and you learn what you are told. This information is stored, and you have no reason to question it. The people who care for you take you to school and you go. Through the process of transference, you assume the teachers are telling you the truth, as they further imprint your mind based upon what they are given. The teachers, in turn, trust these materials given to them by their authorities. The cycle continues to perpetuate itself because each person is imprinted to respect, obey, and trust whatever authority is above him/her.

Everyone is imprinted that those in authority are here to help the masses, from parents, teachers, politicians, to spiritual leaders; that these leaders all have nothing but the magnanimous good of the people at heart. With this imprinting in mind, you hold within you a certain level of trust in the information that you receive. You build your belief system and your perception of yourself and the world around you by trusting that this information is correct. There is a part of you that subconsciously models yourself and your goals based upon what the outer world imprints upon your conscious mind. You do not have a reason to question it. With this information, you build and define your world.

As you mature, your perception changes as you gather a different set of facts. This new set of facts allows you to reach new conclusions to old experiences. Does this mean that the first conclusion was incorrect? Or does it simply mean that you reached a correct conclusion for one layer of experience, and now you are into a second layer of the same experience? Is the second conclusion more correct? And if so, does this mean that there might be a third layer with different facts which will bring you to a third conclusion? And so on.

When you have a thought or feeling that will not go away, or continually pops up now and then, this is a thread that you can follow into another layer of yourself. Place this thought at your pineal gland, or third eye area, on a background of royal blue, and hold it there. Bring the bigger picture to yourself by holding the clue that you have in focus.

As the picture grows, use a journal to write down your findings. Remember, no matter how young you were, there is a part of you that knows exactly what happened, by whom, how, and why.

Breathe yourself into your center, anchor yourself in your Oversoul and God-Mind, and go within. If you become traumatized in any way, ground yourself in brown, and give everything a rest.

If you come upon a layer of trauma, this may be a way of stopping you on your search. Go slowly if you need to, but go. Allow yourself to see what you need to see, a step at a time, releasing as you go. Be aware that many people who have been through traumatic experiences have "masked memories." This means that what you think is trauma from one experience, is really trauma from another. Or there may be an underlying trauma that is being suppressed while you deal with what you think is your core issue. The deeper you go inside your issues, the more you find out who and what you are. Multidimensionality becomes an active part of your learning process as you realize that every experience that you have is multi-layered.

In the same way, realize that the outer world is also multidimensional, with many layers of experience. You are accustomed to seeing the world the way you did as a child, trusting the information that you received as well as the people who imparted it. It is inconceivable to that part of yourself that anyone could be passing on suspect information unknowingly, much less knowingly.

However, on your multidimensional, multi-layered exploration of the outer world, think about what you studied in school to formulate your own conclusions. All the information that you are taught via the outer world is suspect. At one time, everyone was taught that the world was flat. Now, this thought seems ludicrous. But at the time, the flat Earth theory was acceptable and the thought of a round Earth was ludicrous.

Schools and churches both bring people together for mass education purposes. Is this for the good of the people? Explore the hierarchy of leadership and see where it leads you. Who sets the precedents, and why? Use your own abilities to formulate your own conclusions. Explore the energy behind the words. Put people, places, and experiences up to your pineal gland, surround them in royal blue, and look for yourself. And, when you are satisfied with your answer, look again, because most likely there is another layer that is buried beneath that.

Life has a way of layering itself in such a way that you cannot even identify the layers, much less sort which facts belong to which layer. This is purposefully programmed within you to squelch the inner and outer quests, sometimes knowingly and sometimes unknowingly. As long as your attention can be diverted outward and held there, you will be diverted from inner exploration and peeling the layers of mind-control and programming. The only way to really know who you are is to sort out who you are not.

Chapter 2
Compartmentalization

Physical realities are the natural Self-Compartmentalizations of God-Mind exploring Itself. In True Reality, God-Mind can never separate from Itself, only create this illusion for the purpose of exploring Its own totality. Physical realities provide a vehicle for this Grand Internal Dissection.

Every species of plant, animal, mineral, and physical being that exists is a compartmentalization/subpersonality of God-Mind. A part of God-Mind becomes the species to understand and know Itself through experiential exploration. Every individual within the species is a cell within God-Mind, each one unique with at least one differentiating characteristic from all others. God-Mind "isolates" Itself, cell by cell, for Self-Exploration. In this way, each subpersonality within God-Mind continually explores and defines Itself.

For example, there are 20,000 known species of butterflies alone. Within each of these 20,000 known species, there is every variation that can possibly be imagined. This species is really a compartmentalization of God-Mind, twisting and turning on a Self-Exploratory journey.

Physical beings are merely another compartmentalization/subpersonality of God-Mind.

Every type of physical being that you can imagine exists some-where, someplace. In Its quest for Internal Knowledge, physical beings are continually compartmentalized into more subperson-alities of God-Mind so that It can continue Its Self-Exploration.

On the soul-personality level, this compartmentalization is enhanced via the illusion of separation. As a cell within a subper-sonality of God-Mind, the individual stays focused in its own com-partment via this illusion. Within this illusion, the soul-personality asks the following questions: What is separation from God-Mind? From my Oversoul? From my parents? From my family? From myself? From a physical body? From others? How many ways can I separate from others? How many ways can I separate from myself? How many ways can others separate me from myself?

Keeping this in mind, understand that group or individual mind-control is a continuation of the compartmentalization process. Mind-control is another way that the illusion of separation is perpetuated so that compartmentalization can occur. When you think that you cannot compartmentalize/separate anymore, you find out that you can. The sub-personality of God-Mind must explore Its ability to compartmentalize until It cannot compart-mentalize any more. Every cell must compartmentalize until there are no more ways left to compartmentalize. Only then can Its exploration be complete.

Consider the following simplified model:

God-Mind compartmentalizes into Oversouls

Oversouls compartmentalize into soul-personalities

Soul-personalities compartmentalize into subpersonalities/alters

Subpersonalities/alters compartmentalize ad infinitum

Each compartmentalization perpetuates the illusion that it is separate from the whole. These compartmentalizations allow all aspects of God-Mind to continually experience Itself via the illusion of separation. In this artificially created scenario, the soul-personality becomes angry and despondent as it seemingly wanders further and further away from its Source. It is so fully immersed in the illusion that it looks to find its way "back" to God-Mind.

When the soul-personality is compartmentalized as much as it deems necessary, either by self or others, then it is time to create another illusion—that of "unification." The reverse process happens. As each piece "reintegrates," each cell brings its own unique set of knowledge to add to the whole. Now, the "pieces come together" and the whole understands the totality of Itself through unification.

Consider this simplified model:

Subpersonalities/alters unify with other subpersonalities/alters

Subpersonalities/alters unify with main soul-personality

Soul-personality unifies with Oversoul

Oversoul unifies with God-Mind

This is the natural rhythm of the Universe, or the Breath of God-Mind. As God-Mind breathes Itself out, the soul-personality feels itself moving "away" from God-Mind. As God-Mind breathes Itself in, the soul-personality rides the breath "back" to its Source. As a microcosm of the macrocosm, the physical body replicates this breathing in and out.

Compartmentalization occurs on the Out-Breath. Unification occurs on the In-Breath. Both answer the same question from a different perspective. Together, they are the answer. In True Reality there is only One Soul. This One Soul can never separate from Itself. Compartmentalization via the illusion of separation is the best that It can do. Unification is only an illusion as well, as God-Mind can never separate from Itself in True Reality.

Have you ever heard someone say that he/she is "only a novice" or a "beginner" when it comes to metaphysics? Or, "I wish I could communicate with my Oversoul and/or God-Mind?" These people are definitely "into" the illusion of separation! *There are no novices or beginners!* Everyone is in communication with his/her Oversoul and God-Mind! *There is no separation!* Only illusion that allows the continual, fascinating process of Self-Exploration.

Chapter 3
Nowhere to Hide but Deep Inside

<u>**Part I**</u>

Because the imprinting of the mind-pattern in this reality most often occurs by the age of five, a child does not usually have tools to deal with any trauma that he/she experiences. When a child experiences trauma, he/she cannot just walk away, get in a car, or leave. The child has no conscious choice but to remain in the circumstance and fully experience it. Left without tools to deal with trauma, he/she retreats in the only way he/she knows how—and that is to mentally close out the outer world and emotionally retreat inside. Keep in mind that a child's perception of trauma may be quite different than an adult's.

This emotional retreat may be expressed in a variety of ways. Physically, these expressions might show as the following symptoms with the corresponding mind-pattern:

» Accidents/broken bones— a release and rearrangement of pent-up anger
» Bedwetting/bladder infections—being angry/"pissed off" about outer circumstances
» Chills - fear
» Colds - confusion and doubt, congestion about outer circumstances

» Earaches— not wanting to hear what is being expressed in the outer world
» Fevers— internal angers
» Sore throats—suppressed words that need to come out
» Vision/eye problems—not wanting to see what is going on around

Without proper tools to deal with outer circumstances, these are common childhood reactions to internalizing emotional trauma.

When a child is continually pushed into traumatic situations, the child retreats inside at increasingly deeper levels until he/she actually compartmentalizes a part of the personality. This effectively isolates and shields various aspects of the personality from emotional harm. Through a natural process of self-preservation, the child develops "alters" that he/she calls upon to deal with life on an as-needed basis. This suppression may enhance another aspect of the personality that can more effectively deal with the outer world, such as an anger or hostile subpersonality/alter. An adult faced with severe trauma may also react by compartmentalizing the self in the same way with the same results.

Think of the personality as a self-contained plastic bubble filled with gel. When one side is pushed down, or suppressed, the other side expands because the gel has to go somewhere. The self-altering, literally, rearranges the personality so that it can survive. Without this self-rearrangement, the only other choice would be for the bubble to burst, metaphorically speaking. Literally, the soul-personality would vacate the physical body.

This is a natural form of self-compartmentalization as the soul-personality begins to explore itself in this lifeline. This illusion of division within self is a natural reflection of the illusion perpetuated by God-Mind that within physical reality everything is separate. As a reflection of the macrocosm, the child creates the illusion within him/herself that he/she is separate from him/herself. In True Reality, there is no separation in God-Mind. In True Reality, the child cannot separate from him/herself, just as the macrocosm cannot separate from Itself.

The consequence of this illusion of separation means that as the child develops more conscious tools to deal with life, the alters are not used and become forgotten. They stay tucked away deep inside the child without opportunity to grow and evolve along with the rest of the soul-personality. These alters are not "reintegrated" into the system, but are merely left behind and overshadowed.

Like all things that are suppressed, these alters may occasionally pop out on their own. This is why sometimes you are doing really great with your personal work when suddenly, you find yourself self-sabotaging and reacting with such emotions as stubbornness, willfulness, anger, resistance, fear, etc. You may wish that you could get through these walls, but you simply cannot. This is because the walls actually exist. You built them long ago in a time now forgotten to your conscious mind.

Or, you may speak to someone thinking that you are in total agreement, or reach a great understanding, only to find later that this was not the case. You may have spoken to a subpersonality of that person who in the sense of illusion, is separated from him/herself.

This is also why you may need to repeatedly explain a certain concept or viewpoint to someone, or you find this happening on occasion with yourself. Each alter within, and there may be a myriad of them, are literally having the conversation for the first time.

Until you reach all involved subpersonalities/alters and either bring them into agreement, or integrate them into the system, you will find these discrepancies of understanding. This is why it is a good idea to always speak to someone on the Oversoul level first. Remember that you only speak to your own Oversoul, and it is your Oversoul who does the rest of the work. This way, your Oversoul is able to reach all subpersonalities/alters that are involved in the situation. When you realize that you also may have subpersonalities conversing with others' subpersonalities, you understand the more intricate levels of communication. You may both be flip/flopping around. You may not really know who is speaking to whom.

To reintegrate the system, it is important that all the "splits" from your childhood years, or from adult trauma, merge back into the main personality. All alters suppressed deep inside must have a voice and be allowed to speak. This will tell you where the imprinting occurred so that you can effectively integrate them. By doing this on the Oversoul level, you give these parts of yourself a voice.

No longer suppressed, alters can finally say and/or do on the Oversoul level that which they had no power to do many years before. This brings growth and awareness to the rest of the "system" so that it can successfully reintegrate. Use the merger symbol below at the pineal gland to help with successful integration. Subpersonalities are also discussed in detail in my book, *Decoding Your Life*.

You have worlds hidden within worlds of your soul-personality, all a reflection of the activity within God-Mind. The trauma that is experienced in the outer world is a tool used for self-exploration. Challenging lessons that push you into the core of who and what you are. Are you up to the challenge?

Part II

Everyone is targeted for mass programming, but it is estimated that approximately one to two million people, or ½% of the total US population, are specifically targeted due to genetic/DNA heritage. If you are part of this target population, then it is especially important that you work on merging your subpersonalities/alters with the "main system."

For those of you who have received specific individual programming, extreme trauma is purposefully induced to enhance the natural ability of the soul-personality to compartmentalize. With severe trauma that is inescapable, a child or adult, goes continually deeper and deeper inside until a compartmentalization, or "split," occurs.

These compartmentalizations are carefully orchestrated and guided with drugs, hypnosis, mantras, words, lights, pictures, sound, and implants to achieve the programmer/controller/handler's goal. The subpersonality/alter is taught to rely on the controller rather than on the soul-personality from which it is split. The physical brain is altered so that the neuro-network is purposefully distorted. This keeps the alters from finding their way to the surface, or to each other. In this way, the natural ability of the mind to compartmentalize is used to create definite alters for specific purposes.

These programming experiences are "piggy-backed" upon natural behaviors, inclinations, and existing environments. If, for instance, there was/is discord in the home the target's natural feelings of confusion and low-self worth might purposefully be enhanced by the controller. Messages from angels, aliens, ascended masters, and/or guides may be overlays of the controller's messages, often referred to as "masked memories." Missing time, or periods in your life that you simply cannot remember, are often symptoms of specific programming. A memory of sexual abuse by a parent might actually be covering sexual abuse perpetrated by a programmer/controller/handler.

What you think may be an out-of-body experience brought on by being "spiritual" may be the result of being forced out through sound, drugs, trauma, etc. Thinking that you are having a "spiritual experience," you may even help the experience along by moving into it rather than working to stop it.

Without conscious memories of these experiences, suppressed memories, experiences, and feelings rise to the surface, often resulting in behavior that without explanation may appear irrational. People with obsessive-compulsive behaviors are often highly programmed. Feelings of extreme low self-worth and self-esteem may be enhanced through these suppressed memories, as may be depression and any suicidal tendencies. Unexplained nighttime vomiting may be the body's way of expelling programming drugs, or as with bulimia, trying to vomit out emotional pain and trauma. Promiscuity, or the suppression of natural sexual expression, may be the result of programming. Gender identity and sexual orientation issues are often a result as well.

Whatever happens, or happened, during programming, a part of you knows, and knows well. Being separate is only an illusion. "Not knowing" is an illusion. Using the merger symbol, you can begin to reintegrate these parts into the main personality.

With the programming continually rising to, or pushing upon, the surface, and alters flip/flopping around, it is difficult to progress in any area of your life. Natural mind-patterns of self-sabotage have been enhanced. It may be difficult to live a "normal" life with "normal" relationships and careers. With enhanced self-sabotage routines hidden within yourself, you may continually set yourself up for failure without ever understanding the depth of all that affects you.

Because these programs/memories/alters are hidden so deep and well, it is important to assimilate all conscious mind-patterns so that you can find and integrate the deeper ones hidden away. Start with today, cleaning out the conscious mind of all that is no longer necessary. Then, as a natural process, the memories hidden in your subconscious mind will start surfacing from the multi-layers and levels below. This must be done in a way that can be integrated, understood, and emotionally handled.

Taking notes is important, as this will later help you go back and put the pieces together. In the beginning, you might not be aware of any patterns. But as the notes grow, patterns begin to emerge. Even if you begin with a phrase here, or a shadowy memory there, this is still a release of information. This tiny release starts the pattern, allowing more and more information to rise up. Soon the trickle begins to grow as more information has an outlet.

Keep in mind that all experience is energy comprised of color, shape, form, consistency, and weight. The suppressed information is energy that is compressed into the soul-personality. Removing anything begins the act of decompression, providing an "escape valve" so that the energy now has a way of releasing itself. Just like opening up anything that is under pressure, it must be opened gradually, or it will blow up. You do not want to be a kettle that explodes, so proceed with caution, slowly and gently.

It is important to begin to understand your programming so that you can begin to control it rather than it control you. If you continually start something positive and worthwhile only to end it with a self-sabotage routine, you can begin to recognize what you are doing, how and why you are doing it, and you can finally get to the imprint that creates this. You take control of your life, rather than some suppressed subpersonality/alter controlling you from its hiding place within.

When you are specifically targeted, keep in mind that the programmer knows you better than you know yourself. Inside and out, strengths and weaknesses. Strengths may be hidden or "countered" while weaknesses used against you for control.

Remember, all mind-control/programming is only an enhancement of what already exists within you. If someone outside of yourself has molded, shaped, and compartmentalized you further into the illusion of separation, you can mold, shape, and reintegrate yourself back into your True Form.

If you can do this in a proactive way, there is less chance that it will pop out on its own and surprise you, putting you into the reactive mode. No "deprogramming" process is easy, whether it is from general mind-control or if you are/were a specific target. However, the soul-personality obviously has deep lessons to learn, and it is important to understand the underlying themes of knowledge woven into these intricate experiences. As a microcosm of the macrocosm, self-exploration is ultimately Oversoul/God-Mind exploration.

Chapter 4
Exploring the Darkness

All that is going on in the outer world is a reflection of some part of yourself. The undercurrents of society are rising from their hiding places, coming increasingly out in the open. This means that your own personal undercurrents are ripe for exploration.

Most people explore their daily life, because this is what most affects them on an ongoing basis. Often times, this leads to exploration of the middle layers of experience when people begin to question habits, relationships, personal trends, and responses to determine their origins. There are usually a lot of issues to explore, and this layer can keep you busy for years and years.

Beneath this middle layer, you find the undercurrents that exist within even deeper layers of your being. They are not usually easily identifiable, yet they propel the middle layer and daily living.

To explore these hidden areas, it is important that you align Self with your Oversoul and God-Mind. To do this, take a look at how far your auric field extends from your physical body. Then, pull it in close to your body and place it in a bubble. Now you have boundaries that state where you start and stop. Use your breath to find your center. Breathe in from the top of your head to the base of your spine, exhaling in reverse, sending your breath all the way up into your Oversoul and God-Mind. Work with your breath until you feel centered.

Now that you are centered, breathe in the strength of your Oversoul and God-Mind, exhaling all that no longer belongs within your being. Breathe in the strength, exhale all that you no longer need. As you do so, feel yourself sinking deeper and deeper inside of your Self. Acknowledge that Self is anchored deep within the strength of your Oversoul and God-Mind. Feel and know the depth and strength of this inner connection.

Allow your consciousness to sink further inside, into depths that until now you did not even consciously know existed. Allow yourself access to the deepest levels of Self-knowledge that you can, with the least amount of discomfort. If at any time you feel traumatized or upset, put yourself in brown for grounding and conclude the exercise.

Go as deep within yourself as you feel led to explore. If you feel strong enough, place a clear black color at your pineal gland. The positive aspects of black represent depth, mystery, and the hidden. By using the positive aspects of black, you can use this color to go deeper inside of yourself. Then, surround yourself in a layer of royal blue, then a layer of violet, then a layer of gold.

However, if you have a tendency to toward depression or un-stableness, it is best to avoid use of the color black as a color code at this time. If you try to use it, your consciousness will want to use it in the way that it is most familiar, and it may be difficult for you to come out of it. Continue to work with the alignment of Self, Oversoul, and God-Mind, to identify, feel, and operate within/from your center. Surround yourself with the layers of royal blue, violet, and gold without using the black at the pineal gland.

When that feels comfortable, simply work on feeling the strongest strength in existence—that of Self, Oversoul, and God-Mind. Use that strength to explore within. Only use a clear black as a color code when you feel that you can use it as a positive exploration tool of Self.

Before you conclude your work, understand that you can breathe yourself into alignment and touch into the strength of Self, Oversoul, and God-Mind at any moment necessary, ultimately knowing that the alignment and strength are already always there. Simply focusing upon it brings it into your conscious mind.

Realize that the true test of your abilities lie in the outer world. It is easy to be a "perfect person" when you are alone, but how about in a busy, hectic world? You may wish that you lived where it is quiet so that you can mediate more and connect even deeper within. Yet, if you can do this in a noisy environment, you can do this anywhere!

The same with a family that you feel is unsupportive; or coworkers that "push your buttons." What can you do within an environment that is designed to pull you down? How strong are you? Can you walk through the darkness of the outer world stronger and better for the experience, or do you allow outer circumstances to pull you down and into them? Can you keep yourself clean no matter how deep the mud and muck? Can you maintain and retain your personal integrity regardless of the degradation of society and its attempts suck you into its pits? Just because "everyone does it," do you have to join in? Do numbers of people make something correct? Are you strong enough to be your own person regardless of how many people fight against your right of personal self-expression?

There is a reason why you chose to be here at this particular time, with the increasing undercurrents of darkness that are rising to society's surface. This is a perfect opportunity for you to allow your personal undercurrents of darkness to do the same. Is the darkness negative? Or is it simply dark? Why does it exist within you? Why does it exist within society? Take all your findings up to your Oversoul and ask for explanation. You already know. Now it is time to bring that knowledge into focus. When you understand the depths of your own being and take the time to penetrate the multi-layers/levels, you will in turn take the knowledge into your understanding of the outer world.

Self-knowledge also reflects back to you in the outer world. If you cannot clearly define your own center, how can you possibly know when others are off-center? If you do not understand your own boundaries, how can you know when others step outside of theirs? If you do not understand the depths of your own inner levels, how can you identify the deeper levels of others?

Do not confuse darkness with "bad." The darkness is really the hidden part of yourself. Or, more accurately, that part of Self that is not in your focus at this moment. Everything serves a purpose; everything is a part of, and defines, God-Mind in Its Self-exploration.

Does the exploration of undercurrents and darkness bring fear to the surface? Anchor yourself in your center, and allow the fear to rise up in a way that you can handle. This is your opportunity to face fear and walk through it. Whatever is hidden, whatever you are avoiding, develop your center and strength so that you can bring it out in the least uncomfortable way. Then, explore and release it on up to your Oversoul, giving thanks for the lessons learned and assimilated.

Using society to reflect these dark undercurrents usually means that the circumstances control you until you can find a way to turn the tables. This puts you in a reactive position. Consciously choosing to explore the dark undercurrents of Self puts you in a proactive position. A proactive position means you have a greater chance of controlling the situation before it controls you. Keep this in mind. You can choose to create your own inner catalyst to bring out your issues, or you can choose to let the outside world do it for you.

Chapter 5
Red, White & Blue...Are These Triggers for You?

Red, white, and blue are three of the most common colors presented to the public.

At a very early age, young children are imprinted to love and honor these colors through the guise of patriotism. They are taught to stand at attention for these colors, to pledge allegiance to them, and even to fight for these colors should it become "necessary."

Fashion focuses on these colors, often showcasing the trio together. Interstate roadways and highway information signs use the red, white, and/or blue themes. Since the World Trade Center event, red, white, and blue are the trendy colors to display in every way imaginable. Some people have several flags displayed between home, work, and vehicles. Flags are being given away for free at parades, rest areas, and public events.

The public explanation of these colors is that the red stands for those who died for this country, white is for purity, blue is for the blue skies above, and there is a star for every state. The subliminal imprint for red is that it opens you sexually for programming, white blinds you from the truth, and navy blue represents aggression in the future.

You might notice that the majority of successful chain stores use these colors to attract business, such as Lowes, Wal-Mart,

K-Mart, Target, Office Depot, Office Max, T.J. Maxx, Sam's Club, and Costco, with a little bright yellow thrown in for ELF (such as McDonald's and Wendy's). Because you are so programmed with a love for these colors, it is easy for them to capture your attention, and your dollars. You automatically patronize these larger stores because you are programmed to do so. The small independents, which cannot compete because of volume purchases, are soon out of business. Then, of the three or four industry chains that are left, one or two go out of business leaving the consumer with little buying choice, and the small independent business owners are gone with the wind.

Personal service and responsibility are now out the window as well. No one assumes responsibility, and no one cares. Why should they? Apathy is rampant. Business is compartmentalized. It is difficult for anyone to "fight the system" as it is too large and onerous for anyone to navigate, even when you find a person who sincerely wants to help. Employees within this type of system have less incentive to function with a work ethic and pride. They have no power, their superiors have no power, and with "minimum wage" paychecks, they barely make ends meet.

Banks, utilities, schools, and hospitals are more examples of corporations, both public and private, that are utilizing these colors. Make note of who stays in business and who does not. Watch what happens as the shake-out of small business owners leaves fewer and fewer choices. Notice the colors of the "survivors." You can begin to pinpoint them now. These decisions occurred privately a long time ago. Now, they are becoming more obvious to the public.

Because the Illuminati are adept at cryptology, they know how to layer several levels of meaning into these public color displays. For them, the red represents Satanic ritual and ceremony, the crux of their religion. The white represents their ability to "white wash" whatever is necessary. The navy blue is the color of the Reptilian pineal gland area. The star is really a pentagram, which is a sacred symbol within the Satanic mind.

You will see the continuing proliferation of these colors. Currently, approximately 25% of the world's nations' flags encompass some combination of red, white, and blue, with most of the "newer" countries using this combination. At least another 50% of those remaining countries have either red, white, or blue flags, or a combination thereof. This will make them easy transitions into a global red, white, and blue flag. As an interesting aside, you might notice that the flags of most public buildings are fringed with gold, a universal military signal that the country is under occupation.

Red, white, and blue are triggers for suicide programming and fighting to the death for a cause. They also trigger people to pledge total loyalty to those who control the colors of the flag and not to think for themselves.

Red, white, and blue...what do these colors mean to you?

Chapter 6
Do Unto Others...The Reptilian Balance

Almost every child at some point in his/her development, is told to think about how he/she would feel if he/she were in another person's shoes. This is the usually the first introduction to the "Golden Rule" that says: ***Do unto others as you would have others do unto you.*** In other words, "How would I feel if this situation happened to me?"

The Golden Rule is a good beginning principle that challenges little children to think outside of the "me" box. Yes, there is someone else out there besides "me." Someone else has feelings that I must consider during my interactions with the outside world.

The imprint of the Golden Rule carries forth into adulthood, where people continue to think, "What if it were me? How would I feel? I will do x, y, and z for that person because that is what I would like done for me."

What people often do not stop to realize is that once they understand the Golden Rule, there is another rule that spirals out from it. This one says: ***Do unto others what they need/want done unto them.*** In other words, what does the other person actually need or want, rather than what would you need or want if you were the one in his/her situation.

Many people buy gifts according to the Golden Rule: "What would I want?" And that is what they give. People often give advice this way. "What would I want to know?" People continue on through life using this Golden Rule without realizing that at some point it no longer honors the other person. Instead, it becomes a way of enforcing your own thoughts and desires onto someone else.

Perhaps that person wants his/her house in a mess and does not want your help in straightening things out. Perhaps he/she needs a relationship that is abusive. Perhaps that person that you think you "should" call really does not want a phone call from you. Go up to the Oversoul level to find out what he/she really does want before you impose your "what I would want" onto someone else.

With the Golden Rule as the original imprint, many people extrapolate this into a misunderstanding of others. When you say, "how can he/she do that?" you are really saying, " I could not do that." You put yourself in the other person's shoes (again) and then you try to imagine yourself doing whatever. But, you just cannot imagine this because you are not that person. In this reality of separation, for all intents and purposes, that person is an entirely different entity than yourself. So, to understand the actions of another, you must go to the Oversoul level and ask that the other person be explained to you. Succinctly put, you must learn how the other person thinks to understand his/her actions.

In the same way, when someone questions the motives of the hybrid/Reptilians as well as the Reptilians themselves, then it becomes important to address this question on the Oversoul level. You cannot think like a human and understand a Reptilian. You must think like a Reptilian.

What kind of a soul-personality would be drawn into a Reptilian body? What would that soul-personality need to learn in order to achieve its personal balance within God-Mind? As a finger of God-Mind exploring Itself, what knowledge/information would a Reptilian bring into the total picture?

Reptilians represent the antithesis, or balance, to the mass population. God-Mind is always in balance, regardless of what that form may take, and how the human mind may perceive/judge it. If humans are about emotion, then Reptilians are about logic.

If you had access to all the resources in the world, what would you do with them if you were an emotionless Reptilian? Why should you not have a slave race working to meet your every need? Why should you not move them about like pawns on a chessboard? Why should you not eliminate the troublemakers? Why should you not introduce your religion? Why should you not use every available means to control the masses that have the potential to outnumber you? Why should you not keep the "secret information" away from them to protect yourself?

Understand who and what they are. Their logical minds have taken the time to learn who and what you are. They know you better than you know yourself. They understand your emotions on all levels. They know what motivates you, what makes you angry, what makes you passive. They know what food is good for you and what food is not. They know your strengths and your weaknesses. They are a collective hunter that has studied its prey. Learn from their example.

The Reptilians are the antithesis to humans in this reality. They provide the balance within God-Mind. Victim/oppressor. Freedom-seeker/enslaver. Emotion/logic. Outer Earth/Inner Earth. Straightforward communication/cryptic communication. Nonmaterialism/materialism. Short-term goals/long-term goals. Use your imagination to continue the thoughtstream.

The Reptilians, like everything else that exists in this physical world, are a reflection of you. They could not exist in the outer world if they did not exist somewhere in your inner world. Likewise, you are a reflection of the Reptilians. You could not exist in their outer world if you did not exist somewhere in their inner world.

In the big picture, the group consciousness of the Reptilians is centered in the brainstem, which is fight or flight, which correlates to logic because they have to know when to stay and when to run. The group consciousness of the humans is centered in the right brain (emotion). The Reptilians seek total domination of the right brain of emotion, while the humans seek total domination of the left brain of logic. While within the group consciousness there is some deviation on either theme, the collective consciousness on both sides is in agreement. Together, they represent a balance within God-Mind.

The Golden Rule is a good starting point when you are a child, just beginning to understand that the world consists of more than just "me." But those days are long past. Understand the thinking process of others via the Oversoul level. Recognize that regardless of your perception or judgements, God-Mind is always in balance. Whether you like what you see is inconsequential. Are you up to the challenge?

Chapter 7
Wake-Up Call

What you draw to yourself is an absolutely amazing and perfect depiction of what exists within your mind-pattern. From the moment that you are conceived until your departure from this plane should you so choose, you are the center of your universe and everything does revolve around you!

The power that is in your mind is astounding! Even without conscious direction, the power that flows through the instrument of your body creates and shapes everything that exists in your world. Your thought power brings everything to you.

Without conscious guidance, your power can create through building or destruction. Most people are great at building through destruction, because this is exactly what happens when your mental capabilities run rampant and unchecked.

Visualize yourself standing still, with a volcano of never-ending, undirected lava flow-like fountain of power pouring out every pore of your being and into the world around you. Where does it go? What does it touch? What does it do as you stand there, silently observing? What kind of havoc are your undirected, misunderstood mental powers wreaking upon your personal world?

As you stand there, observing the very world that you have participated in creating, from world geography and political structure to your health, home, relationships, and finances, what do you see? Everything that exists is somehow touched by you and what you have allowed to exude through your being, whether conscious or unconscious. And, now you complain because of what your life is?

Well, this is your wake-up call, loud and strong. The more undirected energy is "dumped" into the world, the worse it becomes and the harder it is to extricate yourself from this personal and global situation. You have a responsibility to clean up yourself, thus reining back in all the undirected and misdirected energy that has spewed forth from you.

This is not an easy task for most people. Pulling back in all that you have cast out means reviewing all to which your energy was attached. This can happen with the strength of one thought, or you can spend eons of time moving through this. It is always your choice.

Most people like to look at what they have done and the damage that has ensued. Regardless of their words, they enjoy their discomfort and wallowing in the products of their creations. This is what they know and this is what they keep. The strength of the mind-pattern that created the seeming chaos and mess holds it to them, and on some level people purposefully keep it that way.

Stay in the drama, yell "woe is me," blame the world, wallow in self-pity, cry endless tears of inner pain, curse God and humankind alike, along with a few aliens, hybrids, and Reptilians just because you know they exist, too. How low can you sink, how much suffering can you tolerate, knowing that it is inescapable? Even with physical death, if this is your mind-pattern, your life will follow you beyond this plane, eternally haunting you with increasingly more viciousness and destruction!

The closer you are to crashing through your own self-imposed ceilings, the louder the internal cries that stop you from making your getaway into a liberated plane of existence. You create your own mental traps, you allow the self-sabotage, you accept the self-doubts that rear their ugly heads, you stage the outer world to appear as though it is unnavigable.

What happened to your faith in Self, Oversoul, and God-Mind? Who "took" it from you, or rather, who did you willingly give it to and why? Who is really your worst enemy? Would you dare point the finger at yourself??

When you have had enough of it all, you will pull in your un-checked, misguided energy and power. You will loosen its hold on all that is around you. You will pull it into your self to examine exactly where this energy went and why. You will do this so that you never, ever have to experience this again. You have done it once, so why continue to repeat the patterns? You will do this so that you can explain to your Oversoul and God-Mind what happens to un-directed flow of God-Mind – what happens to it, how it transforms as it exudes and is "tainted" as it passes through every cell of your being on every level.

You give it all to your Oversoul and God-Mind so that it can be recast and you can follow it upward for a change instead of allowing it to pull you down into your own seemingly self-destruction. You know what happens with chaos, so now you can explore order. You know what happens with self-destruction, so now you can explore self-enhancement. You know imbalance, so now you explore balance.

You can go into your genetic structure and remove all that your soul-personality no longer needs. You can break the genetic chains that you have chosen to enslave you so that you are no longer at their mercy. You can open the DNA that holds your rightful heritage. Learn about who and what you are. Know that no one and no thing can put you down or "make you be a certain way." Reaction is totally your response – no one "makes" you behave or feel a specific way.

Are you willing to take responsibility for conscious directed power that flows through the instrument that is your physical body while on this plane? Are you willing to throw off the cloak-and

– dagger mentality in exchange for the creative, talented, mantle that is rightfully yours?

No one can stop you from creating the path that you desire except you. The world is your oyster. Accept nothing less than the best, physically, mentally, emotionally, spiritually. Make what was once your ceiling now your floor. Consciously make your choices, be unstoppable in reaching your goals, align yourself with your Oversoul and God-Mind to clean up the "past" and set your "future" in motion.

Put all your abilities to positive use, create your path, refuse to let the outer world stop you. Move forward with the strength and determination that puts you firmly and sure-footed on your narrow, focused, refined path into continually deeper levels of existence within the Mind of God, and thus within yourself.

Chapter 8
Who's Going to Win?

The release of technology to the public means that people have increasing receptors in their homes, automobiles, and even on their persons to receive ELF (Extra-Low Frequency) for mind-control purposes. This technology allows ELF bombardment of the masses, while specifically targeted people get an extra dose. Is this knowledge something that should frighten you and create paranoia within your mind-pattern? How "should" you respond?

First, you have to think about "the adversary" and why it is even in your life. What part of you keeps inviting it in? Take a look at what you could possibly like about this mind-numbing process that ELF bombardment creates. Could it possibly be that it is simply easier to let others take responsibility for you rather than you take responsibility for you?

Everyone complains about a dictatorship, yet that is the most efficient form of control. You do not have to take responsibility for one single thing. You can just sit there and complain while doing what you are told. Without choices, navigating life is much less complex. You know what to do and when to do it. You do not have to think about anything. You can use your extra energy to complain while being led blindly about.

So, you passively open yourself up to receive the ELF, then complain because it affects you. You may think that you are "fighting it" but who is winning the battle? Passive resistance is the best modus operandi. Always keep in mind the woven "Chinese handcuffs" played with by children. You put one finger in each end and pull. The harder you pull, the stronger the hold on your fingers, and the less likely you are to escape. Relax your fingers, and they come right out.

Yes, you can use sea salt baths, protection techniques, and a myriad of other crutches that aid your developing mind-pattern. But when it comes right down to it, you need to find out why you let the ELF in!

Think about what you do that allows it in. While there are other points of entry, the basic door into your system is through the root chakra. Anything that opens the root chakra opens you to ELF. Drinking alcohol, smoking, illegal and legal drugs (including prescription and over-the-counter), and even some herbs open the root chakra. Anything that sexually stimulates the root chakra area opens you up, ready to receive ELF and the programming that it contains. This means anytime the genitalia responds to anything you are a candidate to receive programming, from advertisements to movies and books, to sexual activity.

When you know that you are open, use the "crutches" that you know. However, recognize that the goal is to correct the mind-pattern so that you do not continue to allow the ELF in on any level. Which takes you back to your initial quest—why do you allow it in the first place??

Only you know the answer to this one. You can whine and carry on, throw a temper tantrum, and even threaten suicide, but no one does anything "to you"—you always do it to yourself. The "attacker" only attacks when you allow it in. Say you decide to throw in the towel and actually do away with your physical body—do you think the journey of the soul-personality that inhabited the body actually has it any easier? Think about it—you set up a test for yourself, you whine because you have to take it, then you simply extricate yourself from the situation so that you can take an even more difficult test. What's wrong with this picture? And, who wins? Certainly not you!

If you are angry at "them," who does the anger hurt? "Them?" If you are frightened of them, who does it weaken? "Them?" So what is the point of being angry and frightened? Release it up, be done with it, take your test. You are here for a reason—you chose to be here. You only journey through this reality once in this particular way. As difficult as you may find your life, choose to find the easiest path through the challenging times. One exists, or you could not imagine it. With the strength of your mind-pattern, pull it to you, and put yourself firmly upon it.

While you are sitting around moaning and complaining, feeling angry and frightened, destroying and weakening your body, and building negative mind-patterns, "they" are having a field day. They are enjoying their lives, plotting and planning, and celebrating each achieved goal. You aid their cause! You play right into their hands! You do just as they wish, caving in as the stakes and challenges grow. One by one, then by the dozens, hundreds, and thousands, they crush their adversaries in victory. And you just lie down and let them.

At minimum, you can choose to be a formidable opponent. What happened to the fire in your belly? Have you allowed it to completely burn out and die? What if the oppressors came, and there was no one who could be oppressed? What happens when someone stands up to a bully?

Choices, choices...you always have more than you can choose from. You may not like the options at the time, but they still exist. And, one or more will get you to where you need to grow.

Who are you betting on to win? "Them"? Or you? You know darn well who **they** are betting on. "Whiners never win, and winners never whine," so goes the old saying. Take a deep breath, do your balancing, grounding, self-to-Oversoul connecting. Survey your kingdom, and march forward to your own personal victory. After all, you are the only thing that this reality is about.

Are you going to continue to spend your energy in a nonproductive way for you, thus a   productive way for "them"? Or are you going to put on your brakes and reverse the situation? One person, one ripple into the collective unconscious can make a major difference. Two people, two ripples…what kind of ripple do you choose to send out?

Chapter 9
Becoming Invincible

What if all the outer threats to your inner security were suddenly wiped away tomorrow? Regardless of the outer world situation, you would still be the same person inside. So what would happen? Eventually, your thought process would manifest itself in the outer world in much the same way as today, except perhaps with a few variations.

People who are ill and go in for surgery to cut the illness out very often recreate a similar situation in the body. People who leave one relationship without fixing the inner self most often recreate the original relationship over and over again. And so it goes. Changing the outer world may sound like an idyllic way to move on into something better, but the reality is that your mind-pattern will just have to recreate the situation over again. Twice as much work, half the reward.

Rather than worrying about the outer activities and how you should respond to them, focus your attention on your inner activities in full conscious awareness. Knowing that the outer world only exists as a reflection of yourself, what can you do to improve your inner quality to become invincible?

For example, what if someone tried to…

…give you poison, but your mind-pattern would not allow your body to accept it?

…put a bullet in your body, but your mind-pattern allowed the bullet to pass right through without damage?

…put a microchip in your body, but your mind-pattern neutralized its effectiveness, or even expelled it from your cellular structure?

…alter your brain with drugs, but your mind-pattern neutralized their effectiveness?

The Life and Teachings of the Masters of the Far East, written by Baird T. Spalding in 1924 (*DeVorss & Co*) is said to be a report of his true encounters with human-type beings living in the Himalayas in the late 1800s. These beings, Jesus among them, were reportedly no longer subject to the "every day rules" of most humans. For example, they could materialize and dematerialize themselves and objects at will. They knew how to separate their cellular structures so that they could walk between the molecules of walls. The stories go on and on, leaving much controversy about the veracity of the books. But, regardless of whether you view them as fact or fiction, they open your mind to the potential of humankind.

Think about all your challenges and how you feel about them. Do you get tired and weary of them? Do you wish that they would just go away? When you get tired enough and weary enough, you will find a way through them to the other side. Part of your mission here is to exhaust the knowledge of every experience until there is absolutely nothing left to gain from that experience. You can complete an experience mentally, or you can go one step further and actually outpicture it for physical experience. Your choice.

Once you learn the current rules of existence, then you may travel up the spiral to learn the next set of rules. Only then are you ready to let go of your current challenges, including the over-all outpicturing of the group consciousness, including violence, hatred, war, etc. Some part of this is a reflection of yourself out of balance. If there you see violence, then somewhere inside of you there is violence. If you see hate, then somewhere inside of you is hatred. Even if you "hate" for the "correct" reason, this is still hate inside of you.

You can choose to stay in and participate in the collective, or you can choose to move beyond it. But you do not give that choice to yourself until everything is in place. You cannot build upon the rules until you know the rules upon which to build. A two-edged sword, but nonetheless, one that exists and must be traversed.

Right now, the human body only operates at approximately 4% of its capacity. Imagine the possibilities if you just doubled that to 8%! How strongly do you want to experience the 100% potential of the human body and therefore the capacity of the brain and the mind to create through it? What are you willing to give up for the deepest, most secret knowledge? Are you too anchored into this reality as it now exists, to give it up to build something else? What are you holding onto, mentally and physically, that prevent and distract you from changing this reality into a better one?

What would you need to accomplish to become invincible and how would you do it? What mental challenges exist in the outer world for you to create this kind of reality? A true athlete continually pushes him/herself. For example, if he/she runs one mile, he/she will strive to run two miles. Once the two mile limit is reached, he/she will continually push to reach the next milestone. A true athlete is proactive in his/her pursuits.

In the same way, strive to surpass what you can mentally accomplish. What can you mentally face and move through with grace and dignity? Accept the challenge of facing the most difficult personalities and circumstances that confront you. Align Self with Oversoul and God-Mind. Anchor yourself in the strength of the Triad. Anchored in this strength, there is absolutely nothing that you cannot face. Become the objective observer. Control yourself so that the outer people and circumstances do not. The outer challenges only exist to balance your lack of inner challenges. Become proactive and greet your deepest challenges with open arms.

Accept all mental challenges as courageously and fearlessly as possible. Know that you will be tested over and over again to determine the depths of your true mental capabilities. Become a mental athlete—proactive and self-challenging, balanced and in control of yourself. It is the mind that directs everything else. Create an invincible mind and all else follows its lead. As always, your choice to decide how far, how fast, how deep. Change the world by changing yourself. Without doing so, the world will be forever the same.

Chapter 10
Practical Tips & Affirmations

Blocking Triggers

Many people feel triggered as a result of increased ELF and personal deprogramming work. This ranges from short tempers to suicidal feelings. Many people feel jittery, nervous, and constantly on edge, as if "something" is about to happen. It is especially important to be aware of your reactions to both internal and external stimuli so that you can be in control if it instead of it being in control of you. Be extremely diligent in keeping your T-Bar archetype balanced and spinning your chakras to help keep you centered and calm.

Affirmation: *I balance my T-Bar and spin my chakras to help block internal and external triggers.*

It is especially important that you keep the brown merger archetype at your pineal gland on a background of royal blue every second of every day and night. Use a template under your pillow while sleeping and keep one on your body facing toward you to give you an extra boost. Spend time drawing it, or tracing it with your finger if necessary. Mentally place any known triggers behind it so that the trigger merges with your personality and you control it, rather than allowing it to control you.

Affirmation: *I creatively use the brown merger archetype to block internal and external triggers.*

The silver infinity archetype represents your connection to your Angelic Frequency and Oversoul. When you feel especially depressed or in despair, this archetype pulls you up to your Oversoul level. Use it as necessary in all chakra bands as well as above your head. In addition, surround yourself and your surroundings in heavy violet.

Affirmation: *I use the silver infinity archetype to elevate me beyond my internal and external triggers. I surround myself and my environment in heavy violet for additional protection.*

Sea salt helps to counter the effects of ELF and grounds the physical body. Put a few tablespoons in your bath, and even set small bowls around your house. A small bowl under your bed can aid your protection techniques during the night. A light sprinkle of sea salt on your food helps to stabilize the physical body.

Affirmation: *I use the frequency of sea salt as an aid to block all internal and external triggers.*

Use tones to shatter the parts of yourself that accept and allow internal and external triggers. Then, create tones to put everything back together in a new way that does not allow any trigger to penetrate the mind-pattern.

Affirmation: *I use tones to block any trigger from taking effect within my mind-pattern.*

When you feel like you are responding or beginning to respond to triggers of any kind, use food to pull yourself into your body. Eat heavy meats, starches, and grains to ground yourself down into the body. Use the color "brown around yourself for grounding.

Affirmation: *I surround myself with brown and eat grounding foods to block all internal and external triggers.*

Whether you are specifically or generally programmed, continually do your release work. The only way a trigger can affect you is if there is some part of you that allows it in. Proactively search for holes and vulnerabilities within your own mind-pattern so that you can correct it before someone else finds it and uses it against you. This is already happening. You are the only one who can correct it.

Affirmation: *I release all internal and external trigger-accepting mind-patterns up to my Oversoul and God-Mind.*

Compartmentalization

The powers-that-be are intent on compartmentalizing every aspect of society. As the "whole" is sliced away, they find the weak areas to use as weapons against society. Become aware of the compartmentalization within society. You must become aware of something before you can change it.

Affirmation: *I become aware of the attempts to compartmentalize society and thus myself.*

Careers are increasingly compartmentalized in an attempt to make the workplace more "efficient." This is one reason why so many people want to work for themselves. Being one's own boss is not necessarily so great and/or easy, but it is an attempt for people to bring wholeness into their lives once again. Can you see how the workplace is compartmentalized? How many examples can you think of?

Affirmation: *I become aware of the attempts to compartmentalize the workplace and thus myself.*

Families are compartmentalized. The family unit is being told that if you are unhappy, leave it; leave your spouse, leave your children. Find yourself, find happiness. Tools in society for fixing the family unites are not as easily accessible as the tools to pull the family apart. Much is said and written about bringing the family together, however, this is more talk than action. Observe what is said and written, comparing this to what is actually being done. This is how they fool you. You hear one thing, while something else is really happening.

Affirmation: *I become aware of the attempts to compartmentalize the family structure and thus myself.*

Observe how the latest trend in the media is to flash a series of scenes in front of your face. Before you have a chance to adequately focus, another scene is flashed. This is a way of keeping your thoughts defocused and scattered–another way of shattering the whole.

Affirmation: *I become aware of the attempts to defocus and scatter my whole.*

Observe how the media plays on your emotions–the sexual nature of advertising, the fear in the news, anger fed toward others–all attempts to take a variety of base emotions, feed them, and grow them into something that can be used against you. Open sexual chakras allow specific information to be programmed into the populace. People who are afraid willingly give up their freedoms. Angry people, especially a group of angry people, do things as a group that they most likely would not do as individuals.

Affirmation: *I become aware of the attempts to control my emotions in a negative way.*

Food sources are likewise becoming increasingly compartmentalized. Whole foods are less and less available, and increasingly expensive. People are trading whole foods for convenience in a scattered world. Take the time to eat whole foods, symbolizing our acceptance of the whole you. Convenience works once in a while, but feed your body and mind the best whole nourishment that you possibly can.

Affirmation: *I ingest whole foods, symbolizing keeping myself whole.*

Continue to observe yourself to understand where you are scattered and defocused; how this is happening; who and what is doing this to you; and what part of yourself allows this. Take the time to pull your thoughts, emotions, and lifestyle to the center of your being. Now that you are aware of the puposeful compartmentalization process, you can make conscious decisions to stop it.

Affirmation: *I consciously make the decision to keep myself whole and complete.*

ELF

ELF means "extra low frequency" and affects everyone every day. ELF is primarily transmitted through communication devices, such as telephones, radios, computers, and satellites. The degree to which you are affected is a direct result of many factors, from your location to your personal receptivity of these waves. ELF can disrupt your personal energy field, physical health, and mental capacities. It is important to be aware of its existence. Today, focus on all the electronic devices that surround you on a daily basis. Focus on the device that you see, and the communication transmissions through it that you do not see.

Affirmation: *I am aware of the extensive ELF in my environment.*

ELF transmissions usually show as bright yellow in the auric field. Anything in that particular hue will help to pull ELF into your energy field. For this reason, it is important to avoid this particular shade of yellow in your environment, including clothes. Prescription medications and often Chinese herbs also place a bright yellow, ELF color in an individual's auric field. Review your environment to determine if you have anything that might attract and hold ELF that is possible to eliminate.

Affirmation: *I allow only pale yellow into my auric field and environment.*

The frequency of violet will help reduce, and can eliminate, ELF receptivity. Keep a violet bubble with a mirror on the outside around yourself to deflect ELF transmissions. Or, you may put yourself in a violet tetrahedron (three-sided pyramid) which is in turn inside a violet octahedron (four-sided pyramid on top, four-sided pyramid on the bottom).

Affirmation: *I effectively deflect all ELF transmissions.*

Routinely flush your environment with violet to flush out the residual effects of ELF. Use violet around the electronic devices in your home and office to help neutralize any ELF transmissions coming through them. Also use violet protection techniques on any transportation modes you use, home, workplace, etc.

Affirmation: *My environment is free of all ELF transmissions.*

Taking sea salt baths (or swimming in salt water) will help negate the effects of ELF. Sea salt will also help stabilize the auric field, and draw toxins out of the body. If you crave salt for any reason, you may want to look at this. For example, salt cuts mucous in the body as well as helps neutralize the internal effects of ELF and radiation poisoning.

Affirmation: *I release external and internal ELF residual effects.*

If you are receptive to ELF, there is a part of your mind-pattern that is allowing it in. The most important part in keeping it out is correcting the mental imbalances that allow it to enter into your auric field in the first place. Like so many things, the basic mind-pattern behind allowing in ELF is a victim mentality, so continue your release work.

Affirmation: *I release the need from every part of my being to accept ELF transmissions.*

Recognize that you are the master of your own ship. Everywhere you turn, others are trying on some level to push you overboard. It is up to you what you decide to accept. Sometimes the decisions are not easy. You are the only one who can save you. No one else can. Be aware of all that exists around you so that you can make choices that are correct for you. ELF is always trying to bring you down. This is just another test for you to walk through unscathed and unaffected.

Affirmation: *I only accept that which enhances my mental and physical capacity.*

Mind-Control

While many people are becoming increasingly aware of the mass mind-control that is thrust upon society, more and more people are coming into the realization that they are/have been personally targeted for specific reasons. Most people do not publicly speak about their experiences because they fear repercussions from others. When these experiences are not voiced because of fear, the fear holds the power, not you. Is there someone with whom you can share your experiences? If so, it may be time, as he/she may have something that can be shared in return. If not, get a journal and write it down, no matter how small. Acknowledging the experience in some way is the first step.

Affirmation: *I acknowledge and share my "strange experiences."*

Some people hear voices, noises, sounds, tones, and/or buzzing, especially between the waking and sleeping state as you fall asleep, or during the night. These may be satellite transmissions and/or ELF pulses that directly affect the brain, and/or interact with the brain waves during the sleep state. These may even be strong enough to force you out of your body. When this happens, use a pale yellow frequency line to trace the source.

Affirmation: *I identify the source of strange voices and noises.*

If you feel extremely depressed, aggressive, and/or are filled with fear and paranoia, this can be the result of mind-control. Flood your entire being with violet, flushing all that you no longer need up to your Oversoul. Be sure to keep your T-Bar archetype balanced and spin your chakras daily, per *The Healer's Handbook*.

Affirmation: *I keep myself balanced and protected to counter mind-control effects.*

If you have been subjected to mind-control, you may find that you easily disassociate yourself from others and the environment. You may feel that you easily flip between personalities, or your mood easily changes. If this is the case, use the brown merger symbol at the pineal gland to bring all parts of Self together. If you are uncertain, use the brown merger symbol above your head. If it moves to the pineal gland, then leave it there. If it stays above the head, leave it there.

Affirmation: *I merge all parts of Self into one.*

You may notice sudden behavior changes in yourself, others, or even children. These may strike you as odd or unusual. If so, use the violet protection techniques as well as the balancing techniques. On the Oversoul level, ask for permission to use these techniques on others. Also ask permission to consciously share this information with those that need it.

Affirmation: *I utilize the violet protection techniques to counter mind-control effects.*

If you have any unusual body markings, moles, or growths that suddenly appear, use castor oil on them to counter the effects. Mentally, flood them with violet.

Affirmation: *I observe and neutralize unusual body markings, moles, and/or growths.*

Blurred vision, vision changes, or even facial features changing may be a sign of mind-control, as may "blank faces" and/or vacant stares. Observe when you feel these things occur and write it down.

Affirmation: *I keep a journal of my unusual experiences.*

Programming

Nightmares and dreams often reveal specific programming codes as they sometimes come to the surface during the dream state. Keep these in your journals, as the patterns may eventually reveal themselves to you.

Affirmation: *I remember and record all significant dreams.*

Obsessive-compulsive behavior may be the result of specific programming. If this is a factor in your life, trace this back to the time period that this began and begin looking at the memories that surface. Any time anything traumatic surfaces that you cannot handle, immerse yourself in brown, and bring yourself out of the experience.

Affirmation: *I identify the origins of any undesired, controlling behavior.*

Some people turn to drugs and/or drinking to deaden the pain of programming experiences that they cannot face. Trace these behaviors back to the time that they began, and begin exploring that time period. Any time anything traumatic surfaces that you cannot handle, immerse yourself in brown, and bring yourself out of the experience.

Affirmation: *I bravely face all unpleasant memories.*

If you cannot remember your childhood, or details are sketchy, there is a good chance that some sort of programming occurred that you are blocking out. Lack of childhood memories is often an indicator that someone was severely traumatized. To unlock the closed memories, immerse yourself in dark green, and focus on what you can remember. Then, mentally explore your memories from there. Write down whatever comes up, regardless of significance. This is your starting place and your key for further exploration. If at any time you become traumatized, immerse yourself in brown, and come out of the experience.

Affirmation: *I unlock previously inaccessible childhood memories.*

Program codes are sometimes present in any "doodles" that you may draw. If you have something that you constantly draw or see, there may be more to it than meets the conscious eye. Write these down in your journal and study them. Mentally put them in pale yellow to see what knowledge you absorb from them.

Affirmation: *I pay attention to all unconscious information.*

Programmed people have specific triggers that activate them into specific modes of behavior. Whenever specific behavior happens, realize that something happened to create that. Write down what happened just before these changes came on. Eventually, you may be able to identify your specific triggers, thus gaining more conscious control of your behavior.

Affirmation: *I identify my specific triggers.*

Continue to keep your mind and body protected using the balancing and protecting techniques. Use your internal exploration and knowledge of self-awareness to deactivate your personal programs so that you have more control than they have. Keep a journal of all activity so that you can literally piece your personal story together. These notes will deepen your self-understanding.

Affirmation: *I deactivate outside programming.*

Glossary

Activation: when a program is brought to full function.

Alien: a physical being from another planet.

Alter: a subpersonality which can be programmed.

Archetype: glyphs and symbols emanating from mind-patterns.

Astral plane: the border zone between physical reality and hyperspace.

Chakras: along the human spinal column there are several nerve bundles called "ganglions" which are esoterically called "chakras," a word which means wheels in Sanskrit. They form along the "S" curve of the spine which looks like a snake. For this reason, the chakras system is referred to as "Kundalini," the Sanskrit word for snake.

Construct: similar to a physical object created in the programming matrix to work with the alter in a specific function.

DNA sequences: this refers to the DNA sequences opening up in the body which is a form of Kundalini activation. DNA codes are the instructions that tell your body what to do and be. Some instructions you are running at birth. These dictate that you will have blue-eyes, two legs, two arms, etc. Others activate later in life, such as health conditions, ability to play music, sing, etc. When the chakra centers along the spine open up, this is referred to as Kundalini activation.

Direct Awareness: to know by experiencing the knowledge.

Energy: a physical substance consistng of shape, weight, consistency, and color.

ELF (Extremely Low Frequency): energy waves that influence body and mind.

ET (Extraterrestrial): borderline physical/nonphysical beings not bound to our reality.

Frequency: resonance of a particular nature.

Function: a programmed action.

God-Mind: neutral energy; All That Is.

Guardian alter: keeps watch over an alter section to ensure adherence to a program.

Hyperspace: a region of consciousness which exists out of linear space and time.

Illuminati: 13 families that control the Earth.

Internal Programmer: a programming representative of the human programmer; monitors the entire 2, 197 compartments within the matrix; programmed into each specifically programmed person.

Know by knowing: to understand through direct awareness; to understand the feeling of an experience.

Language of Hyperspace: the Original Language that emanates from the Mind of God consisting of color, tone, and artchetype.

Linear Time: Physical method of measuring centuries, one after another.

Matrix, programming: the structure in the mind that facilitates mind-control; 13x13x13 which equals 2,197 compartments.

Meditation: the listening from which information is gathered; centered in the right-brain.

Merovingian: first Illuminati family.

Mind-pattern: a blueprint of a person's thought.

Montauk Project: mind-control project.

Neural Linguistic Programming: a programming tool using words and actions to mask or trigger a thought or action.

New World Order: global government.

New World Religion: global religion.

Oversoul: neutral energy that comes out of God-Mind: your Oversoul is to you what your Earth parents are to your body; your point of origin out of God-Mind.

Pineal Gland: organ at the center of the head.

Prayer: the request that affects the results of meditation; centered in the left-brain.

Radionics: a practice whereby sensitive individuals diagnose and treat a patient through the use of an electronic device or template.

Reptilians: a species from the Draco star system who colonized Lemuria.

Sexual Magick Ritual: sexual activity combined in a specific way to achieve specific results using thought-form projections.

Sex-Slave: a programmed person used in Sexual Magick Ritual.

Shapeshifter: a person who physically changes from one species into another.

Simultaneous existence: all lifetimes occuring at the same moment in the Eternal Now.

Soul-personality: individual strand of an Oversoul.

T-Bar: archetype emanating from the pineal gland relating to balance.

Trigger: sensory input that opens a program.

True Reality (actuality): the absolute state of being.

Visualization: creating a mental scenario that can be manifested either mentally or physically; centered in the pineal gland.

Index

Expansions Publishing Company, Inc.
Products and Services

www.expansions.com

Addressing The Issues

Montauk: Alien Connection

Blue Blood True Blood: Conflict & Creation

True Reality of Sexuality

Stewart Says…

<u>Additional Books</u>

White Owl Legends: An Archetypal Story of Creation

Belief Systems Shattered

Belief Systems Shattered…Again

Expansions Publishing
Presents

LEVEL I SERIES

Level I Includes:
- The Language of Hyperspace
- DNA Galactic History & You
- Dream Analysis & Intermediate Color Codes
- Simultaneous Existence
- Basic & Intermediate Color Therapy
- Triad Healing

Dream Analysis & Intermediate Color Codes

DVDs

DNA, Galactic History & You

Simultaneous Existences

History of Mind-Control

Mind-Control & Programming Parts I & II

Deprogramming for Counselors

Sexuality, Ritual & Relationships

Illuminati & Montauk

Montauk: One Man's Story

Conspiracy Con: From Mind-Control to Mind-Patrol & The Reptilian Agenda

By Stewart A. Swerdlow
and Janet D. Swerdlow

Finding The Solutions

Healer's Handbook: A Journey Into Hyperspace

Hyperspace Helper: A User-Friendly Guide

Decoding Your Life:
An Experiential Course in Self-Reintegration

Additional Books
Practical Tips for Everyday Living
Volumes I, II, III

Life Support Group ™ Manual
Self, Members, or Leaders

Expansions Publishing
Presents

LEVEL I SERIES

Level I Includes:
- The Language of Hyperspace
- DNA Galactic History & You
- Dream Analysis & Intermediate Color Codes
- Simultaneous Existence
- Basic & Intermediate Color Therapy
- Triad Healing

Dream Analysis & Intermediate Color Codes

DVDs

Language of Hyperspace

Dream Analysis & Intermediate Color Codes

Basic & Intermediate Color Codes

Triad Healing

Nonhuman Communication

Nonhuman Chakra & Energy Systems

Scanning

Survivor/Surpassor

Mind/Body Correlations

Intuition Intensive

Level II Includes:
- Nonhuman Communication
- Nonhuman Chakra & Energy Systems
- Scanning
- Survvor/Surpasser

Level III Includes:
- History of Mind-Control
- Mind-Control & Programming Part I
- Mind-Control & Programming Part II
- Deprogramming Techniques for Counselors
- Sexuality, Ritual, & Relationships
- Mind/Body Correlations

Personal Consultations with Stewart & Janet

Monthly Newsletters

Janet's Planet

Stew's News

Visit
www.expansions.com

Read the Newest Cutting-Edge Information

Daily Practical Tips

Current Events & News

Q & A Column

Articles by Janet and Stewart

Newsletter Subscriptions
Stew's News
Janet's Planet

Latest Books, DVD's, & Products

Seminars, Lectures, & Events
...and Much More!

Notes

Notes